Attack On Yamamoto

The Doolittle Raid
Round-the-World Flights
From the Wright Brothers to the Astronauts
The Modern U.S. Air Force
The Compact History of the U.S. Air Force
Doolittle's Tokyo Raiders
Four Came Home
Air Rescue! (with W. F. Moseley)
Helicopter Rescues
The Complete Guide for the Serviceman's Wife
Grand Old Lady (with W. F. Moseley)
Our Family Affairs
The DC-3: The Story of a Fabulous Airplane
Lighter-Than-Air Flight
Polar Aviation
Minutemen of the Air
The Legendary DC-3
The Wright Brothers: Pioneers of Power Flight
The First Book of the Moon
Jimmy Doolittle: Master of the Calculated Risk
The Saga of the Air Mail
Air Mail: How It All Began

Attack On Yamamoto

CARROLL V. GLINES

ORION BOOKS/NEW YORK

Published by Orion Books, a division of Crown Publishers, Inc., 201 East 50th Street, New York, New York 10022

ORION and colophon are trademarks of Crown Publishers, Inc.

Manufactured in the United States of America

Library of Congress Cataloging-in-Publication Data

Glines, Carroll V., 1920–
    Attack on Yamamoto / Carroll V. Glines. — 1st ed.
      p.   cm.
    Includes bibliographical references.
    1. World War, 1939–1945—Campaigns—Bougainville Island. 2. World
War, 1939–1945—Aerial operations, American. 3. Yamamoto, Isoroku,
1884–1943—Death and burial. 4. Bougainville Island—History.
I. Title.
D769.99.B68G55   1990
940.54'26—dc20   89-77025
                                                                 CIP

ISBN 0-517-57728-3

Book Design by Shari DeMiskey

10 9 8 7 6 5 4 3 2 1

First Edition

DEDICATED

to

Colonel John W. Mitchell

*Leader of the Longest Fighter
Intercept in History*

CONTENTS

INTRODUCTION

THE SQUADRON OF LOCKHEED P-38 LIGHTNING FIGHTERS TAX-
ied out for takeoff from Guadalcanal's Fighter Two airstrip, their
twin Allison engines straining, anxious to be airborne. Long-
range gas tanks were strapped under the wings of each aircraft.
In the lead was Maj. John W. Mitchell, an easygoing Mis-
sissippian with a slow southern drawl that belied the fact that he
had already blasted eight enemy planes out of the sky during his
combat tour with the Army Air Force in the South Pacific.

Mitchell's mission this day was one that, if successful, would
do down in the history books. Its importance had been driven
home to him the day before. He was ordered to take his personally selected squadron and intercept and destroy an enemy
bomber containing Adm. Isoroku Yamamoto, commander in
chief of the Japanese Combined Fleet, the man who had masterminded the "infamous" attack on Pearl Harbor.

Knowing the admiral was punctual to a fault, American intelligence sources had learned from intercepted and decoded
radio messages that he would depart Rabaul on the northern
coast of New Guinea and arrive at an airfield on the southern tip
of Bougainville on the morning of April 18, 1943. He would be
flying in a Betty bomber escorted by six Zero fighter planes.

The admiral, true to his reputation, was on time. However, there were two bombers instead of one, accompanied by the six Zeros. Mitchell led his squadron of sixteen P-38s into the attack with twelve of the planes to act as high cover for the remaining four, which he designated the attack or "killer" flight.

As Mitchell had told his men before takeoff, he led the high-cover planes in a rapid climb. Meanwhile, the killer flight went after the two bombers. In the ensuing melee, which lasted less than ten minutes, both bombers were shot down. None of the escorting Zeros were downed.

One of the pilots in the killer flight was lost. It was later confirmed that Admiral Yamamoto had indeed been in one of the bombers and had died that day.

These are the facts. But the story does not end with the demise of the Japanese naval officer whose name is linked forever with the attack at Pearl Harbor. The interception became a classic air action in the annals of the U.S. Air Force. Precisely planned and led by Major Mitchell, the mission was the longest successful fighter intercept mission ever flown by American fighter planes. A daring, powerful enemy leader, revered by his people, had been eliminated. It was a terrible blow to Japanese morale and an extraordinary morale boost for Americans fighting the enemy in the Pacific.

With the hindsight of history, the admiral's death was a symbolic episode in the history of the war in the Pacific. It marked, if not the beginning of the end, the end of the beginning, for 1943 was the year in which the Americans turned from defense to counterattack. A grand strategy against the superpowerful Japanese war machine had been worked out between the two American naval and ground force commanders—Adm. Chester W. Nimitz and Gen. Douglas MacArthur. America's industrial power was producing the weapons of war in enormous quantities. By the spring of 1943, the war had taken a definite turn in favor of the Allied forces.

The American fighter pilots who participated in the Yamamoto mission were understandably elated, especially the three survivors of the four-man killer flight. After these three men returned to Guadalcanal, however, a controversy developed among them that continues to this day. The basis of the quarrel: Who *really* shot down Yamamoto?

It may not seem of any real consequence today who actually fired the shots that downed an enemy bomber. What is important is that the mission was planned and carried out in the finest tradition of the U.S. Air Force. The anonymous cryptographers who decoded the enemy messages and learned the admiral's itinerary, the Army Air Force squadron commander who planned the interception, and the pilots who participated in it deserve prominent mention in the World War II military aviation history books.

Most of the participants of the mission were content to leave it that way. However, one pilot, Capt. Thomas G. Lanphier, Jr., claimed *he*, and only he, was the pilot who fired the fatal shots, and his version has prevailed in all World War II accounts of the mission written thus far. However, his story has been actively challenged in recent years because of evidence from the crash site of Yamamoto's aircraft where the wreckage still rests, testimony from a surviving Japanese Zero pilot and a high-ranking passenger on the second Japanese bomber who survived, military intelligence information which has recently been declassified, newly discovered Japanese war documents, and recollections of the surviving killer flight members. After reviewing the evidence presented up to 1972, the air force decreed that Lanphier and Rex T. Barber, Lanphier's wingman, should share the credit for the Yamamoto shootdown and that is the "official" decision at this writing.

It is the purpose of this book to review the known facts, provide a behind-the-scenes look at the intelligence breakthroughs that made the interception possible, examine new evidence discovered in recent months, analyze the statements made by Japanese and American survivors, and consider the question of who deserves the credit for bringing down an enemy leader whose demise certainly helped shorten the war.

Thomas Lanphier died in November 1987. However, he produced enough written and recorded materials in an attempt to justify his claim that there is no doubt what he would say today. He was a man with a capricious, mercurial personality, often brilliant, ambitious to a fault, articulate, and driven to desperation in his desire to defend his version of a brief combat shootout that put his name in the history books. He was an exceptionally aggressive, sometimes reckless, fighter pilot who was respected by his contemporaries for his willingness to tangle with the enemy at great risk to himself. His bravery under fire has never been questioned; his imprudence has.

Rex T. Barber, the other pilot who claims credit, is a contrast in personality. Quiet, unassuming, and unpretentious on the ground, but a vigorous, aggressive fighter pilot in the air, he has no aspirations for greatness. A native of Oregon, he remained in the air force flying fighter planes after World War II. He flew jet fighters during the Korean War and retired as a colonel after a full air force career.

Barber disputes Lanphier's claim and presents much evidence to support his own right to the distinction of having participated in an exciting moment in history. This book is the first opportunity he has had to tell his side of the controversy since the uncovering of information from Japanese and other sources.

The author has the difficult task of trying to reconstruct a short aerial engagement that took place nearly a half century ago and, perhaps, to rewrite history. The yellowed pages of reports of combat actions seem indisputable and there is always the temptation to take them at face value. However, as the reader shall see, they are not infallible, and too often are written in the passion of war by persons who were not on the scene and who tend to take the words of returning warriors as fact. Or, they may have been written by the combatants themselves, perhaps to their personal advantage and glorification.

Who *really* shot down Yamamoto? The reader may decide after reading the following pages.

CARROLL V. GLINES
McLEAN, VIRGINIA

Attack On Yamamoto

1

"TALLEY HO! LET'S GET THE BASTARD!"

*I*N THE EARLY HOURS OF APRIL 14, 1943, A Japanese coded message concerning the forthcoming itinerary of Adm. Isoroku Yamamoto, the Japanese navy's commander in chief, was simultaneously intercepted by NEGAT, a U.S. Navy radio intercept station in Washington, D.C., FRUMEL (Fleet Radio Unit, Melbourne, Australia), and FRUPAC (Fleet Radio Unit, Pacific), the communications intelligence unit for the U.S. Navy's Pacific Fleet at Pearl Harbor. The three stations had an exclusive radio circuit and could exchange information quickly. They pooled their efforts and agreed on the contents.

Capt. Roger Pineau, a naval historian who assisted in the writing of the navy's official World War II history, relates what happened next:

> At FRUPAC, this "puzzle" first reached the hands of Marine Lt. Col. Alva B. Lasswell, one of the navy's most experienced cryptanalyst-linguists.
> "Red" Lasswell had studied Japanese in Tokyo from 1935 to 1938. After communications intelligence duty at Cavite [in the

Philippines] and Shanghai, and seven months in San Diego, he had reported to Pearl Harbor in May 1941.

From his very first worksheet on this message, Lasswell saw it was important. Lt. Cmdr. John G. Roenigk, another linguist, recalls that Lasswell leaped to his feet and shouted, "We've hit the jackpot!"

All hands pitched in. Traffic analysts Tom Huckins and Jack Williams reworked the addressee information; cryptanalysts Tommy Dyer and "Ham" Wright worked to recover new additives and code groups; and Jasper Holmes's estimate section searched for area designators. Joe Finnegan, Roenigk, and other linguists dug for collateral information in other messages.

At Stations NEGAT and FRUMEL, too, all hands scrambled to solve the message. Cmdr. Redfield Mason, in charge of translating in Washington, saw the raw message the minute it came in. Chief Petty Officer Albert J. Pelletier, who car-pooled with him, remembers Mason's shouting, "I want every damned date, time, and place checked and double-checked."

Mason poured over every squeaked-out recovery, saying, "Good!" and Mason's "Good!" was very high praise. Pelletier recalls thinking and saying, "I hope we get the S.O.B."[1]

A top secret coded dispatch was immediately sent to the headquarters of Admiral Chester W. Nimitz, commander in chief, U.S. Pacific Fleet also at Pearl Harbor, as well as to the commander, South Pacific and the commander, Seventh Fleet. It was a fragmentary translation of a Japanese message, dated April 13 from the Japanese commander in chief, Southeastern Area Fleet to several addressees on Bougainville Island:

ON 18 APRIL CINC COMBINED FLEET WILL VISIT RYZ, R___ AND RXP IN ACCORDANCE WITH THE FOLLOW-ING SCHEDULE:

1. DEPART RR AT 0600 IN A MEDIUM ATTACK PLANE ESCORTED BY 6 FIGHTERS. ARRIVE AT RYZ AT 0800. PROCEED BY MINESWEEPER TO R___ ARRIVING 0840. (___ HAVE MINESWEEPER READY AT #1 BASE.) DE-PART R___ AT 0945 IN ABOVE MINESWEEPER AND AR-

RIVE RXZ AT 1030? (_____) DEPART RXZ AT 1100? IN
MEDIUM ATTACK PLANE AND ARRIVE AT RXF AT 1110.
DEPART RXP AT 1400 IN MEDIUM ATTACK PLANE AND
ARRIVE RR AT 1530.

2. AT EACH OF THE ABOVE PLACES THE COM-
MANDER IN CHIEF WILL MAKE SHORT TOUR OF IN-
SPECTION AND AT ———— HE WILL VISIT THE SICK AND
WOUNDED, BUT CURRENT OPERATIONS SHOULD CON-
TINUE. EACH FORCE COMMANDER _____. IN CASE OF
BAD WEATHER THE TRIP WILL BE POSTPONED ONE
DAY.[2]

The communications staff member who prepared the intercepted message added:

COMMENT BY FRUPAC: THIS IS PROBABLY A SCHEDULE
OF INSPECTION BY CINC COMBINED FLEET. THE MES-
SAGE LACKS ADDITIVES, BUT WORK WILL BE CONTIN-
UED ON IT.[3]

A few hours later, the Pearl Harbor and Washington communications units dispatched more complete translations of the
same message. The message had been sent from the Japanese
commander in chief, Southeastern Air Fleet, to subordinate
commanders in Air Flotilla No. 26, Air Group No. 204, and the
Solomons Defense Force, located at Rabaul, and to the Ballale
garrison commander on Bougainville. The communications intelligence staffs continued to decode, translate, and verify the
information. Since they did not have the latest Japanese additives and code books, they had to pass the intercepted code
message between a few traffic analysts, cryptanalysts, and linguists in order to come up with the basics contained in the
message.

From this message, it seemed certain that Admiral Yamamoto, Nimitz's opposite number in the Pacific, planned to make an
inspection tour of his forces on Bougainville. If this visit came off
as apparently planned, Yamamoto would come closer to the
American forces in the combat zone than ever before.

Comdr. Edwin T. Layton, Nimitz's chief intelligence officer, took one look at the message, whistled softly, and went quickly to Nimitz's office to brief his boss on what the communications intelligence personnel had learned. Admiral Nimitz walked to a huge wall chart of the Pacific Ocean and checked the distances between Guadalcanal, where there were army and navy fighters under Adm. William F. "Bull" Halsey's command, and Yamamoto's possible destinations on Bougainville.

Nimitz calmly read the partial decryption that still had some blanks. "Do we try to get him?" Nimitz asked Layton.

There was no doubt in Layton's mind that shooting down Yamamoto would be a serious blow to the enemy. Aside from the emperor there was no one held in higher regard by the Japanese public than Adm. Isoroku Yamamoto. His men idolized him. Comdr. Mitsuo Fuchida, leader of the planes during the Pearl Harbor attack, wrote later: "If, at the start of the Pacific War a poll had been taken among Japanese naval officers to determine their choice of the man to lead them as Commander in Chief Combined Fleet, there is little doubt that Admiral Yamamoto would have been selected by an overwhelming majority."[4] Commander Layton thought his death would demoralize the Japanese navy and shock the nation. A navy intelligence profile on the enemy leader described him as "exceptionally able, forceful, and quick-thinking."[5]

In his memoirs, Layton confirmed this assessment and added: "There was no one to replace him. Admiral [Tamon] Yamaguchi had gone down with the carrier *Hiryu* at the Battle of Midway, and during our review of who might succeed to the command of the Combined Fleet, Nimitz proved surprisingly well informed of the reputations and qualifications of the senior Japanese naval staff. In a final summary I assured him that there was indeed only one Yamamoto. 'You know, Admiral Nimitz, it would be just as if they shot you down,' I said. 'There isn't anybody to replace you.' "[6]

Nimitz smiled but didn't reply to the compliment. He said, "It's down in Halsey's bailiwick. If there's a way, he'll find it. All right, we'll try it."[7]

U.S. Navy task force commanders in the Pacific were immediately informed:

INDICATOR JAPS TO HOLD CONFERENCE SOON CON-
CERNING OPERATIONS AND DEFENSE MEASURES FOR
NEW GUINEA SOLOMONS BISMARK AREA X. . . . X
YAMAMOTO HIMSELF ARRIVING BALLALE SHORT-
LAND AREA AT 10 HOURS ON 18TH VIA BOMBER FROM
RABAUL X ESCORTED BY 6 FIGHTERS X TO RETURN
RABAUL (WE HOPE NOT) DEPARTING KAHILI 16
HOURS SAME DAY X ALL DATES AND TIMES ARE LOVE
[LOCAL] X IF BAD WEATHER TRIP POSTPONED TILL
19TH X[8]

Nimitz had met Yamamoto in 1937 when Nimitz had been a
guest at Emperor Hirohito's game preserve. Yamamoto had
hosted a duck hunt for a group of American, British, and Dutch
naval officers, all of whom knew that the top enemy naval leader
was compulsively punctual; he adhered to his schedules virtually
to the split second.

The date of Yamamoto's proposed visit to his forces on
Bougainville—April 18—had a familiar ring to it. It was on that
same day the year before that a sixteen-ship task force under the
command of Adm. William F. Halsey had launched Lt. Col.
James H. "Jimmy" Doolittle and his sixteen B-25 medium bombers on their morale-boosting raid against Tokyo and four other
major Japanese cities. Doolittle and his Raiders departed the
carrier *Hornet* then under the command of Capt. Marc A.
Mitscher, now assigned as Commander, Air, Solomons (COM-
AIRSOL) with the rank of rear admiral. The interception would
be assigned to his command.

Naval communications units at Pearl Harbor and Washington
sent out more complete translations of the original itinerary
message and filled in most of the blanks that confirmed the
admiral's plans. RR was Rabaul; RXZ was Ballale, an island off
the southern tip of Bougainville; RXP was Buin, a nearby base
on Bougainville Island. The fourth place to be visited was later
identified as Shortland Island. This information was sent to
Adm. William F. Halsey, Commander, South Pacific. Halsey
forwarded the known basic information to his subordinate task
force commanders in the Pacific:

. . . DURING HIS TRIP THE CINC WILL LOOK INTO EXISTING CONDITIONS AND MAKE VISITS TO THE SICK WARDS X SOME BLANKS IN THIS PARAGRAPH # IN CASE BAD WEATHER SHOULD INTERFERE WITH THIS SCHEDULE IT WILL BE POSTPONED ONE DAY X COMMENT: IT WILL BE NOTED THAT THE ONE UNKNOWN PLACE IS 40 MINUTES BY SUBCHASER FROM BALLALE X THE ROMAN DIAGRAPH "XP" IN BUIN IS NOT CONFIRMED BUT LOOKS GOOD AS IT IS 10 MINUTES BY AIR FROM BALLALE X H [HALSEY] COMMENT: TALLEYHO X LET'S GET THE BASTARD X[9]

As the navy cryptographers and translators in Hawaii continued to monitor for confirming messages about Yamamoto's visit, another Japanese message had been intercepted by FRUMEL in Australia which gave additional instructions to subordinate commanders:

SOUTHEAST AREA FLEET/CONFIDENTIAL TELEG. NO. 131755—MILITARY SECRET HA-1 CODE

THE INSPECTION TOUR OF THE COMMANDER IN CHIEF TO BALLALE, SHORTLAND AND BUIN ON APRIL 18 IS SCHEDULED AS FOLLOWS:

1. 0600 DEPART RABAUL BY MEDIUM ATTACK PLANE (ESCORTED BY SIX FIGHTERS); 0800 ARRIVE BALLALE. IMMEDIATELY DEPART FOR SHORTLAND ON BOARD SUBCHASER (1ST BASE FORCE TO READY ONE BOAT), ARRIVING AT 0840. DEPART SHORTLAND 0945 ABOARD SAID SUBCHASER, ARRIVING BALLALE AT 1030. (FOR TRANSPORTATION PURPOSES, HAVE READY AN ASSAULT BOAT AT SHORTLAND AND A MOTOR LAUNCH AT BALLALE.) 1100 DEPART BALLALE ON BOARD MEDIUM ATTACK PLANE, ARRIVING BUIN AT 1110. LUNCH AT 1ST BASE FORCE HEADQUARTERS (SENIOR STAFF OFFICER OF AIR FLOTILLA 26 TO BE PRESENT). 1400 DEPART BUIN ABOARD MEDIUM ATTACK PLANE; ARRIVE RABAUL AT 1540.

2. INSPECTION PROCEDURES: AFTER BEING BRIEFED ON PRESENT STATUS, THE TROOPS (PATIENTS AT 1ST BASE FORCE HOSPITAL) WILL BE VISITED. HOWEVER,

THERE WILL BE NO INTERRUPTIONS IN THE ROUTINE
DUTIES OF THE DAY.

3. UNIFORMS WILL BE THE UNIFORM FOR THE DAY
EXCEPT THAT THE COMMANDING OFFICER OF THE
VARIOUS UNITS WILL BE IN COMBAT ATTIRE WITH
DECORATIONS.

4. IN THE EVENT OF INCLEMENT WEATHER, THE
TOUR WILL BE POSTPONED ONE DAY.

On April 15, more complete translations of the original intercepted message were sent. Later that day, another message
was disseminated which had been intercepted by FRUMEL
(Fleet Radio Unit, Melbourne, Australia). It was sent to an
unidentified addressee and made reference to "the special visit
of Yamamoto." This was further confirmation that the Yamamoto
visit was pending. It added "in view of the situation regarding air
attacks on the post," certain precautionary arrangements were
requested, including the moving of the post to a new location.
The message also requested: "Give consideration to construction
of slit trenches and other defense devices" and "Cause the 13
millimeter machine guns to be brought up."[10]

Attached to the translation was a comment by the unknown
cryptographer who forwarded the message:

"GI COMMENT: CATCH HIM IN THE AIR."[11]

Meanwhile, Halsey relayed the elements of Nimitz's messages to Adm. Aubrey Fitch, Commander, Air, South Pacific
[COMAIRSOPAC], and Adm. Marc A. Mitscher, Commander,
Air, Solomons [COMAIRSOL], located on Guadalcanal. After
conferring with his staff and receiving an assurance from Admiral
Mitscher that the Army Air Force P-38 fighters on Guadalcanal
had the range to make the interception, Halsey relished going
after the Japanese naval leader. Halsey had said many times that
Yamamoto was "No. 3 on my private list of public enemies,
closely trailing Hirohito and Tojo."[12]

On April 17, Commander Layton prepared a top secret message to Halsey for Nimitz's approval:

> SUPER. BELIEVE SPECIFIC EFFORT WORTHWHILE. IN
> ORDER PROTECT R.I. [RADIO INTELLIGENCE] SUGGEST
> PILOTS BE TOLD COASTWATCHER RABAUL AREA SIG-
> NALLED OUR SUB TO EFFECT UNKNOWN HIGH RANK-
> ING OFFICER MAKING TRIP TO BALLALE OR SOME
> SUCH SOURCE. SUGGEST EVERY EFFORT BE MADE TO
> MAKE OPERATION APPEAR FORTUITOUS. IF FORCES
> YOUR COMMAND HAVE CAPABILITY SHOOT DOWN
> YAMAMOTO AND STAFF, YOU ARE HEREBY AUTHO-
> RIZED INITIATE PRELIMINARY PLANNING. OUR BEST
> WISHES AND HIGH HOPES GO WITH THOSE INTERCEPT-
> ING HUNTERS.

Nimitz approved the message but added a personal note for
Halsey: "BEST OF LUCK AND GOOD HUNTING."[13]

There seems to be no doubt that Nimitz, ever mindful that he
should not conduct the naval war in the Pacific without the
knowledge of his superiors, made sure that his decisions on
important matters were relayed to Washington. He sent information copies of significant messages to his superior, Adm.
Ernest J. King, commander in chief, U.S. Fleet, in Washington,
and it can be assumed that information copies of message ex-
changes about the Yamamoto mission between Nimitz and his
subordinate commanders would be included. There is no indication, however, that Admiral King, if informed, ever reacted to
any of Nimitz's messages about Yamamoto. Layton is reported to
have stated that the decision to shoot down Yamamoto was
Nimitz's alone and did not require the approval of higher authority in Washington.[14] In his own memoirs published later,
however, Layton reports that "Nimitz . . . had already received
the president's approval for the operation via the secretary of the
navy . . ."[15] He cites no documentation to substantiate this
statement and none has ever been found.

A number of other writers and historians have also alleged
that Nimitz received personal approval for the Yamamoto interception from both Secretary of the Navy Frank Knox and
President Roosevelt. One writer reported that Knox was so
concerned that the assassination of such an important enemy

leader might have political repercussions that he insisted on getting an opinion from the navy advocate general as to the legality of such a mission, from religious leaders about its morality, and from Army Air Forces Gen. Henry H. "Hap" Arnold as to whether such a mission was possible. However, the author cites no documentation other than the books of two other writers who themselves offer no documentation.[16]

Thomas G. Lanphier, Jr., one of the pilots on the mission, always claimed that the message he read when he first learned of the mission had come directly to Guadalcanal from Secretary of the Navy Frank Knox and was signed simply "Knox." After interviewing Lanphier, one author asserted in 1969, without further documentation, that this was the message:

SQUADRON 339 P-38 MUST AT ALL COSTS REACH AND DESTROY X PRESIDENT ATTACHES EXTREME IMPORTANCE THIS OPERATION[17]

A British writer in a book published two years later states the following message was sent:

SQUADRON 339 P-38 MUST AT ALL COSTS REACH AND DESTROY YAMAMOTO AND STAFF MORNING APRIL EIGHTEEN STOP AUXILIARY TANKS AND CONSUMPTION DATA WILL ARRIVE FROM PORT MORESBY EVENING SEVENTEENTH STOP INTELLIGENCE STRESSES ADMIRAL'S EXTREME PUNCTUALITY STOP PRESIDENT ATTACHES EXTREME IMPORTANCE THIS OPERATION STOP COMMUNICATE RESULT AT ONCE WASHINGTON STOP FRANK KNOX SECRETARY OF STATE FOR NAVY STOP ULTRA-SECRET DOCUMENT NOT TO BE COPIED OR FILED STOP TO BE DESTROYED WHEN CARRIED OUT STOP.[18]

These messages are considered to be fictitious. Frank Knox was secretary of the navy; there was no "Secretary of State for Navy." Neither Lanphier nor anyone else has ever been able to produce such a message. Knowledgeable military researchers and official government historians seriously doubt that Secretary

Knox would have sent such a message over the heads of Nimitz and his subordinates specifically directing an Army Air Force fighter squadron to participate in a combat action.

Although this purported message, with its catch words "reach and destroy," has been cited and repeated often by still other writers, no researcher has yet been able to find any record or proof of any discussion or exchange of communications about Yamamoto or personal approval of the ambush between Admiral Nimitz, Secretary Knox, or President Roosevelt in any navy or presidential files.

Capt. Roger Pineau, noted naval researcher and historian, stated:

> Naval archives, the National Archives, and the FDR Library at Hyde Park reveal no record that Roosevelt's approval was requested, or, in fact, that there was any communication on the subject between Washington and Nimitz.
>
> President Roosevelt left Washington by train on 13 April for a sixteen-day tour of southwestern states. During that time, his only related messages from Washington were on 18 April telling of Japanese planes downed in the Shortland area, and a follow-up message next day noting that Yamamoto may have been in one of the planes.[19]

While the messages flowed back and forth between Pearl Harbor and Nimitz's subordinate commanders in the South Pacific, Mitscher enthusiastically tackled the assignment to get Yamamoto. He knew that eight members of two of Jimmy Doolittle's crews had been captured, tortured, and starved by the Japanese and then three of them had been executed; one died later of starvation. Several of Halsey's own pilots had been captured and had also been treated cruelly. The opportunity to shoot down Yamamoto in retaliation for Japanese cruelty was a rare one that could not be lost.[20]

But there were many other decisions that had to be made before assigning the mission. What type of aircraft could fly the distance from Guadalcanal to Bougainville, engage in a fight, and return? How many would be in commission? What type of aircraft would Yamamoto be flying in—the Betty medium bomber or the older Sally? What about the hundred or so Zero fighters at Kahili? Would a number of them be sent up from Kahili to escort their leader to Ballale as American fighters had flown out to escort Secretary of the Navy Frank Knox when he had made an inspection visit to Guadalcanal the previous February?

According to Admiral Mitscher's biographer, Mitscher called marine Brig. Gen. Field Harris, his chief of staff, and told him to draft a plan for the interception. Harris brought into the operations dugout Comdr. Stanhope C. Ring, deputy chief of staff for operations, to make preliminary time-and-distance calculations. Next, marine Col. Edwin L. Pugh, of Fighter Command, was summoned to discuss the type of plane to use on the attack. More staff members were brought in, among them: Army Air Force Lt. Col. Aaron W. Tyer, base commander on Fighter Two; Comdr. William A. "Gus" Read, assistant chief of staff for administration; and marine Lt. Col. L. Samuel Moore, Pugh's assistant. Mitscher's biographer tells what happened next:

"All conceivable holes were plugged. Read, who did not know about the broken codes, suggested that, since the information about the Yamamoto visit might have been picked up from gossip in Rabaul and therefore unreliable as to detail, the surest method might be to strafe the small boat in which the admiral would ride after landing. Harris said such an idea had been considered and dismissed."[21]

Mitscher recalled that Read was concerned that the Japanese might be enticing the American fighters into an ambush. Mitscher rejected that notion promptly because of the source of the coded top secret message sent to Yamamoto's subordinate units.

The official history of Marine Corps aviation in World War II tells a slightly different, self-serving story:

Admiral Mitscher called in the exec of his ComAirSols Fighter Command, Lieut. Colonel L. S. Moore. "Sam," he said, "work me up a plan to get this bird." Some officers wanted to nail Yamamoto in his launch as he motored to Ballale after the arrival at Kahili; but this was discarded in favor of an aerial kill. Moore assigned to the job 18 P-38s—the longest-legged fighters in the Command, the 6 best shots in the "trigger section," 12 more as cover—commanded by

Maj. John W. Mitchell, USA. The job of plotting a course from Henderson Field to southern Bougainville was handed to Fighter Command's operations officer, Maj. John P. Condon.

Condon's course sent the Army flyers outside The Slot, along the coast of New Georgia. Moore instructed the pilots to fly at 50 feet, off the coast of New Georgia, to try to avoid radar detection. The instructions read: "Destroy the target at any cost." That, said Moore, meant ramming Yamamoto's Betty if necessary. "And," he said seven years later, "I believe they would have done it if necessary."[22]

Arguments ensued as navy and marine officers on Mitscher's staff came and went, each giving their opinions. There seemed to be consensus on only one point: The P-38s of the Army Air Force's 339th Fighter Squadron based on the Fighter Two strip about two miles away were the only fighter aircraft available that could fly the distance, make the intercept, engage in combat for a short time, and return. And that was possible only if at least one large 310-gallon belly fuel tank was installed on each aircraft, together with the regular 165-gallon tanks. It was agreed that the 339th's squadron commander should be assigned the mission. Army Air Force Maj. John W. Mitchell, the 339th's commander, already an ace with eight victories to his credit, was summoned to Mitscher's operations dugout.

2
THE CODEBREAKERS

*T*HE SUCCESS OF THE MISSION ABOUT TO BE assigned to the 339th Fighter Squadron on Guadalcanal would depend on the validity of the information gleaned from the coded "whispers" exchanged between the commander in chief of the Japanese Combined Fleet and his subordinate units. How reliable was the information? How was it possible that U.S. Navy cryptographers could decipher and translate the enemy's top secret code so accurately and quickly?

It is generally agreed among military historians that reading the secret messages of an enemy is the most important form of intelligence information that a nation can have. It is more accurate than information provided by spies and it has been shown to have great influence on a nation's strategy and politics in both war and peace.

As one author observed,

. . . the key figures of World War II intelligence were seldom mysterious agents lurking in the back streets of Tokyo or Singapore. More often it was the hollow-eyed, unshaven cryptologists or photo reconnaissance analysts deep in a basement or windowless room, surrounded by the clack of IBM sorters and tabulator machines or the stench of darkroom chemicals—it was men (and women) of this sort who were the intelligence aces of World War II. Far from the fighting fronts, in Pearl Harbor, Melbourne, New Delhi, and Washington, small groups of seldom-seen, overburdened, relentlessly driven men and women labored over the greatest intelligence feat of the war: the recovery, decryption, and analysis of coded messages.[1]

And so it was that almost all of the messages flashed between the top Japanese naval units and their leaders after Pearl Harbor were intercepted and read by the U.S. Navy's outstanding codebreakers. Their work, unheralded and still mostly classified, was the secret weapon that could be said to have won the war in the Pacific; certainly, it gave the Americans unprecedented access to enemy plans and unit movements. Without a shadow of a doubt, this knowledge shortened the war and saved many lives on both sides. America owes much to a small band of dedicated men and women who were content to remain anonymous and fight a secret war on which the fate of the country rested.

Americans were relatively inexperienced in decoding diplomatic and military messages. For three centuries, from 1540 to 1844, the British government had three linked organizations—the Secret Office, the Private Office, and the Deciphering Branch—that opened letters, deciphered their contents, resealed them, and passed them on to their addressees. During the reign of Queen Elizabeth I, less than fifty years after the offices had been set up by Henry VII, it caused Mary, Queen of Scots, to literally lose her head. Intercepted letters between Mary and Antony Babington indicated that they were discussing Queen Elizabeth's assassination, a conspiracy punishable by an executioner's ax.

Early in the eighteenth century, the interception of mail was legalized and approved by the English courts when there was deemed sufficient cause to suspect that treasonous acts were being contemplated. The practice continued until 1844 when the three offices were closed. It was not until 1914 that a message-reading office was opened again in London known simply as Room 40 O.B. This organization's ability to intercept and decode German communications played a vital role in winning World War I for the Allies.

The post–World War I years saw the development of several kinds of cryptographic machines that assisted in enciphering and deciphering coded messages in the United States. In the winter of 1917–18, an employee of AT&T, Gilbert Vernam, proposed an ingenious way to encipher messages by "scrambling" them in the transmission process. Another AT&T employee, L. F. Morehouse, improved on the basic patent.

The man who truly advanced the state of the art in coding and decoding was William F. Friedman, a dapper genius whose primary interest was genetics. An American, he trained a few cryptographers in Great Britain before World War I ended and played a significant role in solving one of the most famous field ciphers in military history—the ADFGVX cipher used by the German high command in March 1918.

Employed by the U.S. Army in the States in the early 1920s, Friedman solved the secrets of several cipher machines and perfected a way to test them by statistical and mathematical means. He also conceived a principle by which the wiring of a coding/decoding device could be reconstructed.

Meanwhile, the U.S. State Department had its own secret organization whose roots went back to the John Quincy Adams administration under the title of Committee of Secret Correspondence. In 1867, the first code room was established in the State Department and in 1882, the Navy Department established the Office of Naval Intelligence (ONI) to keep the department informed of the characteristics, ships, installations, and policies of other navies. By 1910, the State Department had twenty-nine clerks and "telegraphists."

It was during World War I that the name of Herbert O. Yardley entered the code-breaking saga. Born in the Midwest, the son of a railroad agent, he became exceptionally adept with the Morse code and practiced for hours on end in slack time at his father's station. When he graduated from public school he became a Western Union telegrapher and moved to Washington in 1913 as a civil service telegrapher in the State Department at $17.50 a week.

Yardley became interested in the coded messages that crossed his desk and began reading everything he could find in the Library of Congress about ciphering. He learned quickly and began deciphering State Department messages for the fun of it and was amazed at how quickly he could do it.

Yardley left the State Department and joined the Signal Corps of the army. He proposed the establishment of a supersecret cipher bureau under the intelligence division. The idea was quickly adopted and an office was created under the title of Military Intelligence Service (MIS). Yardley was put in charge and organized MIS into five subsections which included encoding outgoing and deciphering incoming army messages. One subsection, called the Code and Cipher Solution subsection, was formed to crack the codes and ciphers of the country's enemies, the first organization of its kind to be firmly established within the U.S. government.

When World War I was over, MIS was disbanded; that is, all except the supersecret Code and Cipher Solution office. However, funds were nearly impossible to come by, especially to run an army organization that had to remain hidden if it was to preserve its underground status. The solution was to place the office under the State Department and move it to New York City. Yardley chose to refer to the organization as the "Black Chamber" while others referred to it as "Yardley's bureau."

In 1919, Yardley was asked if he could unravel Japanese codes. It was obvious then that Japan was becoming a potentially strong adversary in the Pacific and should not be allowed to build a threatening military establishment without Americans knowing about it. A confident man, Yardley promised he would do so within a year or resign.

Although he could not read or speak Japanese, Yardley broke the Japanese diplomatic code and on January 12, 1920, forwarded the first translation of a decrypted Japanese message to Washington.

It was at this time that the Navy Department's ONI gained respected status. Five ONI agents broke into the office of a Japanese consul and photographed the Japanese top secret naval code book. Just as Yardley had succeeded in breaking the Japanese diplomatic code, the navy now had possession of the Japanese naval code. It was contained in the "Red Book," named for the red binder in which the navy kept the code book's photographed pages. This code was given the official designation of "JN-1" because it was the first Japanese navy code obtained by the Americans.

It took five years before the Red Book's contents were fully decoded. Much credit goes to Lt. Comdr. (later Rear Adm.) Ellis M. Zacharias, the U.S. Navy's most capable Japanese linguist. Meanwhile, in 1923, navy Lt. Laurence F. Safford was assigned to Washington and placed in charge of the newly created Research Desk of the Code and Signal Section in the Office of Naval Communications. Safford was known as a "promoter" with a penchant for invention and gadgetry but had no cryptographic skills or experience.

Safford's job was to construct machines and systems to protect the security of the fleet's communications. After a year in the job, Safford persuaded his superiors to let him set up listening stations in key locations to intercept Japanese radio transmissions and thus put the Red Book to practical use. As a result of his initiative, the first Pacific electronic monitoring station was set up on Guam. A small staff of cryptographers was hired and the Navy thus established its own "Black Chamber."

One of the civilians hired was a "Miss Aggie" whose full name—Agnes Driscoll—was kept secret for many years. She succeeded in breaking the Japanese flag officer (admiral's) code system. This was designated the "AD Code" to distinguish it from the "JN" system. A noted historian reports:

"The importance of Miss Aggie's feat cannot be overstated. Since it was the system the Imperial Navy reserved for the concealment of its admirals' dispatch traffic, the messages it was supposed to cloak contained data of the utmost secrecy and confidence. The compromised code, thus became, in Safford's words, 'our main source of information on the Japanese Navy.' Its solution was the crowning achievement of the Navy's entire cryptological effort, and it was especially astonishing and gratifying since it came so early in the game."[2]

After this breakthrough, the navy improved and extended its

monitoring facilities to listen in on Japanese transmissions closer to the source. In those between-wars years, radio transmissions were poor between ship and shore and between ships. There were numerous gaps or "skip zones" which made it impossible to communicate with all stations and ships at all times. Interception of those transmissions was likewise difficult.

Additional monitoring stations were set up in the Philippines and Shanghai, in addition to Guam. In 1927, Commander Zacharias conceived the idea of "ambush by radio" during Japanese naval maneuvers by continuously monitoring all the Japanese messages while he was on board the Marblehead, a navy destroyer. Using the stations on Guam and Shanghai as backups, he had continuous surveillance over the maneuver messages, even when the Japanese suddenly switched to a new code just before the maneuvers began. Working around the clock, Safford's crew in Washington broke the new code quickly and coverage was uninterrupted.

American cryptology suffered a setback when Secretary of State Henry L. Stimson, serving in the Hoover administration, was briefed on the Black Chamber and Yardley's ability to read Japan's secret radio transmissions. On the eve of the arms limitation parley in London in June, 1930, he was appalled at the thought and rebelled in outrage. He told his staff that "the way to make men trustworthy is to trust them." He felt that the whole concept of message interception was a violation of this principle and declared that "Gentlemen do not read each other's mail!" He ordered the State Department funds promptly withdrawn from all of Yardley's activities.[3]

Disillusioned and bitter, Yardley was out of a job. He contacted the Japanese ambassador Tsuneo Matsudaira in Washington and offered to sell the secrets he had so painstakingly learned for seven thousand dollars. The Japanese thus obtained all they needed to know of Yardley's codebreaking methods, his work sheets, and solutions to other codes, including those of Great Britain.

Stimson's decision to kill all cryptological work included the navy. The cryptographic office in ONI was closed and its budget transferred elsewhere.

Meanwhile, the U.S. Army did not feel any restraint and

suddenly became interested through the initiatives of William F. Friedman, the man who had coined the word *cryptanalysis* and had been quietly working in the War Department at his specialty since returning from England after World War I. Friedman lobbied successfully for recognition of his codebreaking abilities and in the spring of 1929, the Signal Intelligence Service (SIS) was created. Its purpose was clearly spelled out and included "interception of enemy radio and wire traffic, the goniometric [a goniometer is an instrument for measuring angles] location of enemy radio stations, the solution of intercepted enemy code and cipher messages, and laboratory arrangements for the employment and detection of secret ink."[4]

The cryptoanalysis community was jarred badly in 1931 when Yardley published a book entitled *The American Black Chamber* which revealed many of the codebreaking secrets he was privy to during his tenure in the business. He rationalized that he was being patriotic by writing the book so that the United States "may protect herself from the prying eyes of skillful foreign cryptographers." In the preface, he stated, "It is my aim to unfold in a simple dispassionate way the intimate details of a secret organization that I fostered for the American Government; an organization which, at its height of power, employed 165 men and women."[5]

The government did not indict Yardley for any security violations; he later published other books about his experiences in codebreaking. Apparently, the government never found out about his arrangements with the Japanese.

In 1932, Friedman invented a cryptographic system that he patented. He followed this with other patents and the end result was a machine that became one of the most used deciphering devices of World War II. He also invented a new machine which incorporated a message-authenticating system with a keyboard, perforated card control, and a mechanism like an adding machine. It was the first machine to use an IBM card for cryptographic keying purposes.

Although this machine was yet another technological breakthrough in the science of cryptology, the shortage of funds before World War II prevented its being manufactured in any quantity. In collaboration with his navy counterparts, however, Friedman was able to get the machine built by Teletype Corporation in Chicago under the name of ECM Mark II for the navy. The army called it Sigaba. In *The Man Who Broke Purple*, author Ronald Clark describes the machine:

> It was large, making up three separate 300-pound loads, consumed much electricity, and could be moved only by truck. It was used in all theaters of operations at the highest levels of command, and even by President Roosevelt in Washington. So great was the importance attached to it that none of America's allies was allowed even to see it, let alone have it, not even the British, who operated their own electric cipher machine known as Typex. However, in order to ease communications between U.S. and British forces, adapters were developed so that messages could be sent in cipher between Sigaba and Typex.[6]

In 1935, another cryptographic breakthrough occurred. ONI sleuths obtained information that allowed the Research Desk to construct a copy of the Japanese cipher machine dubbed the "Red Machine." This machine reduced the work of cryptanalysts and speeded up the decoding process. By this time, Comdr. Safford, after a stint of sea duty, had returned to Washington and was placed in charge of the Communications Security Section in the Office of Naval Communications, labeled simply OP-20-G on the organizational chart.

Safford's job was to develop a machine-based crypto system to ensure the security of the navy's own secret messages. In addition, he was to continue to keep up with the Japanese naval code system. His section was given increased personnel and better facilities.

In the army, William Friedman and his staff remained small. However, in 1938, it became increasingly clear that army and navy cryptographers should compare notes when the Japanese introduced a new cipher which was tied to a machine radically different from the Red Machine. Safford and Friedman shared information with the approval of their military superiors. The understanding between ONI and SIS was that Friedman and his staff would concentrate on solving the new Japanese cipher and construct the machine. The navy fed the intercepts to the army and shared what it knew about the Red Machine. However, nothing seemed to work; the new code seemed impossible to break.

Finally, a casual remark by a young cryptologist opened up a possibility that led to the solution and construction of a crypto machine in a mere forty-eight hours. The breakthrough on this, designated the Type No. 97 machine, was of extraordinary importance and is a tribute to the ingenuity and dedication of America's codebreakers. Ladislas Farago commented:

"It was nothing short of miraculous that they succeeded in building a machine the prototype of which they had never seen and whose cryptographic principles and components were unknown to them. They did it from the laboriously gained clues of the cracked cipher the original machine had produced. Henceforth, this strange new gadget, which was given the designation Purple, would do the job that it would have taken dozens of men and women weeks, if not months, to achieve without the machine."[7]

The word *Magic* was chosen as a cover name for the entire operation involving all of Japan's diplomatic crypto systems—the Red Machine, Purple, and the other series of codes and ciphers which the army and navy had cracked previously. Farago explains:

" 'Magic,' when used with a capital M, denoted the whole operation in all its various phases; 'magic' with the lower case 'm' stood for the decrypted intercept which it produced. The term was also designed as a security classification, higher than 'Top Secret.' In the quaint vernacular of the project, the handful of people cleared for 'Magic' were dubbed Ultras."[8]

The Magic operation was a closely guarded secret within the military. Gen. George C. Marshall, army chief of staff, restricted access to the decrypted dispatches only to those who had genuine need to know the information contained in the "ultrasecret" intercepts. Magic was the exclusive property of the War and Navy Departments. Neither the White House nor the State Department was given access, probably because of the fear of leaks by political appointees who were not security conscious. Even Gen. Henry H. "Hap" Arnold, chief of the Army Air

Forces, was not told about it. The sole civilian in the navy cleared for Ultra was Secretary of the Navy Frank Knox; only six navy officers were cleared for access.

Four Purple machines were constructed in late 1940 and set up in a special section in the Navy Department. They were so successful that cryptographers were decoding Japanese messages sometimes before their own clerks could do so at the Japanese embassy a few blocks away. The operation really owed its success to the cooperation between personnel of the Army Signal Corps and the Navy Communications Office which enabled both services and their stations in the States and Hawaii and the Navy stations overseas to ensure continuous coverage and message interception.

In the summer of 1941, the U.S. Navy's codebreaking capabilities in the Pacific were focused in the basement of the administration building of CINCPAC headquarters at the submarine base at Pearl Harbor. Comdr. Joseph J. Rochefort was in charge of a radio intelligence unit designated Fleet Radio Unit, Pacific, more commonly known as FRUPAC. In addition to deciphering enemy messages, Rochefort's unit kept track of all ship movements in the Pacific and weather information and forecasts.

After the attack on Pearl Harbor, FRUPAC settled down for a long war. OP-20-G assigned ten officers and twenty enlisted men to FRUPAC to attempt to crack all Japanese naval codes. About sixty men were assigned to outlying stations. This relatively small cadre kept the operation going twenty-four hours a day throughout the war without letup. One author noted that the men were "all people of quick intelligence, absolute devotion to their task, and—almost always—of highly idiosyncratic temperaments. . . . Like troglodytes, they inhabited a kind of underworld cellar, approached only by two locked doors and in a permanent state of shabby disorder amid which heaped files and the ejections of IBM machines struggled—as the occupants were indeed doing—for survival."[9]

The personal attributes of a good cryptographer, according to W. J. Holmes, who served on the FRUPAC staff, were: "He needs only time, patience, an infinite capacity for work, a mind that can focus on a problem to the exclusion of everything else, a photographic memory, the inability to drop an unsolved problem, and a large volume of traffic."[10]

There was a time after Pearl Harbor when neither FRUPAC nor OP-20-G could read enough of the enemy's messages. The JN codes had been changed many times since the original JN-1 code of the Red Book days. By December 7, 1941, the Japanese naval code signal series were now up to JN-25. FRUPAC, assisted by Hypo, a station on Oahu, Station George on Guam (before its capture by the Japanese), Cast on Corregidor (before the Philippines fell), and Belconnen in Australia all had contributed to the eventual JN-25 interception and decoding. The ability to intercept, decipher, and interpret the enemy's top secret naval messages, plus the fact that the Japanese believed their top naval code could never be broken, were prime factors in the eventual outcome of the war in the Pacific.

As the war progressed, so did the capabilities of FRUPAC in Hawaii and OP-20-G in Washington. The navy and marine officers assigned remained anonymous and could not discuss their work until many years afterward. The list includes W. J. Holmes, Joseph J. Rochefort, Alva B. Lasswell, Wesley A. Wright, Thomas H. Dyer, Edwin T. Layton, Joseph Finnegan, and others. Each played a vital role in improving the units' capabilities. By the beginning of 1943, their expert analysis and their decryption of Japanese naval messages, assisted by the navy's worldwide communications intelligence network, gave Admiral Nimitz a nearly perfect view of where the enemy naval forces were located and what their intentions were.

The protection of a codebreaking capability is just as important as protecting the results of codebreaking. Any mention in the American news media of the military's capability to read the message traffic of the enemy was closely monitored by the FBI, navy, and army communications security agents. After the Battle of Midway, it was feared the cryptographic secrets of both services were in jeopardy when on June 7, 1942, the Chicago *Daily Tribune* published a news item by Stanley Johnston on its front page headlined: "NAVY HAD WORD OF JAP PLAN TO STRIKE AT SEA. KNEW DUTCH HARBOR WAS A FEINT." The article continued:

> The strength of the Japanese forces with which the American navy is battling somewhere west of Midway Island in what is believed to be the greatest naval battle of the war was well known in American naval circles several days before the battle began, reliable sources in the naval intelligence disclosed here tonight.
>
> The navy learned of the gathering of the powerful Japanese units soon after they put forth from their bases, it was said. Although their purpose was not specifically known, the information in the hands of the navy department was so definite that a feint at some American base, to be accompanied by a serious effort to invade and occupy another base, was predicted. Guesses were even made that Dutch Harbor and Midway Island might be targets. . . .

The article contained a very accurate listing of the enemy forces involved. Although the article contained no mention that the United States had broken any codes, there was such a detailed account of what the U.S. Navy knew beforehand that security experts felt sure that the Japanese would learn that their top secret naval code had been compromised. To anyone with even a slight knowledge of navy affairs, the association was clear.

Johnston had been unwisely shown Nimitz's intelligence dispatch about the Japanese forces being assembled for the Midway operation by an officer aboard the cruiser *Chester*. The navy called for a grand jury investigation but finally agreed that it should be called off in the interest of secrecy. However, when the episode appeared to be forgotten, a U.S. representative made a speech in the House of Representatives admonishing the *Chicago Tribune* for publishing the story. He said that somehow the navy had secured and broken the secret code of the Japanese navy and American boys would die as a result of the revelation. *American Legion* magazine commented that "Navy officials, after they recovered from apoplectic fits, held their breath again. And again Japan either missed the item or simply failed to believe it."[11]

Although the Japanese JN25 naval code was changed on August 1, 1942, it was determined that this was a regular, planned code change. There was never any indication that the change was due to the newspaper's revelation.

By the beginning of 1943, the skills, determination and dedication of a few army, navy, and marine codebreakers had honed the science of cryptology to a fine point; the U.S. Navy had a definite edge over the enemy in the Pacific.

The need to protect the fact that an enemy code had been broken often presented a dilemma. Should the information obtained through a message decryption be acted upon if the action would reveal the capability to decode?

Admiral Yamamoto's fate rested on Admiral Nimitz's answer to this dilemma. Since he had answered in the affirmative by approving an aerial ambush of his enemy opposite number, he had indicated he was willing to take that risk.

3

A MILLION-TO-ONE MISSION

MAJ. JOHN W. MITCHELL, NEWLY APPOINTED commander of the 339th Fighter Squadron, was lying on a cot in his squadron's headquarters tent on Guadalcanal's Fighter Two airstrip trying to get some sleep between missions on the afternoon of April 17. He had never really adjusted to the heat, humidity, and insects of Guadalcanal even though he had been born and raised in Mississippi. In addition, he had occasional bouts of the "trots" as did all the pilots of his unit on the beleagured, blood-stained island.

The 339th was Mitchell's first command. In spite of the less-than-humble living conditions on Guadalcanal, he enjoyed the responsibilities of leading a band of competent, aggressive fighter pilots and the thrill of combat. Strong-willed, confident, efficient, and direct in manner, the soft-spoken pilot with the strong southern drawl was widely liked and respected by all who served with him.

Pilots flying fighters from Guadalcanal in 1942–43 had special problems to contend with because of a shortage of supplies. They lived in tents without floors. The food was far from appetizing and in short supply, as was fresh water. There were no refrigeration units available; consequently, there was no way to preserve fresh meat.

"And there was no whiskey for combat pilots," Mitchell reported. "There was whiskey on some of the islands, but we didn't seem to be able to get hold of much for some reason. I think a certain amount is all right. After a day when the boys have had a pretty tough job, when they are ready to go to sleep they can take two or three shots and get a much better rest."[1]

The mosquitoes were as much an enemy as the Japanese. Malaria was fairly widespread. There was a continual shortage of ammunition, aircraft parts, and instruments; oxygen, so vital to the P-38s on long, high-altitude missions, was not always readily available.

The pilots flew on overwater missions for months without inflatable rubber dinghies to use if they were forced down in the shark-infested ocean. When a few dinghies arrived on the island, the pilots would cut cards to see who would get them. The assumption was that if someone without a raft went down, another pilot would circle and throw his raft out to the downed pilot.

Pilots did not have jungle packs with survival materials in the backs of their parachutes. These packs had a fishing kit, machete, nonmeltable chocolate, a waterproof matchbox, and a small pocket knife. Mitchell had heard of them but never saw one during his Guadalcanal days.

As Mitchell drowsed, Lt. Col. Henry Vicellio, 347th group commander, poked his head under the tent flap.

"Mitch, they want you over at the 'Opium Den' [the pilots' name for the Fighter Command dugout] at Henderson. They've got something for you."

Mitchell got in his jeep with Lieutenant Colonel Vicellio beside him, picked up Maj. Louis Kittel, and drove to the pilots' bivouac area. Vicellio and Mitchell told the group of pilots lounging around to lay off the drinking that night because they had a big mission coming up the next day.

Just as they started to pull away, Vicellio said to Capt. Tom Lanphier, "Why don't you go with us over to Henderson because you'll probably be on it." Lanphier nodded and got aboard.

Mitchell drove carefully over the rutted coral road from Fighter Two to Henderson Field two miles away. Henderson, codenamed Cactus, had been the scene of bitter battles for weeks as the Japanese tried desperately to hold on to this strategic island at the southeastern end of the Solomon Islands. They had finally been blasted off Guadalcanal in February 1943, yet continued to stage frequent air raids, sometimes in great numbers, trying to blunt the growing threat to their southern perimeter which was being continually squeezed and pressured by American air and naval power. Now firmly in American hands in the spring of 1943, Guadalcanal had three airfields which were bases for Army Air Forces, navy, and marine aircraft. Henderson was used by the transports and bombers. Fighter One, southeast of Henderson, was used by the Marine fighters. Fighter Two, northwest of Henderson, was for the Army Air Force fighters and sometimes the marines.

Mitchell, Vicellio, and Lanphier entered the small, stuffy dugout crowded with navy, marine, and army officers. Lanphier recalled that every "brass hat" on the island was there and they had to elbow their way in. The dugout, unsophisticated as it was, was the operations center for Adm. Marc Mitscher, raw-boned veteran of several naval battles who had commanded the *Hornet*, which had launched Jimmy Doolittle the year before on his celebrated raid on Japan. Mitscher as commander of all air operations in the Solomon Islands area was responsible for planning and dispatching all air strikes against the Japanese. Among those present were top members of Mitscher's staff, all with their own ideas of how the mission should be flown and how and where Yamamoto should be intercepted and assassinated.

"When we got there," Mitchell recalled,

the dugout was crowded and everybody seemed to be talking at once. Maj. John P. Condon, a marine officer, handed me a radio message from Admiral Halsey. The message said that Admiral Yamamoto, commander in chief of the Combined Japanese fleet, was going to make a trip from Rabaul to one of their bases at the southern tip of Bougainville, a trip of 315 miles. It gave the exact time he was going to land at Ballale, a small island just off the southern tip of Bougainville, on the morning of the next day. He was going to visit his men there and travel to Shortland Island, a nearby troop base, by submarine chaser before returning to Rabaul. He would be flying in a medium bomber, probably a Betty, and be escorted by six Zeros. Known for his punctuality, there was no doubt that Yamamoto would be on time. Capt. William Morrison, an army officer, had lived in Japan and assured us that the admiral was widely known for holding to a precise schedule once it was set.

There was a big discussion—a real hassle—as to how to get Yamamoto. The reason we were called in was because we were flying P-38s, the only fighter planes that could fly the distance from Guadalcanal to Bougainville and back. The navy and marine pilots would never have let us army pilots in on a mission like that if any of their F4F and F4U fighters could have made the trip.[2]

Mitchell couldn't get too many words into the discussion while the navy and marine pilots were arguing back and forth how they thought Mitchell should fly the mission. The argument boiled down to two concepts: intercept Yamamoto's plane in the air or try to dive-bomb and strafe him on the submarine chaser en route to the island outpost. Most thought Mitchell should strafe and bomb the subchaser after Yamamoto was aboard.

"Being an air force type," Mitchell told the author,

I didn't know one boat from another, a subchaser from a sub. When I finally got a chance to put a word in, I told them that and added a second reason for not trying to get him on a boat: Even if we sank the boat, he might survive and take to a raft or swim to shore. Besides that, the Japs had seventy-five fighters only about fifteen miles from where Yamamoto was supposed to land. We would have to be over the target too long trying to get in trail to strafe a boat in the water. If they sent up fighters to escort the admiral, we'd be in a poor position to defend ourselves at such a low altitude and still get any hits on the target, assuming we could identify it in the first place.

The debate went on for a long time. I argued against the

navy guys and gave my reasons for trying an air intercept. Lanphier backed me up. There was an obvious stalemate. Finally, Admiral Mitscher, who hadn't said much up to now, shushed everybody up and said, quietly, "Since Mitchell's got to do the job, let's let him do it his way." That ended *that* discussion.[3]

Mitchell was told that 310-gallon drop tanks were being flown in that night from air force units at Port Moresby, New Guinea, to replace the 165-gallon drop tanks normally carried under the wings of the P-38. There would not be enough to put two on each aircraft but there would be at least one for each plane which would be mounted under one wing opposite the smaller tank on the other wing.

When Mitchell was asked if there was anything else the navy could do for him, he replied, "Yeah. Get me a good compass. The fluxgate and the magnetic compasses in the P-38 aren't reliable and can't be trusted because they can't be swung properly. The only time we know if they're anywhere near accurate is when we line up for takeoff because we know the runway heading."

He was told not to worry, a good ship's compass would be sent to Fighter Two and promptly installed in his aircraft.

Mitchell was briefed on the antiaircraft emplacements on Bougainville. There were about seventy-five Zero fighters stationed at Kahili on the southern tip of the island and it was possible that a large number of them might take off to escort their boss to Ballale. When Secretary of the Navy Frank Knox had visited Guadalcanal the previous February, the units on the island had sent their fighters out to maximum range to escort him in. When he left, they escorted him as far as they could go. The Japanese could be expected to do the same thing for the ranking man in their navy.

Mitchell was given the weather forecast for the next day: clear with haze limiting visibility to a few miles over the water.

It was late afternoon when Mitchell let Lanphier off at his living quarters and drove to his squadron operations tent to figure out the details of a mission that, if successful, would go down in the books as the longest aerial intercept in military aviation history. Mitchell didn't know much about Yamamoto except that his quarry was the top man in the Japanese navy and a brilliant strategist who had masterminded the attack on Pearl Harbor. He knew that he was considered one of America's "Most Wanted" war criminals. It was a mission certainly worth the risk.

"I was full of confidence in those days," Mitchell told the author,

> and tackled this job as just another mission to be flown. I had, on several occasions, asked to take a fighter sweep up to the southern tip of Bougainville as we often had reports that there were usually a number of flying boats and lots of shipping in the harbor. My requests had always been denied as it was felt the risk of losing some of our precious P-38s was too great.
>
> While I was aware of Yamamoto's position in the Japanese naval heirarchy, my thoughts at this point were that our chances of getting him were *very* slim. I was more excited about the possibility of running into a bunch of enemy planes than the possibility of downing Yamamoto.[4]

Joined by Lt. Joseph E. McGuigan, a navy intelligence officer, and Capt. William Morrison, his army counterpart, Mitchell laid out a map of the Solomon Islands on a table in the mess tent and studied it by lamp light. There were many questions to be answered: What route should they fly? What altitude? What time should they take off? Was the weather forecast going to hold? How could they avoid radar contact and the Japanese coastwatchers? Who should fly the mission? What tactics should they use at the interception point? Would Yamamoto's flight be flying direct from Rabaul to Ballale or on a dogleg course to avoid possible interception? How long could the P-38s loiter in the area if Yamamoto was late? How would they handle the situation if those enemy fighters at Kahili came up to greet the admiral and escort him to his destination? Would those large fuel tanks arrive at Fighter Two in time? If so, could the P-38 mechanics get them fitted in time? How many aircraft would be in commission?

Mitchell had been handed a small strip map with course lines drawn on it by Maj. John P. Condon, a marine air staff officer, but he didn't trust the airspeed, distance, and time figures. Condon didn't fly the air force P-38s and didn't know at what indicated airspeed Mitchell would set his throttles for long-range cruise, nor could he know then at what altitude Mitchell planned to fly.

By taking Yamamoto's takeoff and arrival times, Mitchell approximated the airspeed of his bomber at 180 mph or 3 miles a minute and presumed it was a Betty bomber. "Strictly a guess," he says, "because no one seemed to know for sure." He then backed off that speed and calculated the point, about 30 miles from Yamamoto's landing point at Balalle, where he wanted to intercept the flight.

Mitchell figured the P-38 zero-wind ground speed using long-range cruise control at 200 mph. With a wind drift correction, based on a quartering 5-knot wind "off the port bow" on the first leg as he had been told to expect, he estimated they would average 197 mph to the target area.

There had been some talk about circumventing the island chain so they wouldn't be seen or heard and thus avoid detection by Japanese coastwatchers or radar. Mitchell agreed that the flight should be entirely over water and out of sight of any land areas but neither Condon nor anyone else at the meeting was able to make a reliable flight plan that Mitchell could accept. Several had tried and made rough sketches but Mitchell wasn't satisfied. None of them were P-38 pilots and therefore they were not familiar with the plane's performance capabilities.

The small strip map showed the area from Guadalcanal to Bougainville but the scale was so small it didn't show many details of the land areas. Besides, they would be flying at least fifty miles offshore of any Japanese-held territory. As Mitchell said, "each wave looks like another one." There would be no landmarks to use as checkpoints; it would have to be dead reckoning all the way—flying only by airspeed, clock, and compass until landfall off the Bougainville coast.

Mitchell told the author, "At that time, I figured the odds at about a thousand to one that we could make a successful intercept at that distance. Today, after years of thinking about it, I'd make that a million to one."

One thing that bothered Mitchell was how anyone knew for

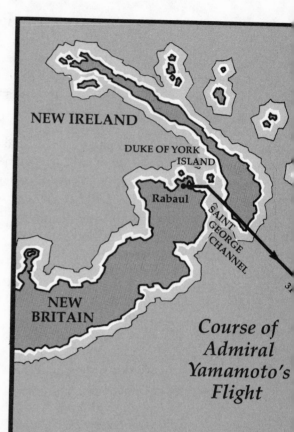

NEW IRELAND

DUKE OF YORK
ISLAND

Rabaul

SAINT GEORGE CHANNEL

NEW BRITAIN

Course of Admiral Yamamoto's Flight

SOLOMON SEA

Major Mitchell planned five legs for the interception of Admiral Yamamoto's bomber. Four legs with times, headings, and distances are shown above. The fifth leg on a 90-degree heading was to have been followed by the top flight of twelve aircraft after crossing the coastline. They were to climb and circle then continue on the east side of the island in case the Yamamoto bomber chose that route to the destination. (Illustration by Wayne Shipp)

Leg No. 1 – 265⁰ - 183 mi = 55 min.

Leg No. 2 – 290⁰ -88 mi. = 27 min.

Leg No. 3 – 305⁰ -125 mi. = 38 min.

Leg No. 4 – 020⁰ -16 mi. = 5 mi. + 16 min. for climb

Leg No. 5 – 090⁰ - 69 mi. = 21 min.

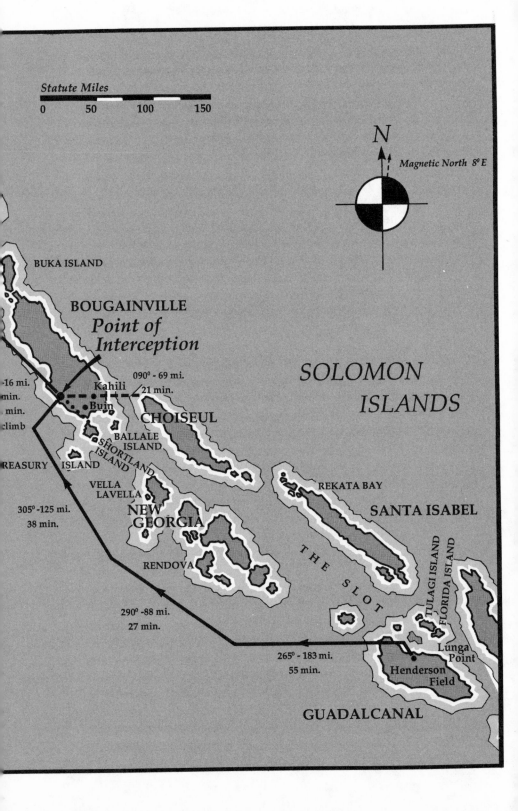

Statute Miles

0   50   100   150

N

Magnetic North 8⁰ E

BUKA ISLAND

BOUGAINVILLE
*Point of
Interception*

SOLOMON
ISLANDS

-16 mi.
min.
min.
climb

090⁰ - 69 mi.
21 min.

Kahili
Buin

CHOISEUL

BALLALE
ISLAND
SHORTLAND
ISLAND

TREASURY ISLAND

VELLA
LAVELLA

305⁰ -125 mi.
38 min.

NEW
GEORGIA

REKATA BAY

SANTA ISABEL

RENDOVA

T H E   S L O T

290⁰ -88 mi.
27 min.

265⁰ - 183 mi.
55 min.

TULAGI ISLAND
FLORIDA ISLAND

Lunga
Point

Henderson
Field

GUADALCANAL

sure that Yamamoto would be at or near the place he wanted to intercept him:

"The only assurance we had was from Captain Morrison, the army intelligence officer who had lived in Japan for a number of years. He reiterated a number of times that the Japanese were noted for their punctuality and that Yamamoto was well known publicly for keeping precise schedules, that it was an obsession with him. He said the one thing we could count on was that Yamamoto would be on time."[5]

Mitchell labored over the map while McGuigan and Morrison carefully drew lines and double-checked Mitchell's estimates. Ignoring Condon's map, Mitchell plotted the outbound courses and calculated the best intercept point to be about thirty miles or about ten minutes flying time for the bomber out of Ballale. Since the admiral was due at Ballale at 0945, the interception should take place at 0935 Guadalcanal time, 0735 Japanese time. He guessed that the bomber would be flying a direct course from Rabaul and that the bomber with the escorting fighters would be descending from about five thousand feet at that point. "If I had followed Condon's route," Mitchell told the author, "we would have been forty to fifty miles offshore from where I wanted to be."[6]

Mitchell divided his flight plan into five legs. Working backwards from 0935, Guadalcanal time, the estimated time of interception, he calculated that takeoff from Guadalcanal would have to be at 0720 next morning. Allowing fifteen minutes for join up in formation, the flight should depart the island area at 0735 Guadalcanal time.

As Mitchell and McGuigan worked, they were joined in the operations tent from time to time by 339th pilots who had heard that something big was going on. "Everybody wanted to go," Mitchell said. "If there was going to be a big show, they all wanted in on it—typical fighter pilots."

The last question he had asked himself was the easiest to answer. He had learned there would be eighteen P-38s in commission. That meant eighteen pilots. Mitchell went down the list of about forty pilots available and chose eighteen. They were men he had flown with from Fiji and New Caledonia with the 12th and 70th Fighter Squadrons and who were now assigned to the newly activated 339th under his command. All three squad-rons were assigned to the 347th Fighter Group headed by Lt. Col. Henry Vicellio.

Maj. Louis Kittel, seeing that his former 70th Squadron pilots weren't as well represented as he thought they ought to be, asked Mitchell to consider other names. Mitchell let Kittel select seven other men besides himself to fly in the cover flight.

The tactics would be simple. All eighteen aircraft would fly the entire route at about 50–100 feet off the water. When they made landfall, a "killer" section of four aircraft would attack the bomber, which would be protected by the six Zeros. The other fourteen planes would climb immediately to about 18,000–20,000 feet to provide top cover against the Zeros expected to come up from Kahili.

Mitchell worked by lantern and flashlight until he had all his questions answered. When he finished, he spread the word that he wanted all 339th pilots to be awakened at 5:00 A.M., get breakfast, and report to the operations tent at 6:00 for a briefing. Mitchell arose at 4:30, rechecked his flight plan, and ate a small breakfast. When the pilots assembled, he told them the es-sentials of the job the squadron had been assigned, who the target was, and that the mission was highly classified.

"I told them it was to be an all-volunteer mission and, as I expected, everyone kept asking if they could go," Mitchell said.

I listed the names of the pilots I had selected on a blackboard. I told them the strategy I was going to follow and the dogleg route we would follow entirely out of sight of land. When we made landfall at Bougainville, we would skin off our drop tanks and a killer section of four aircraft would seek out the bomber and the six fighters. The rest of us would climb rapidly to altitude to be top cover for the killer section and also be ready to bounce any of the seventy-five to one hun-dred Zeros based at Kahili near Buin. I really expected them to send up at least fifty of those fighters just as we had done for Secretary Knox and I anticipated a real turkey shoot.

Guess I was being greedy but I felt sure they would greet their top boss with a big show of an escort force and we'd be able to pounce on them from altitude. I thought we were going to be in for a hell of a good fight and I didn't want to miss it. I could have named myself to lead the killer flight to go after the bomber but I wanted to get after those Zeros.

Besides, I didn't want eighteen ships going in there against only six escort fighters and a lone bomber. That way, there would be too many trying to get the bomber and we would be getting in each other's way. It would be dangerous up there with everybody firing their guns. Those 20mm cannons were pretty lethal and some of the junior pilots would probably get a little excited and fire indiscriminately.

I briefed the pilots on the routes out and said we would come back direct to Guadalcanal when the job was done. We wouldn't linger because we wouldn't have the fuel.

I selected Tom Lanphier to head the killer section of four aircraft. The other three were Rex Barber, Jim McLanahan, and Joe Moore. Besby Holmes and Ray Hine were designated spares and were to fill into any position in the formation for a pilot who had trouble and had to turn back. I then told them we would be cruising at about 200 mph indicated airspeed, to fly off of my lead, stay awake, and not to fixate on the water, which is easy to do on a long mission so close to the waves. I told them why we were flying at that level out of sight of land and impressed on them the importance of the mission and that we were to get that bomber no matter what. That was it. We were not going to shoot up the fighter strip at Kahili or attack any other targets on the ground or water.

If anyone had to abort, I told them to move up in their respective formations by hand signals only. No one was to touch that mike button from the time we took off until we engaged the enemy planes. When the mission was over, we were all on our own to get back to Guadalcanal.

That ended the briefing. There were a few questions but these boys were all well-trained and experienced. Rex Barber was flying Lanphier's wing, and McLenahan and Moore were guys I had trained so I had the utmost confidence in all of them. If anybody could do the job, I knew they could.[7]

The pilots were all given small strip maps and copies of Mitchell's flight plan with the headings and times for each leg listed. Some didn't realize it but the mission they were about to fly would be the most important in their combat careers.

During the night, the long-range drop tanks had arrived at

Henderson aboard B-24 heavy bombers from the 90th Bomb Group at Port Moresby, New Guinea, and trucked to Fighter Two. Despite a heavy rainstorm, the ground crews worked the rest of the night under tarpaulins in the revetments getting them attached. There were just enough tanks for each plane to have one 310-gallon tank under one wing, with the regular 165-gallon tank under the other. Since the tanks were so near the center of the fuselage, the weight differential of the added fuel would make little difference in the P-38's flight characteristics.

At daybreak, the last tank was being attached to the last plane. The navy ship's compass that was promised was installed in Mitchell's cockpit and "swung" (adjusted). Everything seemed to be fitting in place.

4
WHO WAS ADMIRAL YAMAMOTO?

HY WAS JAPAN'S TOP NAVAL LEADER SINGLED out for assassination? What made him so important that the Americans would risk a number of pilots and late-model fighter planes, rare commodities during that phase of the war in the Pacific? Was the mission worth the possibility that the Japanese would discover that their top secret naval code had been broken?

Yamamoto was not his real surname. He was born to the Takano family on April 4, 1884, in the village of Nagaoka in the bleak northwest of Japan's main island. The seventh and last child of a poor schoolteacher and former samurai named Sadayoshi Takano, he was not given a first name for over a month after his birth. Takano's wife, exasperated at her husband's apparent disinterest in the lad, nagged and insisted he give the child a name. Finally, while playing his favorite game of *go*, a form of Japanese checkers, Takano replied, "I was fifty-six years old when he was born. Call him Fifty-Six."[1] In Japanese, the word for Fifty-Six is *Isoroku* and that is the first name given to the man who would later be so feared and hated by American forces during World War II.

Isoroku learned a little English and was exposed to Christian teaching by an American missionary named Newall during his preteen years. However, little is known about what effect, if any, this man had on Isoroku's feelings toward America or Americans. He attended the Nagaoka Middle School where boys were sent on long marches, especially in bad weather, to toughen them up and prepare them for future military service.

"During the winter months," Yamamoto recalled,

> our hours were longer and our tasks were made much harder. [The purpose was] to build endurance. The room was heated only by hibachi. The temperature was half of what would be considered necessary in a foreign home. On the ninth day of the midwinter month, thought to be the coldest day of the entire year, no fire was allowed. We were given a hundred ideographs to write. We must keep at the task until it was finished, no matter if the brush fingers became purple and frozen and there was no feeling from the wrist down. When the work was done we thawed our hands by rubbing them in snow.[2]

At sixteen, Isoroku decided to apply for entrance into the Imperial Naval Academy at Eta Jima at a time when Japan was building a large navy. At the turn of the century, Japan had seventy-six warships in its fleet and the best and brightest of Japan's young males were encouraged to man them. Isoroku placed second among the three hundred who competed for vacancies and entered the academy in 1901.

The course was not an easy one. Biographer John Deane Potter noted that "Cadets were not permitted to drink, smoke, eat sweets, or go out with girls. The lives of these dedicated, monastic youths would be devoted until death to the glory of the sacred Emperor and their homeland of Nippon."[3]

Isoroku graduated seventh in his class in 1904, a time when Japan's leaders had embarked on a strategy of conquest against Russia. War began that year with a surprise attack by a Japanese destroyer against the Russian fleet at Port Arthur. Three Russian battleships were badly damaged and a cruiser was sunk. For the next three months, Adm. Heihachiro Togo, Japan's most famous naval leader, blockaded the port hoping to tempt the Russian ships out of the harbor to fight.

Isoroku was assigned to the cruiser *Nisshin,* one of Togo's protecting ships. The Russians, outgunned and outnumbered, sent a fleet of twenty-seven warships from Europe to attack the blockading ships from behind. It took seven months for the Russians to arrive at the Straits of Tsushima. In a single day— May 27, 1905—the Russians lost twenty-three of their ships; the four survivors struck their colors in surrender.

Isoroku had been in the battle and described what happened to him in a letter to his parents:

"When the shells began to fly above me, I found I was not afraid. The ship was damaged by shells and many were killed. At 6:15 in the evening a shell hit the *Nisshin* and knocked me unconscious. When I recovered I found I was wounded in the right leg and two fingers of my left hand [the middle and index fingers] were missing."[4]

Later, he described the incident differently:

"With a great roar, a shell scored a direct hit on the forward 8-inch gun that still remained. Billows of acrid smoke covered the forward half of the vessel, and I felt myself almost swept away by a fierce blast. I staggered a few steps—and found that the record charts that had been hanging around my neck had disappeared, and that two fingers of my left hand had been snapped off and were hanging by the skin alone."[5]

Thereafter, Isoroku became known in the Shimbashi geisha district as "Eighty Sen" because the regular charge for a manicure of all ten fingers was one yen and his favorite geisha charged him for only eight.

Isoroku was a serious young man on duty and did not drink, smoke, or socialize much with his brother officers. A complex man, he was professional to the core, keenly interested in naval tactics, but he did not shun the pleasures of off-duty life. He visited the geisha houses frequently when ashore. Short in stature (five feet, three inches), he was highly intelligent, sentimental, earthy, blunt in speech, and a passionate gambler. One author who had met him before World War I described him as "leather-faced, bullet-headed, bitter-hearted . . . a hard chunk of a man, hair cropped as short as the bristles on a beaver-tail cactus, lips thick, jowl heavy, chin prominent."[6]

Yamamoto was obsessed with punctuality and harshly berated any subordinate who was not on time for meetings and appointments, an obsession that was later to prove fatal. He went on many training cruises to Australia and the west coast of the United States. There seemed to be no doubt among his colleagues that he was destined for high rank.

After Isoroku's father and mother died in 1913, in accordance with Japanese custom, he was adopted into the more prosperous Yamamoto family who traced their forebears to ancient warriors who had fought in the shogun wars. Such adoptions were common in Japan by families without a male heir. In 1916, he formally renounced the name of Takano in a Buddhist ceremony.

Isoroku Yamamoto remained single until the age of thirty-three when he married Reiko Mihashi, twenty-two, daughter of a rich farmer. Shortly after the 1918 marriage, Yamamoto was sent to Harvard University for a year without his bride. He took an intensive course in English and majored in economics. He learned to play poker and became extremely fond of the game because it required an ability to bluff his opponents and determine what cards they might hold—a skill he identified with naval tactics and strategy.

One of Yamamoto's special interests in his economics studies was the petroleum industry, which he realized was of utmost importance to any navy, especially his own because Japan had minimal oil resources and was greatly dependent on imports. Since fuel was limited, the world's third largest navy was constantly haunted by the specter of an oil shortage. As a result, most of the fleet's training during World War I was restricted mainly to the waters off the Pacific shores of Japan.

As World War I progressed, Yamamoto became interested in the use of aircraft. In an interview with a *National Geographic* writer in 1915, Yamamoto was asked what he considered *the* war vessel of the future. "The most important ship of the future will be a ship to carry airplanes," he replied.[7] As he advanced in the navy, he argued frequently in favor of aircraft carriers. His arguments were strengthened when the Americans began experimenting with launching planes from ships, and the British Royal Navy built the world's first aircraft carrier in 1918. Although thoroughly trained in the strategy and tactics of battleships, cruisers, destroyers, and torpedo boats, he was adamant that in his belief the most important ship of the future would be one that would carry airplanes.

Yamamoto had severe critics. When asked how he could expect to destroy a battleship except with a battleship, he answered, "With torpedo planes" and quoted a Japanese proverb: "The fiercest serpent may be overcome by a swarm of ants."[8]

In 1919, Yamamoto was assigned to Washington as assistant naval attaché for a two-year tour. He was promoted to captain in 1923 while visiting Europe, and the following year, although not a pilot, was made second in command of Japan's first naval air training center at Kasumigaura, presumably because he had developed a reputation as a hard taskmaster and disciplinarian. Upon arrival, he found the pilot trainees to be an undisciplined lot with long hair, sloppy uniforms, and a casual attitude toward authority. To gain their respect, he took flying lessons and soloed, then began to take strong measures against those who deviated from correct officer decorum and flaunted the regulations. As biographer Hiroyuki Agawa noted, Yamamoto was "genuinely afraid that the tendency of fliers to see themselves as specially gifted persons who could do anything by relying on intuition, without paying proper attention to logical method, together with the concomitant tendency to behave like hoodlums, would be bad for the future of aviation."[9]

In 1926, Yamamoto returned to the United States and served as naval attaché at the Japanese embassy in Washington, D.C., until 1928. His duty was to learn as much as possible about the American navy—its history, policies, strategy, tactics, budget, and plans. During this assignment, friendly American naval officers taught him bridge, which he learned quickly. An inveterate gambler by now, he was fascinated by card games. As he explained later, "Our language has no alphabet and each single word or syllable is represented by a character. A Japanese has to keep 5,000 ideographs in his head. After that it is child's play to remember 52 cards."[10]

Japan had been an ally of Great Britain and the United States during World War I. In 1921, at an arms limitation cônference in Washington, as a reward for its support, Japan had been given all the German possessions in the western Pacific north of the equator—the Marianas and the Carolines—which became known as the Japanese Mandates. The Japanese were bound by a 5-5-3 agreement whereby for every five capital ships that either Great Britain or the United States built, Japan could build only three. Japan had pushed vigorously for a higher ratio but the objection of her representatives were to no avail. In the postwar years, Japan built to the limit of the 5-5-3 agreement.

In 1923, Lt. Sunishi Kira, later a vice admiral, made aviation history as the first pilot to land on Japan's first carrier, the *Hosho*. By 1927, the fleet included four carriers. In 1928–29, Yamamoto commanded the aircraft carrier *Akagi*, and his pronaval aviation voice was now being heard at the highest levels of the government. He was selected to attend the Naval Disarmament Conference in London in 1930 and was a leader in obtaining agreement to give Japan equality with the British and Americans in the number of submarines and light cruisers that each could build. After the conference, Yamamoto was promoted to rear admiral and appointed head of the technical research division of the navy where his views about the future of aircraft as an extension of naval power carried great weight. In 1933, he became commander of Carrier Division One. Potter tells of his growing convictions about carrier aviation:

Yamamoto wanted torpedo planes and long-range bombers but most of all he wanted a fast fighter that could fly off the deck of an aircraft carrier. He gave orders to the Japanese aircraft factories to produce their own planes experimentally. Mitsubishi, the big industrial combine, submitted plans for a navy fighter [which became the famous Zero] . . .

At the same time, with the militarists gaining increasing control of the Japanese government, the naval hold-down was more and more actively criticized in Japan. The outcry became so great that it was decided in 1934 to hold another naval conference in London.

The obvious Japanese representative was Vice Admiral

Yamamoto who had already publicly attacked the Japanese naval ratio as "this national degradation." He was named chief delegate with full decision powers. He sailed from Yokohama for Seattle, spending most of his time in his cabin playing poker. When he arrived in the United States he refused all newspaper interviews. He also refused to read the American papers in case any cunning Western arguments might sway him before he could put Japan's case at the conference.[11]

American newspapers took a great interest in him. He was given wide coverage as he traveled across America to New York in a locked train compartment. At the time, Gen. William "Billy" Mitchell, outspoken aviation proponent, was lobbying for greater American military air strength. His view was that American military planes must be designed specifically to fight Japan in the Pacific. Newspapers daily gave prominence to his dramatic statements that war with Japan was inevitable.

When Yamamoto reached New York, he still refused to see reporters. His aides brushed them off, saying, "So sorry, but the admiral does not speak English." This rebuff was never questioned and a record of his years in the United States was apparently not on file in American newspaper offices.

Yamamoto sailed for England, refusing to leave his cabin. When he landed at Southhampton on the morning of October 18, 1934, he called a press conference and, in English, announced that "Japan can no longer submit to the ratio system. There is no possibility of compromise by my government on that point."[12] Thus, the 1934 London Naval Parley was doomed before it began. It was the last attempt to limit naval forces by treaty.

The failure of the London conference marked the beginning of Japanese naval independence and the rise of Yamamoto as a powerful influence in Japanese military affairs. He was appointed vice minister of the navy in 1936 and began to vehemently oppose the battleship admirals who saw no future in the aircraft carrier. By now Yamamoto was firmly convinced that no navy could be successful in a future war if its fleets were not formed around ships carrying planes. Aircraft could act as scouts and bombers and thus take the fight to the enemy before the surface ships were close enough to do battle. Despite strong resistance, Yamamoto won out. When the keels of several new carriers were laid, he commented that battleships are "like elaborate religious scrolls which old people hang up in their homes. They are of no proved worth. They are primarily a matter of faith—not reality."[13]

Although the target of continual criticism, Yamamoto prevailed and expanded his own views on naval aviation to include the manufacture of long-range flying boats that could fly 800 miles with 2,000 pounds of bombs. He encouraged increased production and improvement of the Mitsubishi Zero, which could operate from the new carriers being built.

The Japanese were successful in protecting their growing naval strength from public view as the 1930s were winding down. English-language magazines and newspapers reported that war with Japan was impossible because the country's army and navy had few planes that could stand up against the British and American fighters then being built on both sides of the Atlantic.

Behind the closed doors of the Imperial Japanese defense establishment at the end of World War I, secret documents had clearly indicated that the United States was the leading potential enemy of Japan, with Russia second. Consequently, the navy's war planners envisioned attacking American possessions in the Pacific. Army strategists saw the future as a land war against Russia. Yamamoto was highly skeptical about the formalistic views of the Navy General Staff and Navy Staff College which made assumptions he could not accept: (1) Japan would attack the Philippines; (2) the U.S. Fleet would sail to the aid of the Philippines; (3) Japan would wage a war of attrition in the Marianas; and (4) there would be a great sea battle between the two fleets in which the American fleet would be destroyed.

In the late 1930s, American military strategists began to sense the growing threat to American interests in the Pacific and the U.S. Navy was ordered to strengthen its power base in Hawaii instead of the West Coast. This convinced many Japanese army and navy leaders that the United States was clearly preparing for war against Japan. The Japanese began to think in terms of attacking Pearl Harbor by sea, as had been discussed in military circles for many years. However, the planners did not consider the use of carrier-based aircraft initially.

Concurrently, Hitler and Mussolini urged Japan to join them in a tripartite pact. Japanese army leaders saw this possibility as a strong asset and pressed for approval. However, a number of top naval leaders, including Yamamoto, opposed the idea, and Yamamoto became exceptionally outspoken in his belief that it would be foolish to join with the two dictatorships and thus declare openly that America was a chosen enemy. He wrote in a statement of his views that "A war between Japan and the United States would be a major calamity for the world, and for Japan it would mean, after several years of war already [with China], acquiring yet another powerful enemy—an extremely perilous matter for the nation. . . . It is necessary . . . that both Japan and America should seek every means to avoid a direct clash, and Japan should under no circumstances conclude an alliance with Germany."[14] Despite the opposition, the Tripartite Pact with Germany and Italy was signed on September 27, 1940.

"His outspokenness made him many enemies," according to Potter,

> particularly among the extreme nationalists. They called him pro-American and a traitor to his country and threatened to assassinate him. . . . The only way to remove him from the daily peril to which his outspoken anti-war stand had brought him was to remove him from the political sphere altogether. In mid-August [1939], he was appointed commander of the First Fleet and [in 1940] was given command of the Combined Fleet with the rank of full admiral. . . . The transfer from the dangerous political position as Navy Vice Minister to sea duty meant strict obedience to the Imperial Rescript, "Men of the services should not participate in politics."[15]

Characteristically, Yamamoto threw himself forcefully into his new responsibilities and announced the policy he would follow in the months ahead: First priority was the training of aircraft-carrier pilots. Yamamoto's concern about air crew training was based on the results of a bombing exercise he had ordered in which thirty-six planes bombing level from one thousand feet scored only a single hit on an old battleship being used as a stationary target. However, three dive bombers scored one hit with a bomb and one with a torpedo. Consequently, many of his staff officers thought level bombing should be abandoned in favor of dive bombing; Yamamoto disagreed and ordered more training in both level and dive bombing for all pilots.

Potter noted: "This was two and a half years before Pearl Harbor. It was the first glimpse of an idea for attacking stationary targets such as anchored warships. By the time of the Pearl Harbor attack, Japanese planes had undoubtedly attained the world's highest rate of accuracy in level bombing attacks."[16]

It is not possible to determine exactly when Yamamoto first thought about a surprise attack on Pearl Harbor but it may well have entered his mind from reading a 1925 novel entitled *The Great Pacific War* by Hector C. Bywater, naval correspondent for the London *Daily Telegraph*. Bywater predicted that a war would begin between the United States and Japan with a sneak attack by the Japanese against naval forces of the U.S. Asiatic Fleet cruising off Manila Bay. This book and a previous nonfiction book by Bywater, entitled *Sea Power in the Pacific*, were translated into Japanese and distributed among students at the naval academy and to the officer corps throughout the navy. Being an avid student of naval affairs throughout his career, it can be assumed that Yamamoto read both books.

When the intensive air training program that Yamamoto had instigated paid off in better bombing results, he began to think seriously, albeit reluctantly, that if war came, a long-range pre-emptive air strike against the American fleet at Pearl Harbor would be necessary to remove the threat to Japan's plans for conquest. In the spring of 1940, he casually mentioned the possibility to his chief of staff, Rear Adm. Shigeru Fukudome, aboard the *Nagato*. Yamamoto said, "An air attack on Hawaii may be possible now, especially as our air training has turned out so successfully."[17]

By April 1941, the plan for a surprise attack on Pearl Harbor— now called Operation Z—was being finalized. Concurrently, Japanese army leaders were gathering intelligence information for operations against Hong Kong, Singapore, Java, Sumatra, and the Philippines. The navy concentrated on extensive sea maneuvers which included a simulation of a Pearl Harbor attack.

Despite the preparations, Yamamoto had some doubts. He told Premier Fumimaro Konoye, "If you tell me it is necessary that we fight, then in the first six months to a year of war against the United States and England I will go wild, and I will show you an uninterrupted succession of victories; but I must tell you that if the war be prolonged for two or three years, I have no confidence in our ultimate victory."[18]

One of the reasons for Yamamoto's concern harkened back to his studies of the oil industry at Harvard. In the summer of 1941, the United States, England, and Holland placed an embargo on oil, steel, and scrap iron sales to Japan. As a result, the Japanese navy had only enough oil on hand for an estimated eighteen months of operations. This fact speeded up plans to capture the rich oil fields of the Dutch East Indies.

Assuming that there would be Japanese naval superiority in the western Pacific, the army intended to sweep through the coastal regions of China to the oil-rich areas to the south. Although Yamamoto proceeded with his own plan to attack Hawaii, he remained reluctant and put his finger on a fatal weakness of the Japanese concept of war when he stated: "It is not enough that we should take Guam and the Philippines or even Hawaii and San Francisco. We would have to march into Washington and sign the treaty in the White House."[19]

Yamamoto was thoroughly convinced that the only way he could be successful at Pearl Harbor was to mount a surprise attack by a massive fleet of carrier-based aircraft. With the assistance of Vice Adm. Shigeru Fukudome, Rear Adm. Takijero Ohnishi, and Comdr. Minoru Genda, Yamamoto planned a force composed of Japan's six largest carriers, two fast battleships, two cruisers, and a number of destroyers, tankers, and supporting ships. By May 1941, Yamamoto had accepted the decision to go to war but only on the condition that his plan to attack Pearl Harbor without warning be incorporated into the master plan. He threatened to resign if this was not done. He won the argument.

On November 5, 1941, Yamamoto issued Combined Fleet Secret Operational Order No. 1, a 151-page document that outlined the tactics to be followed for the Pearl Harbor attack and simultaneous assaults on Malaysia, the Philippines, Guam,

Wake, and Hong Kong. The die was cast. Emperor Hirohito agreed to war against the United States on December 1. Hostilities were to begin on the morning of X Day—December 8 in Japan, December 7 in Hawaii, a Sunday.

When the war began, the United States had seventeen battleships, six aircraft carriers, and thirty-two cruisers, distributed about equally between the Atlantic and Pacific. The Japanese had ten battleships, nine aircraft carriers, and forty-six cruisers, all stationed in the western Pacific. This superiority was due to Yamamoto's strong influence in the naval planning process and his input into the formation of national military policy. On the morning of December 7, 1941, his once-controversial views about whether the employment of carrier-based aircraft in a surprise attack would be successful were completely vindicated.

At 3:25 A.M. Tokyo time, the first 500-pound bomb was dropped on Wheeler Field and the one-sided battle began. On board the *Nagato*, anchored at Hashira Jima, Yamamoto received the news calmly. In one hour and fifteen minutes, the American navy lost eighteen ships, including seven battleships sunk or seriously damaged. (Fortunately, the two Pacific Fleet carriers—*Enterprise* and *Lexington*—were at sea ferrying aircraft to Wake and Midway Islands; the *Saratoga* was being overhauled on the West Coast.)

U.S. naval installations were severely crippled. Of the 169 navy planes in Hawaii, 92 were destroyed, 39 damaged. Three Army Air Corps installations were badly damaged. Of the 231 planes assigned to the Hawaiian Air Force, 96 were destroyed. There were 2,403 American military personnel and civilians killed and hundreds more wounded.

At 6:00 A.M. in Tokyo, a joint communiqué by the army and navy was issued on the radio: "Before dawn today, December 8, the Imperial Army and Navy entered upon a state of hostilities with British and American forces in the west Pacific."[20] A few hours later, there was a further announcement: "Before dawn on December 8 the imperial navy carried out a crippling blow on U.S. naval and air forces in the Hawaii area. . . ."[21]

The Japanese lost only 29 of the 353 planes taking part, 1 large and 5 midget submarines, 55 airmen, and 9 submariners. The

Japanese force, led by Adm. Chuichi Nagumo, returned to Japanese waters as heroes. Yamamoto radioed congratulations from the *Nagato*. Comdr. Mitsuo Fuchida, leader of the attacking planes, was invited to the Imperial Palace for an audience with Emperor Hirohito, a rare honor for a junior officer. Yamamoto received a personal letter of congratulations from the emperor and a handsome set of saki cups.

"Before Pearl Harbor, only a handful of American naval officers had ever heard of Isoroku Yamamoto," a British historian commented. "But after 7th December 1941, his name was on everyone's lips. To every American he became the embodiment of Japanese evil, the treacherous aggressor, the man who not only planned the Pearl Harbor attack but who, in his arrogance, was also believed to be planning to dictate terms in the White House."[22]

Adm. Homer N. Wallin, in a book published in 1968, wrote that Yamamoto was "well-schooled" and "well-regarded by American officers, was a sophisticated poker player, given to successful bluffing. He was regarded as bold and venturesome. But, to some he was headstrong and lacking in prudence."[23]

The plans for the surprise attack on Pearl Harbor had been Yamamoto's and his alone. He had supervised every detail, fought for the concept over the opposition of every senior admiral, and saw that the attack was carried out. He had wanted peace but accepted war.

In the days following Pearl Harbor, despite the praise he received, Yamamoto was still pessimistic about the future. He wrote to his sister, Kazuko: "Well, war has begun at last. But in spite of all the clamor that is going on we could lose it. I can only do my best."[24]

To an unidentified friend, he wrote: "This war will give us much trouble in the future. The fact that we have had a small success at Pearl Harbor is nothing. The fact that we have succeeded so easily has pleased people. Personally, I do not think it is a good thing to whip up propaganda to encourage the nation. People should think things over and realize how serious the situation is."[25]

Despite his doubts, the first three months of 1942 were full of

Japanese military successes. The Dutch East Indies were under Japanese control; the large British base at Singapore was in their hands; Americans in the Philippines were fighting in desperate retreat. Yamamoto was a national hero and all future naval planning was now his responsibility. Adm. Osami Nagano, head of the Naval General Staff, theoretically had the power to issue orders to Yamamoto as commander in chief of the Combined Fleet but Yamamoto, because of his Pearl Harbor success, actually planned future naval operations. The General Staff's function became one of refereeing when disagreements arose.

Arguments did ensue over what to do next. Yamamoto had always favored capturing Midway Island to use as a base for more operations against Hawaii and occupying vital points in the Aleutian Islands. However, he met strong resistance from the army and the desk-bound admirals in Tokyo. That resistance crumbled on April 18, 1942, when sixteen American B-25 medium bombers led by Lt. Col. James H. "Jimmy" Doolittle appeared over Tokyo and four other Japanese cities and dropped incendiary and high-explosive bombs on military and industrial targets.

The American sixteen-ship task force, centered around the carriers *Hornet* and *Enterprise*, had been detected about 650 miles off the Japanese coast by the *Nitto Maru*, a fishing boat on picket duty. Yamamoto issued orders to the Twenty-first Air Flotilla to dispatch medium bombers and fighters from their bases near Tokyo but they never saw the invaders. Everyone, including Yamamoto, believed the American planes were carrier planes with limited range. But these were land-based B-25 Army Air Force bombers and thus were believed incapable of being launched from a carrier.

Yamamoto and his staff were unable at first to determine the takeoff point of the bombers and thought it might be Midway or some base in the Aleutians, yet Midway was 2,250 miles away and the nearest American base in the Aleutians was much farther. Jimmy Doolittle and his Raiders had convinced Yamamoto what he should do next: carry out the Midway/Aleutian plan. On May 5, 1942, he issued the orders.

In a letter to Adm. Mineichi Koga dated May 2, 1942, Yamamoto confided how embarrassed he was about the Doolittle raid.

He wrote: "Even though there wasn't much damage, it's a disgrace that the skies over the imperial capital should have been defiled without a single enemy plane being shot down. It provides a regrettably graphic illustration of the saying that a bungling attack is better than the most skilled defense."[26]

On May 8, a naval battle occurred in the Coral Sea where an American task force, including the carriers *Lexington* and *Yorktown*, engaged the enemy and, for the first time, sank a Japanese ship larger than a destroyer. Although the *Lexington* was lost, along with a destroyer and an oiler, the Americans seemed to come off best. The Japanese lost the carrier *Shokaku*, a destroyer, and three smaller vessels.

Later that month, as the Midway attack force, consisting of five carriers and eleven battleships, and the Aleutian force, with two carriers, steamed toward their target destinations, Yamamoto assumed that the American carriers *Hornet* and *Enterprise* were in the South Pacific. They weren't.

On June 3, the Aleutian force struck the Aleutians with a bombing attack on Dutch Harbor and unopposed landings on Attu and Kiska on June 6–7. The Midway force launched 108 planes against the tiny island on June 4.

Unknown to the Japanese, a relatively small force of Army Air Force bombers operating from Hawaii, along with navy and marine fighters aboard the carriers *Yorktown, Hornet,* and *Enterprise,* had been assembled for the expected onslaught by the 350 vessels steaming toward Midway, the largest naval force ever assembled.

On June 6, the enemy was engaged, and when the battle was over forty-eight hours later, the Japanese had lost four of their six carriers, a cruiser, fourteen other ships, and most of their air groups, planes, and pilots, the best in the Japanese navy. The Americans lost only two large ships, the carrier *Yorktown* and a destroyer.

The greatest sea battle since Trafalgar was over. More Japanese died that day than on both sides of any naval battle of World War I. It was the first and last gigantic carrier battle in the history of the world.

Masatake Okumiya, one of the pilots on the Midway operation, commented: "The loss of four aircraft carriers . . . shocked the Japanese people. We could not understand the gravity of the defeat, for these four carriers had played the major role in the Navy's smashing victories across the breadth of the Pacific. An even greater blow, however, was the loss of the irreplaceable veteran air crews and the skilled maintenance crews which went down with their ships."[27]

How could a fleet as large as Yamamoto had organized be turned back at Midway by such a relatively small American force? In addition to the interception of Japanese messages and the capability to assemble a force of Army Air Force and navy fighters and bombers, another reason for the Japanese defeat was overconfidence. The Midway/Aleutian operation was too ambitious; too many objectives over a wide area of the Pacific had been undertaken in too short a time frame; and too many false assumptions about the Americans had been made in the planning process. However, the landings on Kiska and Attu meant that the Japanese occupied American soil for the first time in history. It was small compensation for the losses from the Midway operation.

But there was one major advantage the Americans had that the Japanese thought was an impossibility: The top secret Japanese naval code had been broken by American cryptographers and all radio messages relating to the oncoming attack had been intercepted. This fact and Yamamoto's passion for keeping precise schedules eventually sealed the personal fate of "the reluctant admiral."

5

"BOGEYS! ELEVEN O'CLOCK HIGH!"

PRIL 18 WAS EASTER SUNDAY BUT THERE were no religious holidays on Guadalcanal in 1943. Mitchell hadn't slept well the night before even though there had been no visit from "Washing Machine Charlie," the Japanese bomber that paid occasional night bombing calls on Guadalcanal with his unsynchronized propellers for which he had become notorious. The details of the forthcoming mission kept going through his mind. Although anxious to fly the mission because of the promise of action against a gaggle of enemy planes, he still wondered about the chances of intercepting Yamamoto's bomber. There was a two-hour difference between the Americans' time and that of the Japanese. Enemy forces kept all their operations on Tokyo time while the Americans used local time. If somebody made a mistake in timing, it wasn't his fault. He shrugged, downed a quick breakfast at the mess tent, and rounded up his pilots for the premission briefing.

"I cautioned them about strict radio silence on the trip out," Mitchell recalled, "and told them I would use the usual signals of kicking my rudders to fishtail my plane when I wanted the formation to spread out and wagging my wings to bring them in close. I would use hand signals otherwise. I urged them to check the belly tank installations on their ships during their preflight walkarounds and switch to them soon after takeoff to be sure they would feed."[1]

He also said he wanted them to fly a loose formation and warned again about the dangers of flying only a few feet above the ocean for the two hours or so it would take them to make landfall at Bougainville. "There's a tendency to daydream and get sleepy on a trip like this," he cautioned. "You're going to be hot and it's going to be boring. Don't stare at the water. Your depth perception goes to hell down low like that and you're going to bust your butt if you get careless. Spread out when I give the signal and fly off my lead. I won't surprise you with any sharp turns."[2]

Mitchell strode briskly down the line of Lightnings looking in the revetments, exchanging a few words with the mechanics and crews along the flight line. He greeted his ground crew and asked his crew chief about the belly tank installation on his airplane and the other planes.

"The guys were up all night," the sergeant replied. "Everybody checked their tanks to be sure they'll feed. And that compass the navy sent over from Henderson was put in, so you're all set."

Mitchell nodded, climbed up on the wing of his Lightning, buckled his parachute leg straps, and eased into the cockpit. He checked the installation of the large navy compass and started the twin Allison engines. Acting on his engine start, the other seventeen pilots cranked up and followed him out to the runup position. After checking both engines carefully, Mitchell lined up on the runway. He paused to check the compass to see if it read the same as the runway heading. "It was right on the money," he said. "So I knew it was going to be all right— certainly an improvement over my regular compass. It made me feel better about flying the courses out. If the wind stayed light as predicted, our chances of getting to Bougainville sight unseen and on time seemed better now. It was up to the admiral to do his part."[3]

At 0710, Mitchell held the brakes as he revved both engines

up to full rpms; he released the brakes, checked the compass alignment with runway heading one more, and was quickly airborne. He was followed by Lt. Julius Jacobson, his wingman, then Lieutenants Doug Canning and Delton Goerke. He started a slow left climbing turn to 2,000 feet. Next in line was the four-plane "killer" flight: Capt. Tom Lanphier and Lieutenants Rex T. Barber, James D. McLanahan, and Joseph F. Moore. Barber was flying *Miss Virginia* because his own *Diablo* was grounded for maintenance. Lanphier admitted having "pre-combat stomach" as he taxied out in *Phoebe*, the nickname for his fiancée and future wife, Phyllis.

Lanphier and Barber got off easily but McLanahan had to abort. Just as he was about to reach flying speed, one of his tires struck an upturned piece of the pierced metal planking on the runway and was instantly flattened. His plane lurched and veered off the runway to a stop. He told the author, "It was one of the saddest days of my life. I really wanted to go on that one. I still get mad every time I think about it."[4]

Mitchell continued circling slowly to allow Maj. Louis Kittel leading the remaining planes of the top cover flight to catch up. Kittel, an avid hunter, likened the upcoming mission to a "trophy hunt" and hoped he wouldn't have to abort. He knew how important Yamamoto was, making this a far different mission than others. "We were briefed very thoroughly about strict radio silence," he said. "That seems like a simple instruction but normally there was a lot of chatter when flights are trying to get organized. We all realized this was a special mission."[5]

When the last man was airborne and had joined up, Mitchell began a slow descent toward the water on a heading of 265 degrees. It was now 0725.

As each pilot settled into position and spread out when Mitchell signaled, they switched fuel selectors from internal fuel to the belly tanks. After a few seconds, Joe Moore's engines coughed and he quickly switched back to the mains. He tried again but the belly tanks would not feed. Disappointed, he pulled up beside Lanphier and hand-signaled that he would have to return to Fighter Two.

Lt. Besby F. Holmes and his wingman, Lt. Raymond K. Hine, the spare pilots, were signaled to fill out the attack flight's four-plane complement. Mitchell hoped no one else would have to drop out.

On the night of April 17 at Rabaul, Rear Adm. Takoji Joshima, concerned that the message announcing Yamamoto's itinerary may have been intercepted, pleaded with his superior to cancel the trip. "I have to go," Yamamoto said. "I've let them know, and they'll have got things ready for me. I'll leave tomorrow morning and be back by dusk."[6]

On his previous inspection trips, Yamamoto had always worn an immaculate white uniform. However, on the morning of April 18, he put on a new dark green "simplified" uniform and strapped on his samurai sword.

The Lightnings plodded westward and as they passed south of the Russell Islands, now in American hands, two Betty bombers—tail numbers 323 and 326—departed Vunakanau Air Base at Rabaul for the seven-mile flight to Lakunai Field to await the admiral and his staff. At 5:45, Japanese time, precisely as scheduled, the two Betty bombers with the VIPs aboard roared off the coral strip and climbed to about 6,500 feet. Six Zero fighters followed and formed into two three-ship Vs behind and about 1,500 feet higher on each side of the Bettys. They would follow a direct course southeast for Buin, 315 miles away. The weather was perfect for flying. They would be on time for a landing at Ballale Island at 0945.

The sixteen Lightnings droned on above the unblemished blue ocean. There was nothing to disturb the scene—no ships, no land, no other planes, nothing. Mitchell remembers, "It was hot as hell in those cockpits and I dozed off a couple of times but I got a light tap on my shoulder from the Man upstairs and caught myself."[7]

One of the Lightning pilots got too low and his propeller tips splashed seawater over his windshield. "I know damn well that woke him up," Mitchell said. "He had to clean off his windshield when he got back. I think that's the only thing he had to clean up but word got back to me later that he wasn't able to get back to sleep for a couple of days."[8]

Del Goerke said he was "hot, nervous, anxious; I suppose the word for it was 'scared.' I certainly had faith in Mitch and our ability to be where and when he wanted to be; but there were so many ifs on the part of the Japanese. The odds were against us; but even the slightest possibility of success made the mission worthwhile."[9]

Doug Canning recalled that the ocean was uncommonly calm and there were few whitecaps because there was practically no wind. He spotted several schools of sharks ("I counted forty-eight at one time") and a huge manta ray, which reminded him that danger lurked only a few feet below if any of them went down.[10]

Mitchell kept watching the compass and checked his watch frequently. After flying on a heading of 265 degrees on the first and longest leg for fifty-five minutes, he turned 25 degrees right to 290 degrees. Twenty-seven minutes later, he turned to 305 degrees. This leg was flown for thirty-eight minutes; then to 20 degrees for the forty-mile leg to the south edge of Empress Bay, toward the coast. As he crossed the bay, he turned to 90 degrees and wagged his wings to signal the planes to tighten up their respective formations.

"We were about four minutes out and I was getting nervous then," Mitchell admits.

It was hazy when we made that last turn toward land and the sun was directly in front of us. I couldn't see anything, no land, nothing. I checked my watch, the strip map on my knee pad, and the compass. Could I have been so far off that we weren't near land at all—any kind of land? I was really getting itchy because I hadn't seen a single checkpoint from the time we left. There are some pretty high hills on Bougainville and I couldn't see anything ahead in the haze and sunlight.

I glanced once more at my strip map and then ahead. Out of the haze I saw a beach and there we were just about where I wanted us to be off the southwest corner of Bougainville. It was 0934—a minute ahead of our scheduled time.

Just as I thought "I better do something now," Doug Canning, flying Number 3 in my flight, broke radio silence and said, "Bogeys! Eleven o'clock high!"

I looked up and there they were, five miles away at about

4,500 feet descending—two Betty bombers instead of one and six Zeros behind them about a thousand feet higher. I "rogered" and said "I have 'em."

We were still on the deck then and heading toward them at a 90-degree angle. I turned right, parallel with their track, and firewalled it to climb as fast as we could. I told the guys to "skin off your tanks," pulled my own belly tank release, and watched as Jacobson, Canning, and Goerke dropped theirs. As we reached the level of the Bettys and still parallel with them, Holmes, in the killer flight, radioed that he couldn't get his tanks off and pulled away from the formation back out over the water. That was a mistake as far as I was concerned. Hine, his wingman, rightfully followed him to protect him.

I called to Lanphier, "He's your meat, Tom." Tom acknowledged and the two remaining planes of the killer flight turned toward the eight enemy planes and continued climbing. The rest of us also continued climbing for a couple of miles parallel to the Japanese planes. I have to admit it was very tempting to me to want to level off and pull over to get at them. If I had known they weren't going to send any fighters up from Kahili to greet the admiral, I would have made the attack. I would have taken over, Lanphier or anyone else be damned. I would have gone in first. I selected the high cover because I thought we'd have a field day with at least half of those seventy-five fighters coming at us from Kahili. They didn't send any at all—a big disappointment to me and the rest of the cover flight.

I kept climbing to about 18,000 feet as I had briefed everyone in the cover flight we would do. There was a lot of chatter on the radio. I looked down and saw some black smoke coming out of the jungle. Lanphier said something about a plane going down and did I see it? I told him I saw a pillar of smoke coming out of the jungle but I had no way of knowing if it was a Betty, a Zero, or a P-38. I saw none of the action below.

There was considerable chatter on the radio after I called Lanphier to take his flight in to the attack. I remember Lanphier complaining about Zeros on his tail. I tried to find out where he was but was unable to do so. About that time, I saw Lieutenant Hine's aircraft smoking in one engine, several thousand feet below me. I was then busy for a few minutes knocking this Zero off his tail but never saw Hine again. I have no idea what happened to him. When I couldn't find him, I called the squadron and said, "Let's go home."[11]

The stories of the members of the killer flight differ from the moment Mitchell told his pilots to "skin off your tanks" and ordered Lanphier to do what they had come to do. First, Lanphier's version, which was published in the *New York Times*, September 12–14, 1945:

I angled across in front of Yamamoto's formation, straining to reach at least the same altitude as his formation before being spotted. Major Mitchell was in a rocketing climb, scanning the air for Japanese fighters from Kahili.

Neither Mitch's section, nor mine, was discovered by the Japanese in the tense two minutes after we sighted the enemy. During those two minutes, though, I lost Holmes and Hine. Holmes called out that he couldn't drop his belly tanks. He leveled off and went on down the coast, kicking and slewing his ship in frantic attempts to tear them off. Hine, as his wingman, was compelled to stay with him. . . .

Barber and I got to a point two miles to Yamamoto's right and about a mile in front of him before his Zero cover saw us. They must have screamed the warning into their radios because we saw their belly tanks drop—a sign that they were clearing for action—and they nosed over in a group to dive on us, on Rex and me.

We closed in fast. Three Zeros which had been flying the seaward side of the Yamamoto formation came tearing down between it and us, trying to intercept us before we could reach Yamamoto's bomber.

Right behind them were the three Japanese Zeros from the inshore side of the formation.

Holmes and Hine were off down the beach, out of sight, and Mitch and his group were out of sight, too, climbing with throttles wide toward what they had every reason to believe would be the biggest fight of all, top Japanese cover from Kahili. . . .

I was afraid we'd never get to the bomber that Admiral Yamamoto rode before the Zeros got us. I horsed back on my wheel to get my guns to bear on the lead Zero diving toward me.

Buck fever started me firing before I had my Lightning's nose pointed in his direction. I saw the gray smoke from his wing guns and wondered with stupid detachment if the bullets would get me before I could work my guns into his face.

He was a worse shot than I was, and he died. My machine guns and cannon ripped one of his wings away. He twisted under me, all flame and smoke. His two wingmen hurtled past and I wasted a few bursts between them. Then I thought I'd better get my job done and go away before I got hurt.

I kicked my ship over on its back and looked down for the lead Japanese bomber. It had dived inland. As I hung in the sky I got an impression, off to the east, of a swirl of aircraft against the blue—a single Lightning silhouetted against the light in a swarm of Zeros. That was Barber, having himself a time.

Excitement in a fight works wonders with a man's vision. In the same brief second that I saw Rex on my right, and saw the Zeros I had just overshot, I spotted a shadow moving across the treetops. It was Yamamoto's bomber. It was skimming the jungle, headed for Kahili.

I dived toward him.

I realized on the way down that I had picked up too much speed, that I might overshoot him. I cut back my throttles. I crossed my controls and went into a skid to brake my dive.

The two Zeros that had overshot me showed up again, diving toward Yamamoto's bomber from an angle slightly off to my right. They meant to get me before I got the bomber. It looked from where I sat as if the bomber, the Zeros, and I might all get to the same place at the same time.

We very nearly did. The next three or four seconds spelled life or death. I remember getting suddenly very stubborn about making the most of the one good shot I had coming up. I fired a long steady burst across the bomber's course of flight, from approximately right angles.

The bomber's right engine, then its right wing, burst into flame. I had accomplished my part of the mission. Once afire, no Japanese plane stopped burning, short of blowing up. The men aboard the bomber were too close to the ground to jump.

The two onrushing Zeros saw it, too. They screamed past overhead, unwilling to chance a jungle crash to get me. In that second I realized my impetus would carry me directly behind the Mitsubishi's tail cannon.

My Lightning's belly was scraping the trees. I couldn't duck under the Mitsubishi and I hesitated to pull up over its line of fire because I already was going so slow I almost hung in midair, near stalling speed. I expected those Zeros back, too.

Just as I moved into range of Yamamoto's bomber and its cannon, the bomber's wing tore off. The bomber plunged into the jungle. It exploded. That was the end of Admiral Isoroku Yamamoto.

Right about then, though, I got scared. I'd slowed so much to get my shots at Yamamoto's bomber that I was caught, so to speak, with my pants, and my heart, around my ankles. My airspeed indicator coldly told me I was doing only about 220 miles per hour, or less than cruising speed, and I had only ten feet of altitude.

For the first time on the mission, I pushed my mike button and called Mitchell. I asked him to send down anybody who wasn't busy. The two Japanese Zeros were diving at me again, almost at right angles, to my left.

I hugged the earth and the treetops while they made passes at me. I unwittingly led them smack across a corner of the Japanese fighter strip at Kahili, where Zeros were scrambling in the dust to take off. I made the harbor and headed east. With the Japanese on my tail I got into a speedy climb. At 20,000 I lost them. I was away with only two bullet holes in my rudder. Nothing more, except a year or two off my life.

Mitchell and his flight, responding to my call, came pile-driving down out of the sky and dispersed the Zeros. Contrary to all expectation, Mitch's covering section had met no resistance. Not one Zero had poked its nose higher than 5,000 feet that day. . . .

Going home, Mitchell called out to all pilots. The mission had been accomplished. Everyone in top cover had seen the two bombers crash in the jungle in flames. There was no doubt of their complete destruction."[12]

In addition to the *New York Times* article, a bylined article by Lanphier was distributed by the North American Newspaper Alliance (NANA) in 1945. While there were some similarities in the two stories, the NANA story had a more colorful description of Lanphier's alleged shootdown. After stating he had shot down one Zero and then kicked his P-38 over on its back, he said:

I spotted a shadow moving across the treetops below. I focused on it and found it to be the elusive bomber I was seeking. It was skimming along the surface of the jungle headed once more for Kahili. . . .

He was moving directly across from my left as I, too, flattened out on the treetops and prepared to slide up beside him for a point blank shot. As I moved in on him I began to realize that I had picked up too much speed in my dive and was going to overshoot him unless I slowed down. For the first time since we had sighted the Jap formation, I cut back on my throttles. Crossing my controls, I went into a skid to further brake my speed.

As I did so, the two Zeros I had not spoken to as we passed upstairs, showed up again. They, too, were diving toward the bomber from an angle slightly off to my right. Their intent was obviously to try and get me before I got the bomber. From where I sat, it looked very much like the bomber, the two Zeros and I were going to arrive at the same place at the same time.

We very nearly did. The next three or four seconds became a life-and-death problem in time and distance. I remember feeling very stubborn just then, about making the most of that one good shot I had coming up at that bomber, no matter what the high-priced talent in the two Zeros wanted to make of it.

I applied myself to my gunnery and taking no chances of missing, began firing a long steady burst across the bomber's line of flight from approximately right angles. Long before I considered myself in range, the bomber's right engine, and then his right wing, began to burn. I had accomplished my part of the mission. . . . The two onrushing Zeros shot by just then, apparently unwilling to chance a crash in the jungle in order to get me.

At the same instant they swooped across the top of my canopy. I was having trouble from another source. Out of [the bomber's] tail was puffing a steady series of shots from the cannon lodged back there. My belly already scraping the trees, I could not duck under it. And I hesitated to pull up over its line of fire since I was already going so slow that I would be left hanging in midair in a sitting duck position, near stalling speed—and the bothersome pair of Zeros were undoubtedly scurrying around into position for another pass at me.

. . . Just as I moved into range of its cannon, the bomber's right wing came off and it plunged into the jungle and exploded.

A glance to my left told me that my two Zeros had not forgotten me, they were diving on me once again, this time from almost right angles to my left. For the first time that day, I pushed my microphone button and called Mitchell. I asked him to send down anybody who was not busy at the moment to help me out. I called him once again [to] ask him to verify the burning bomber. He replied that he could see it. I then applied myself completely to keeping myself alive.

Lanphier described how the pursuing Zeros continued to press their attack but failed to hit him. He said he hugged the ground and zipped in and out of the gullies to escape the two Zeros and led them unwittingly across the Kahili airfield. He stated he saw three columns of black smoke rising out of the jungle behind him which were "the burning bomber containing Yamamoto and two of his accompanying aircraft." He climbed to 20,000 feet and left the area. "Except for the anti-aircraft from the harbor below, I was bothered no further." He continues his narrative:

Barber was not quite so fortunate. When I had pulled up into the Zeros on our first contact with the enemy, Rex had bored on in after the bomber coming our way. Ignoring the other three Zeros, who were by no means ignoring him, he opened fire on his target. The bomber passed under his right wing, still apparently undamaged. Despite the fact that he was now the concerted target of all three escorting Zeros, he bulled his way back through their fire and latched onto the bomber once again. *This time he drove his attack perfectly home blasting off the entire tail section of the Mitsubishi, which rolled over on its back and plummeted to the earth far below. No one jumped out of it.* (Italics added.)[13]

Rex Barber, Lanphier's wingman, tells a different story:

Lanphier and I were approaching the Bettys from approximately 90 degrees and still climbing to get to an altitude at least level with the two bombers.

The Bettys started to nose down, evidently starting their letdown to destination approach altitude. I was on Lanphier's

67

right wing when suddenly the Bettys increased their rate of descent markedly. Three Zeros, above and lagging a considerable distance to the right behind the Bettys, suddenly nosed over in a steep descent and jettisoned their external fuel tanks. We had evidently been sighted. Moments later the other three Zeros on the left side and closer to the bomber formation nosed over.

It became apparent that the three Zeros closest to the Bettys on the right side would catch up with the Bettys about the same time as we would turn in on our firing pass and we would be a perfect target.

Just before the time we would break right to fall in behind the Bettys, Lanphier suddenly broke about 90 degrees to the left and started a head-on pass up and into the oncoming Zeros. This was a wise maneuver on his part as it allowed me the opportunity to attack the bombers without the Zeros on my tail. I banked sharply right to fall in behind the Bettys and, in so doing, my left engine and wing briefly blocked out my view of both bombers. As I rolled back, there was only one Betty in front of me. I didn't know if it was the lead bomber or not.

By this time, we were no more than 1,000 feet above the terrain and the Betty again increased his dive in an evident attempt to get to treetop level. My turn had carried me slightly left of the Betty and about fifty yards behind. I opened fire, aiming over the fuselage at the right engine. I could see bits of engine cowling coming off. As I slid over to get directly behind the target, my line of fire passed through the vertical fin of the Betty. Some pieces of the rudder separated. As I moved right, I continued firing into the right engine. The engine began to emit heavy, black smoke from around the cowling. I moved my fire back along the wing root and into the fuselage, then on into the left engine.

By this time I was probably no more than 100 feet behind the Betty and almost level with it. Suddenly, the Betty snapped left. As it rotated, I almost struck the right wing as the Betty had slowed rapidly when it snapped. I looked over my left shoulder as I roared by and saw the bomber with its wing upended vertically and black smoke pouring from the right engine. I believe the Betty crashed into the jungle, although I did not see it crash.

I also saw three Zeros on my tail; the second flight of three

Zeros had caught up and were making firing passes at me. I turned to the right and headed toward the coast at treetop level taking violent evasive action. Luckily, two P-38s from Major Mitchell's flight saw my difficulty and made a head-on pass over me to clear the Zeros off my tail.

I looked inland and to my rear. A large column of black smoke was rising from the jungle which I believed to be the Betty I had shot down. As I headed toward the coast, I saw Lieutenant Holmes and Lieutenant Hine circling over the water at about 1,500 feet. I also saw a Betty very low over the water and just off shore, heading south. The Betty was so low that its props were making wakes in the water.

Lieutenant Holmes also spotted the Betty, and he and Lieutenant Hine, flying very close on Holmes's right wing, peeled off after it. Holmes started firing. His initial bullets hit the water behind the bomber, then walked up and through the right engine. A white vapor started trailing behind the right engine. Lieutenant Hine started to fire but all his rounds hit well ahead in the water. They passed over the Betty and headed south.

I dropped in behind the Betty and as I closed in to less than fifty yards, I opened fire, aiming at the right engine. Almost immediately, the bomber exploded. As I flew through the black smoke and debris, a large chunk of the Betty hit my right wing, cutting out my turbo supercharger intercooler. Another large piece hit the underside of my gondola, making a very large dent in it.

Ahead of me, Lieutenants Holmes and Hine had encountered Zeros which I think had taken off from the Kahili airstrip. Holmes shot one of them down. I saw Hine heading east, out to sea, smoking from his right engine.

A second Zero, which had broken off from Holmes, started to pass under me. I shot it down. I then looked for Holmes and Hine but saw neither one of them. I was particularly concerned about Hine because he had apparently suffered some damage.

I looked out over the water for signs of a crash. There were three oil slicks, one where the Betty had gone in and one each where Holmes's and my Zeros had crashed. I hoped that Hine was heading for Guadalcanal but that was not the case. I was now low on fuel and could not stay in the area any longer so I turned for home.[14]

Besby Holmes, fearful that he didn't have a chance for survival if he tangled with the Zeros with the belly tanks still attached, had turned seaward and nosed down to pick up speed. Lt. Ray Hine stayed on his wing. When Holmes reached about 350 mph, he hauled back on the wheel and kicked hard left rudder. The tanks tore off and he looked back to see what was happening:

It was impossible to tell what turn the battle was taking. Someone, whom I believe to be Lanphier, yelled, "I'm bracketed by three Zeros and can't go anywhere but straight ahead!"

Just then I saw a Betty plunge straight down and explode with a terrific flash. In the fracas I couldn't tell who had clobbered it. Since Lanphier had already called for help I thought that it was Rex Barber's guns that knocked the bomber down.

Looking below I saw a P-38 chasing a Betty and in turn being chased by three Zeros. Ray Hine and I barrel-rolled down with our Allisons wide open to assist the Lightning pilot, who was in a predicament.

The trapped pilot was Barber, not Lanphier. Lanphier wasn't in sight. I was told later that he was chased to the vicinity of Kahili airfield by three Zeros and finally lost them in a cloud of dust being kicked up by the swarm of Zeros scrambling for takeoff to help save Yamamoto. I did not see Lanphier in the fight after that initial attack.

I told Ray Hine to take the Zero on Barber's right wing, and I slid over to get the two crowding him from the left. As I slipped in behind the first Zero, I saw the Betty bomber fleeing in front of Barber's P-38. What a beautiful, easy target, I thought. We had to get that bomber if it was the last thing we ever did, but first we had to knock the three Zeros off Barber's back.

I let the first Zero have a long burst in the tail. The little Japanese fighter, pelted by the deadly, heavy 20mm cannon and .50 caliber bullets, exploded in a sheet of flame. I ducked instinctively as if to ward off the flying debris, then I quickly put my eye back to the gunsight.

The other Japanese pilot was evidently so intent upon getting Barber that he either didn't see me or was too stubborn to break off the fight. I touched my triggers and watched the bullets nibble at the Zero's tail. Seconds later the airplane flamed and fell off into an inverted dive into the sea.

With my airspeed indicating 425 mph, I zoomed past Barber just as Hine clobbered the Zero on Barber's right wing. The frantic Betty was now flying straight ahead, a sitting duck as far as I was concerned.

I pulled up even with it, setting up a classical high side gunnery pass, one which we all had practiced many times. I chose that method of attack rather than go directly at the tail, which contained a couple of deadly heavy caliber stingers. By this time the Japanese gunners on the bomber were all firing at me.

As I closed in on the Betty, which was now flying barely above the water, I fired a short burst of my fifties to get the proper deflection and check the range. There was no need to be in a hurry. There was still sufficient time to shoot the bomber down in my own way. The next burst of fifties kicked up the water just short of the bomber.

"Next time," I said aloud, at the same time pulling my gunsight farther ahead of the Betty.

"Now!"

I touched the trigger. The fifties chattered and vibrated, shaking the whole airplane. Bullets tore into the Betty, showing me that my range and deflection were perfect. I pressed the button to fire my 20mm cannon and listened to the dull POM-POM-POM of the shells as they exploded.

It was the longest burst I had ever fired, and it was having its effect on the bomber. The gunners who had been sniping at me from the Betty stopped firing. Now I could slide in behind for a stern shot.

We were now no more than ten miles from Kahili field and I could see clouds of dust rising from the hornet's nest of Zeros scrambling for takeoff. Right then I knew I had about run out of time. The Betty had to be polished off quickly if I expected to get back to Guadalcanal.

Flying in extremely close, I lined my gunsight on the bomber's right engine and touched the triggers. The bullets tore into the engine and wing root and I could see little tongues of flame leap out. But the Betty wouldn't go down!

I heard myself yelling, "Go down! Go down! Go down or blow up, dammit! What do I have to do to make you go down?"

I continued to squeeze the triggers and sent a long burst into the engine. A huge puff of smoke, followed by orange flame, burst from the engine cowling. I stopped yelling and quickly came to my senses just as I found myself about to ram the Betty's tail.

In my haste and eagerness I had forgotten how fast I was going in comparison to the speed of the bomber. It almost ended the scrap for me right there. For an instant I thought I could pull over the Betty's tail and escape a collision; but that wasn't possible.

Instead, I rammed the controls forward with all the force I could muster. For a split second, the negative G's lifted me off my seatpack. I saw the shadow of the bomber over me, and immediately hauled back sharply on the controls to keep from crashing into the water.

As I pulled up to make another pass, I saw the Betty crash. It hit the water with great force, broke into pieces and scattered over the surface of the ocean. At the same time Barber bored in and fired at the wreckage. Then the Betty sank.

When I called to Barber and Hine to follow me and clear out of the area, I received no answer. My radio wasn't working. Fortunately, both pilots were flying nearby and we headed toward the open sea. I sighed with relief. We had completed the mission, both Bettys had been shot down, I had knocked off two Zeros, and Ray Hine had gotten another. We had the brass ring!

My relief was extremely short-lived. Out of the corner of my eye I saw an object streaking down on Barber's tail from the direction of Kahili. Turning quickly, I saw a Zero roaring in for the kill.

With my radio out, I couldn't warn Rex. I quickly pulled my '38 up and over in the start of a loop, tripped my maneuver flaps, and then checked my airspeed. It showed 350 miles an hour. I wasn't supposed to trip the flaps above 260, but at this stage of the game I didn't care about that as long as the wings stayed on. Unless I could get there fast Barber was a dead duck.

Pulling straight up, I rolled the P-38 into an Immelmann to get into position to snap a burst at the Zero. The enemy pilot saw me, broke off the attack on Barber, and also pulled up. I went up after him, goosing the throttles to get every ounce of power I could squeeze out of the two engines. Up, up we went. I was getting close, practically on his tail, firing as we climbed.

Suddenly, my Lightning faltered. The right engine conked out and the airspeed started dropping off fast. The thought flashed through my mind that if I didn't get this Japanese pilot now he would discover I had an engine out, roll over then split-S out, come up under me, and knock me out of the sky.

I continued firing, knowing that this would be my only chance. My 20mm cannon had already quit firing. How many .50 caliber rounds were left? I kept my gunship glued on his tail by pushing in hard on the left rudder and increasing the pressure gradually until I hit the rudder stop. I saw a burst of flame from the Zero as he went out of control.

I eased off on the rudder and let the good engine pull me over into a hammerhead stall. My airspeed was so low I didn't dare breathe. That beautiful airplane. It made the most perfect hammerhead I've ever seen. As soon as the 38's nose dropped through the horizon, I leveled the wing and considered the situation. I was alone. Hine and Barber were nowhere around. I later found out that they were engaged in another battle in which Hine lost. He was a fine pilot and his loss was keenly felt.

I had never been in a tighter spot. About the only gratification was that I was still alive and had saved Barber's neck for the second time that day. I had also added another Zero to my list of kills, making my total for the day one bomber and three Zeros.[15]

Doug Canning, leading the second element of Mitchell's flight of four, could not see any of the action either since he was keeping his eyes on Mitchell. When Lanphier called for help, he and Goerke followed Mitchell and Jacobson down looking for the Zeros dogging Lanphier. Mitchell, going at top speed, came in behind a Zero and fired a few shots but claims no hits. He zoomed past his quarry and didn't see it again.

Canning recalled:

As Mitchell went down, I broke away when I was able to

line up on a Zero. I was closing in on him when, because of our rapid descent, my windshield misted over in front of the gunsight and I was unable to fire and lost the Zero. I pulled away and when my windshield cleared, I couldn't find Mitch and noticed that Del Goerke, my wingman was gone. I climbed to about 10,000 feet and found I was the last P-38 in the area. I also saw many, many Zeros taking off from Kahili. Being the last one there, and discretion being the better part of valor, I left the scene.

The whole action took, at the most, about ten minutes. On the way back I caught up with Lieutenant Holmes and helped him get into the Russell Islands base as he describes. I didn't see him land because I was now short of gas. I went on to Guadalcanal where I was the last one to land.[16]

Julius Jacobson, Mitchell's wingman, had followed his leader down and also fired a few rounds at the Zero Mitchell had lined up on. Like Mitchell, he doesn't believe he scored any hits.

"I didn't see any of the action before that," he told the author. "And I didn't see any smoke coming out of the jungle or the dust rising from Kahili as others have told about. I was too busy staying on Mitch's wing. That was my job."[17]

The battle was over. The fifteen P-38s headed for Guadalcanal, some in loose formation, others singly. The sixteenth aircraft, piloted by Lt. Ray K. Hine, never returned; he was listed as missing and, after thirty days, was declared dead. His fate remains unknown.

From the accounts of the three surviving pilots in the "killer" flight, the score would appear to be three Betty bombers and three Zeros shot down. However, Lanphier, in his 1945 account, did give credit to Barber for shooting down a bomber over the jungle. Barber stated that Holmes had shot at the second bomber but did not bring it down. No other pilots confirmed any kills.

Unfortunately, the P-38s did not carry gun cameras so none of the action was recorded on film. It was the word of each surviving pilot in the killer flight against another. None of the pilots flying top cover saw any aircraft go down. Mitchell and a few others saw black smoke coming up from the jungle which they thought was possibly from an aircraft fire. Since both Betty bombers were shot down and Admiral Yamamoto was believed to be in one of them, the mission was accomplished.

To most of the men who flew top cover that day, it didn't matter who shot the admiral down. To Lanphier, however, it mattered very much. If he were given credit for a Betty bomber and a Zero fighter, he would be credited with a total of seven aircraft and thus assure his place in the glory list of pilots who were "aces" for having shot down five or more enemy aircraft. However, one of these seven enemy aircraft was a Zero he claimed while riding as a passenger on a B-17 mission. The B-17 crew refused to confirm this kill. No other pilots ever claimed credit for an enemy aircraft shot down while flying as crewmembers on a bombing mission.

Lanphier's serialized account in the *New York Times* and the NANA story were repeated in abbreviated form under the title "I Shot Down Yamamoto" in a December 1966 *Reader's Digest* article. However, the latter version was slightly different from the first two as he described what he did after he shot down one of the six Zeros:

> At that moment, in an almost vertical climb, I kicked my ship over on its back and looked for the bomber I had lost in the melee.
> Sheer panic does wonders for the vision. In one glance I saw Barber tangling with some Zeros even as two other Zeros bored in on me. Then I saw a green shadow streaking across the jungle below—the bomber, skimming just over the trees. I followed it down to treetop level, and began firing a long steady burst. Its right engine and right wing fell off, and the bomber crashed in the jungle.
> By this time, Barber had splashed the other Betty in the ocean.[18]

This latter version, written to win a special "first person" award from the magazine, implies that he shot down the lead bomber from the rear. In his spoken and written accounts before and afterward, he stated that he had made a deflection shot from right angles to the direction of the Betty bomber.

The original Lanphier versions describing the 90-degree deflection shots have been accepted as fact by most writers. Few doubted his veracity or tried to verify the fine points of his accounts. And even fewer have ever contacted John Mitchell or Rex Barber to determine if there might be other points of view.

There were inaccuracies and exaggerations in Lanphier's versions that have been compounded over time and have stimulated grave doubts on the part of knowledgeable pilots, especially the fighter pilots who served in the South Pacific in the freewheeling glory days of 1942–43. He was challenged frequently by his contemporaries, especially during the 1984–85 period, when he sent drafts of his memoirs to Mitchell, Barber, Jacobson, Canning, and other survivors of the mission, as well as to many friends, acquaintances, and publishers, for comment. To those who disagreed with his version, Lanphier would reply extensively and fall back on the "official" 1943 combat report as his defense. It is this basic report, from which all subsequent accounts have been developed, that is open to serious question. The two men in whose names it was prepared and forwarded— army Capt. William Morrison and navy Lt. Joseph E. McGuigan—are deceased. The colorful language used, rare for a combat action report, was typical of Lanphier's style of writing and speaking.

On the other hand few, if any, doubt what Barber has claimed. According to Julius Jacobson, Mitchell's wingman, "At no time ever do I recall anyone doubt what Barber said or what he did. The only thing ever questioned was what Lanphier said. I'm convinced that Barber mortally wounded that airplane and probably killed Yamamoto, but he did not see it hit the jungle. It is possible the plane flew long enough for Lanphier to get it. If he followed it long enough to get a shot at it, he should get some credit for it."[19]

Lanphier wrote and sold his colorful version of an important event in the air history of World War II. The errors and embellishments in his and other accounts will be explored later.

6

"APRIL 18 SEEMS TO BE OUR DAY."

URING THE BATTLE, THERE HAD BEEN VERY little chatter on the radio between the four members of the killer flight. Barber recalls Holmes saying he couldn't get his tanks off and would remain over the water until he could release them. He heard Lanphier call Mitchell during the encounter, but that's all.

Del Goerke, flying in the top cover, recalled seeing a column of smoke rising from the jungle but nothing else. Too busy staying in formation and looking for the Zeros they thought would be flying top cover for Yamamoto, none of the other top cover American pilots saw any action far below them. Lanphier shouted excitedly over the mike and asked Mitchell if he saw one of the bombers go down, but Mitchell said he could see nothing but the black smoke drifting upward out of the jungle.

Lanphier shouted for help when two Zeros ganged up on him and Mitchell asked him where he was. Mitchell picks up the narrative:

> Lanphier didn't know where he was but said he was still over land heading southeastward toward the ocean. I couldn't

see him but I looked toward the south and saw a P-38 flying along straight and level over the water with smoke coming out of his left engine. There was a Zero flying behind him and I could see smoke coming out of his wings so I knew he was still firing at the '38.

I didn't know who it was but I was sure it wasn't Lanphier because he said he was over the jungle. I called in the blind and said, "This is Mitch. All P-38s check your tail. Somebody's got a Zero sitting on his tail!" I'm sure everybody swiveled their heads at that but the P-38 I saw down below just kept going with that Zero still firing away.

I called to Jake Jacobson, my wingman, and said, "We're going down, Jake," and down we went. We got right on the edge of compressibility because my yoke started to vibrate which, in our limited knowledge of P-38 capabilities, was the sign that you couldn't go any faster or the tail might come off.

I kept my eye on that Zero and pulled up behind him. I was going at least 400 mph and decided to start firing long before I was in range, hoping he would see the tracers and get off the P-38's tail. He did and suddenly broke hard right and headed back toward land. At my speed of about 400 mph, compared to his speed of about 200, I knew I couldn't stay with him without pulling six or eight G's so I didn't follow him. Jake took a pop at him but I don't think he hit him and I know I didn't.

I turned back and made a couple of circles looking for an oil slick or somebody floating around in a yellow Mae West. I didn't see anything. At the time I didn't know who it was in the P-38 but it turned out to be Ray Hine, Holmes's wingman. If Holmes did all the didos [trick maneuvers] that he said he did, I don't see how any wingman could have stayed with him. So Hine must have been flying out there all by himself.

At some time during all this I got the word that the second bomber had gone down in the water so since we had gotten the two bombers, I started climbing and radioed, "Mission accomplished. Everybody, get your ass home."[1]

Doug Canning and his wingman, Del Goerke, also came down after a Zero, but just as Canning was lining up into firing position behind the Zero, his windshield fogged over and he lost his target. Somewhere in the ensuing few seconds, Goerke got separated and didn't fire at the Zero. When Mitchell called for everybody to head for home, Canning began climbing alone toward Guadalcanal.

There wasn't much radio talk among Mitchell's top cover pilots remaining at altitude because they had nothing to report. Maj. Lou Kittel, now leading the top cover of eight P-38s, replied with a simple "Roger" when Mitchell gave the order to go home. Disappointed at having had no action, he turned his flight toward Guadalcanal. Since they had remained at about 18,000 feet, their fuel consumption was not as great as those down lower, and none of his flight of eight aircraft was worried about getting back to Fighter Two.

It was different for Besby Holmes. He had thought his radio had failed him during the brush with the bomber but found that the earphone plug had pulled out. Heading home, he checked his fuel gauges and thought the odds were against him making it all the way to Guadalcanal. He was relieved that he could talk with someone and called Mitchell.

"Mitch, I don't think I can make it," Holmes said, with a tight voice.

"O.K., don't panic. We'll spread out and see if we can find you."

"It seemed an eternity until Doug Canning finally found me and settled in close to my wing," Holmes said. He recalled:

"I've got trouble, Doug," I said. "Not enough gas to get back to the Canal."

"How much do you have left?" Canning asked.

"I'll do some quick figuring and let you know."

The recheck wasn't any more encouraging.

At normal fuel consumption I would be out of gas in about an hour and ten minutes. I had already accepted the fact that I couldn't make Guadalcanal. Now my only hope was to get to the Russell Islands, which, according to my calculations, was an hour and 40 minutes away at normal cruising. Obviously I couldn't fly at normal settings and normal cruising speed. I would have to throttle back and use just enough power to keep the old bird in the sky.

Now that Doug Canning was riding close to me I felt a little better. I knew that if I had to ditch, he would pinpoint my position and tell searchers exactly where to look for me; that is, if the enemy didn't find me first.

79

Still flying close to the water, I weaned the Allisons until my airspeed indicated 170, far from the normal cruising speed of 260. I continued in a straight line toward Guadalcanal, knowing that I hadn't a snowball's chance of making it. Nearing New Georgia, we saw a large formation of Zeros a few miles off to our right, heading up the Slot, looking for us. I prayed that they wouldn't see a glint of sunlight off our canopies. Again luck was with us and we passed the fighters unnoticed.

I recalculated. "Doug, I definitely can't make it back to Henderson. It'll have to be the Russells or ditch," I said.

Canning called back. "I'll stay with you. No sweat."

No sweat, he says! For what seemed hours I flew with my eyes glued to those fuel gauges. One tank ran dry. I switched to another. A few minutes later I switched back to the empty tank hoping to drain out the last few drops that had failed to get into the fuel lines. Back and forth, back and forth I switched tanks until there wasn't a drop left except in one reserve tank. It wouldn't be long until I would have to say goodbye to the gallant old airplane. I hated the thought of losing her after what she had been through in the Yamamoto fight.

A faint line appeared on the horizon. It was an island! But which one? I glanced at the map clipped to the leg of my flying suit. The Russells? It had to be the Russells. I knew the marines had started constructing an airfield there several days before!

Pointing to the fringe of coastline, I called to Doug. "There's the Russells! I'm going to land there no matter what condition the field's in!"

"Lead the way," Canning answered. "I'll stay with you."

The fuel level continued to drop until the needle sat near the empty mark. I hoped, prayed, and agonized as the island slowly began to take shape. Now I could see palm trees and coastline. Only a few long miles separated me from land.

"Doug, drag the airstrip and scatter the workers!" I called. "Buzz in low and see if you can make them get that equipment out of the way."

Canning nodded and I saw his throttle hand go forward. He forged ahead of me and roared toward the airfield, cluttered with steam rollers and other heavy equipment. With his props almost dragging the coral, Canning alerted the workers.

When he pulled up, put his wheels and flaps down, and turned in on what appeared to be a final approach, the heavy equipment and all personnel hurriedly cleared the strip—all 1,700 feet of it.

I dropped my landing gear and flaps and hopped over the small knoll that suddenly appeared in front of me. I set the '38 down heavily and rammed the brakes hard. The airplane came to a skidding halt near the far end. When I opened the canopy my flying suit was dripping wet.[2]

Canning didn't land but returned to Guadalcanal. Holmes discovered that he had only about four gallons of fuel left. He checked his guns and found that all his 20mm ammunition was gone and he had only four .50 caliber bullets left. Later that day, a navy PT boat arrived. Since the PTs also had Allison engines installed and burned high-octane fuel, they furnished Holmes with about 120 gallons in 5-gallon cans, enough to return to Guadalcanal a few hours later.

Meanwhile, Barber also returned to Guadalcanal and had sweated out his own gas supply for the final few minutes:

"I landed at Fighter Two almost out of gas," he recalled. "My crew chief showed me four bullet holes through the blades of my left prop and three in the right prop. There were 104 in-and-out bullet holes in the wings, tail section, and fuselage, probably 52 hits, all from the rear to front. This confirmed for me that I was hit from behind by the Zeros, not by the gunners on the Bettys."[3]

Lanphier also barely made it back. A few miles out from the island, he called "Recon," the Guadalcanal fighter director station. Lt. (jg) Edward C. Hutcheson, the officer on duty, responded and Lanphier yelled jubilantly over the radio, "I got Yamamoto! I got the son-of-bitch! He won't dictate peace terms in the White House now!"[4]

In 1988, Lt. Roger J. Ames, one of the cover flight pilots, said, "All I can remember [about the return from the mission] is how upset I was when Tom Lanphier made his statement over the open mike."[5]

Lt. Joseph O. Young met Lanphier's aircraft and recalled that Lanphier was the first to land. "From the aircraft he claimed victory over Admiral Yamamoto in no uncertain terms. His reaction was astounding to me and appeared to be irrational. He was visibly shaken, but very adamant about his victory."[6]

Lanphier said later he wanted to make a pass and victory roll over Henderson and Fighter Two but with his fuel gauge reading empty, he knew he might not make it. He said his left engine quit on the landing roll and he came to a stop near the end of the runway. Ground crews ran out to his plane and swarmed around him as he climbed out of the cockpit. He kept repeating, "I got the son-of-a-bitch! I got Yamamoto!" Everybody patted him on the back as he unbuckled his parachute and got into a waiting jeep.

Lt. Bill Harris, a pilot who did not go on the mission, recalled: "I saw Tom Lanphier coming down the runway in a jeep from where his airplane was parked alongside the runway, and I heard him call out several times, loudly, 'I got him! I got him! I got that son-of-a-bitch.' This was before he reached the tent where some of the other pilots had gathered and were talking about the mission."[7] John Mitchell also recalled after he landed that he saw Lanphier coming down the taxiway in a jeep, "waving and hollering, 'I got Yamamoto!' "

Other pilots confirmed that they remember Lanphier standing up in the back of the jeep shouting over and over again that he had shot the admiral down. Ground crews cheered and milled around excitedly.

Maj. Louis Kittel, leader of the eight top cover aircraft, said that when he parked his aircraft, his ground crew told him of the results of the mission. "Lanphier apparently announced to the flight crew that he had shot the big man down," he wrote the author,

> because when I parked that was the word my crew conveyed to me. At this point, Lanphier had not cross-checked results with the other shooters.
>
> Tom was open and enthusiastic with his discussion of the mission. I could accept his judgment in making a head-on attack with the Zeros, but I had then, and still have now, deep doubts on his ability to catch a diving Betty, much less make an almost 90-degree deflection shot from presumably out of range.
>
> During my career down there, I had three different occa-

sions to shoot down Bettys. In each case, I had to close from the rear to point-blank range before an explosion would occur. On one of these occasions the Betty was contacted while flying on the deck. It walked up to 320 mph and only because I had altitude to convert to speed could I gain the speed to overtake it."[8]

Neither Mitchell nor Barber could believe what they were hearing from Lanphier. How could Lanphier know which Betty the admiral was riding in? No one could confirm that Lanphier had shot down *any* aircraft. Mitchell and the pilots in the cover flight saw nothing but black smoke coming out of the jungle. Barber knew only that Lanphier had turned away from the two Bettys toward the Zeros trying to intercept them and never saw him after that. Barber was sure *he* had shot down a Betty and shared in the kill of another, plus possibly bagging a Zero. Holmes had not returned yet to report his story. And it was probable that Hine had been shot down. The only witnesses to any of the action of the killer flight against the two bombers were Lanphier, Barber, and Holmes, and their stories did not coincide.

Unfortunately, there was no formal debriefing of any of the returning pilots. Paul S. Bechtel, one of the Guadalcanal pilots, remembers postmission debriefings in those days as "informal and confusing." When the returning pilots gathered in the headquarters tent, he said "everyone was talking at the same time and as far as I know, the only records taken were notes that the one or two 'intelligence' officers present made and these were usually concerned with victory claims and confirming information."[9]

"We had no one who could conduct debriefings in those days," Mitchell recalled. "We were uneducated then. We only knew what we had been through and accepted each other's versions of what happened."[10]

Julius Jacobson confirmed what Mitchell said. "I flew 111 missions in the South Pacific," he told the author, "and I was never debriefed even once." He didn't find this unusual after the Yamamoto mission because "it was not common practice."[11]

Lou Kittel also affirmed that he had not had a formal debriefing. He said, "I don't recall there ever being an official gathering of the participants after the mission but we sure were together for a briefing before the mission." However, he added in retrospect, "I do believe someone met me at the aircraft and asked, 'How'd it go?' "[12]

Del Goerke recalled that he was met by a naval officer who asked what he knew about the mission. "It was from this person that I learned that two bombers had been shot down and that the mission was probably successful," he said. "This officer did not spend much time with me as all I saw was a smoke column coming out of the jungle. The only semblance of a debriefing, insofar as I was concerned, was the officer who met my plane."[13]

Brooklyn Harris, squadron clerk for the 339th, also acted as an intelligence clerk. He recalled that "a lot of us out there were civilians in uniform, and knew nothing of military record-keeping. We did not keep mission reports at squadron level before the middle of 1943.

"No one debriefed the pilots," he said. "The unit of pilots and ground crews at Guadalcanal were attached to a Marine squadron for food and quarters. The Marines and Navy had administrative personnel there. If any individual combat reports were taken at that time, it had to be by Marine or Navy staff."[14]

John E. Little was a pilot on Guadalcanal at the time and he believes there was some kind of meeting of the participating pilots, however informal, after Mitchell and his men landed.

"As I recall," he said,

Col. Vicellio told me the pilots were in a debriefing and as soon as they were finished they would tell us their story. It seemed as if it was 30 minutes to an hour before we got to see them.

They came over and stood in two lines, one behind the other. I don't recall who spoke first, probably Mitchell. I do remember that Tom Lanphier wasn't too sure of exactly what he did. I felt sure that Rex Barber was sure of what he had done. There were about 25 to 40 officers and about 50 to 100 enlisted men listening to the pilots tell their stories about the mission.[15]

Mitchell is positive that *he* held no debriefing of his pilots but wishes he had. "I blame myself for not debriefing everybody, especially Lanphier, Barber, and Holmes," Mitchell said.

I should have known better because it was an important mission. We had good debriefings later in the war but we had no formal setup then. If I had done it myself right then and there, we wouldn't have this controversy today about who shot Yamamoto down. It would certainly have stopped a lot of the flak that Lanphier was throwing out that day and ever afterward.

But who was going to argue with him? Rex Barber was the only other one there after the lead bomber. But he wasn't going to say he had shot the admiral down because neither he nor anyone else knew which bomber the man was in. Rex said he shot down two bombers but nobody listened to him. Lanphier said he saw Rex shoot one down over land which is enough for me to want to give Barber the credit."[16]

Nobody questioned Lanphier's claim as he persisted in retelling his story over and over to anyone who would listen while Barber sat back, unable to understand how Lanphier could continue to make such a claim. Finally, Barber had enough. He asked, "How in the hell do you know you got Yamamoto?"

Lanphier shot back, "You're a damn liar! You're a damn liar!"

Barber was shocked at this reaction. "I hadn't made a statement. I just asked a question, but here he was calling *me* a damn liar for asking a question."[17]

Since the mission was so important, the word that the interception had been successful spread rapidly all over Guadalcanal. Although it was supposedly a top secret operation, everyone on the island from Admiral Mitscher down to the lowest ranking cook, mechanic, and clerk knew about it. Lanphier insisted that he had shot Yamamoto down and everyone took his word as gospel. Only Mitchell and Barber questioned his claim; neither wanted to argue with him.

Later that day, the first of several classified operational messages, based on the informal reports of the personnel at Fighter Two, was prepared by Lt. Comdr. William A. Read, an administrative officer on Mitscher's staff who suggested that a good opening line was needed. The following top secret dispatch was sent to Admiral Halsey:

POP GOES THE WEASEL. P-38S LED BY MAJOR J. WIL-LIAM MITCHELL USAAF VISITED KAHILI AREA. ABOUT 0930L SHOT DOWN TWO BOMBERS ESCORTED BY 6 ZEROS FLYING CLOSE FORMATION. 1 OTHER BOMBER SHOT DOWN BELIEVED ON TEST FLIGHT. 3 ZEROS ADDED TO THE SCORE SUMS TOTAL 6. 1 P-38 FAILED RETURN. APRIL 18 SEEMS TO BE OUR DAY. MSG 180229 COMAIRSOLS to COMSOPAC.[18]

In the final sentence, Mitscher was referring to the launching of Jimmy Doolittle's B-25 bombers from the carrier *Hornet* against Japan on April 18 the year before. Mitscher had been in command of the *Hornet*, while Halsey had been in command of the sixteen-ship task force on the *Enterprise*.

A followup message was sent four hours later confirming the earlier report and restated that three bombers and three Zeros had been downed with the loss of one "blue" (Army Air Force) fighter.

"Once the results of the flight were known and the pilots were back on the ground," Lieutenant Commander Read recalled, "I was instructed to prepare recommendations for all the survivors for the Congressional Medal of Honor and for spot promotion."[19]

Halsey was elated when he got the word from Mitscher. "When the news was announced at my regular conference next morning," he wrote in his memoirs, "[Rear Adm. R.] Kelly Turner whooped and applauded. I told him, 'Hold on, Kelly! What's so good about it? I'd hoped to lead that scoundrel up Pennsylvania Avenue in chains, with the rest of you kicking him where it would do the most good!' "[20]

Halsey immediately sent a secret message to Mitscher:

CONGRATULATIONS TO YOU AND MAJOR MITCHELL AND HIS HUNTERS. SOUNDS AS THOUGH ONE OF THE DUCKS IN THEIR BAG WAS A PEACOCK.[21]

It was still April 17 at Pearl Harbor on the other side of the International Date Line when the word came in. There is no record of any extraordinary reaction. Nimitz's summary of the day's activities said simply: "It seems probable that CinC Combined [Fleet] was shot down in a plane over the Buin area today by Army P-38s."[22]

Arriving back at Fighter Two later that day after refueling at Russell Island, Besby Holmes was "mad as hell" that

the victories had been distributed before I could report what Ray Hine and I had accomplished. As a result a few heated words were passed between us.

Lanphier claimed a Betty. So did Barber. Lanphier claimed credit for shooting down Yamamoto. Neither one mentioned my part since Lanphier never saw it, and Barber obviously didn't know who was providing him assistance. . . .

Barber insisted that he had shot down one bomber on the initial pass as did Tom Lanphier. Each of them, by their accounts, received credit for one bomber. But neither could confirm the other's claim, and we did not have gun-camera film. Rex did confirm the bomber and the fighters that I had claimed; but I was only given official credit for one bomber and one fighter, giving me a total of five in the record book.[23]

From the accounts of the three survivors of the killer flight, the score would appear to be three Betty bombers and three Zeros shot down. However, Barber confirmed that Holmes had been shooting at the Betty headed out to sea but not that Holmes's shots had brought it down. Barber claimed his fire had finished it off. The damage to Barber's P-38 from the collision with pieces of the bomber clearly supported his assertion.

It was the word of each surviving pilot against another. None of the pilots flying top cover saw any of the action against the lead bomber three miles below them. Mitchell and several others saw black smoke coming up from the jungle which they believed might be an aircraft fire; that was all.

Since both Betty bombers were shot down and Admiral Yamamoto was believed to be in one of them, "I didn't give a damn," Mitchell said. "We did what we were supposed to do. It didn't make any difference to me who shot the admiral down."[24]

On April 19, the fifteen pilots were photographed by navy still and motion picture photographers. Barber, Holmes, and Lanphier were also photographed separately. Two days later, an extensive secret report on the mission was prepared on Guadalcanal and forwarded to Halsey and Nimitz. After describing the planning and the route flown to the interception point, the report continued:

When Lanphier and Barber were within one mile of contact, their attack was observed by the enemy. The bombers nosed down, one started a 360-degree turn dive, the other going out and away toward the shoreline; the Zeros dropped their belly tanks and three peeled down, in a string, to intercept Lanphier. When he saw that he could not reach the bomber he turned up and into the enemy, exploding the first Zero, and firing into the others as they passed. By this time he had reached 6,000 feet, so he nosed over, and went down to the treetops after his escaping objective. He came into the bomber broadside—and fired his bursts—a wing flew off and the plane went flaming to the earth.

The Zeros were now pursuing him and had the benefit of altitude. His mission accomplished, he hedgehopped the trees and made desperate maneuvers to escape. He kicked rudders, slipped, and skidded, tracers were flying past his plane, but he finally outran them. In all the action he had received two 7.7s in his horizontal stabilizer.

Barber had gone in with Lanphier on the initial attack. He went for one of the bombers but its maneuvers caused him to overshoot a little. He whipped back, however, and although pursued by Zeros, caught the bomber and destroyed it. When he fired, the tail section flew off, the bomber turned over on its back and plummeted to earth.

By this time, Holmes had been able to drop his tank and with Hine, who had stayed in formation with him, came in to ward off the Zeros who were pursuing Barber. A dogfight ensued, but results were not observed. The flight was on its way out of the combat area (in the neighborhood of enemy bases at Kahili, Ballale, and Shortland-Faisi) when Holmes noticed a stray bomber near Moila Point flying low over the water. He dove on it, his bursts setting it smoking in the left engine; Hine also shot at it and Barber polished it off with a burst in the fuselage. The bomber exploded; a piece of the plane flew off, cut through his left wing and knocked out his left inner cooler, and other chunks left paint streaks on his wing—so close was his attack driven home.

Holmes, Hine, and Barber returned home; however, Zeros were coming in on Barber's tail and Holmes whipped up and around and shot one down in flames. Another attempt to draw away ended in another dogfight during which Barber shot down a Zero. During this time, Hine's left engine started to smoke and he was last seen losing altitude south of Shortland Island. It is believed that Hine also accounted for a Zero as a total of three enemy fighters were seen to fall into the sea during this part of the combat. Holmes eventually ran out of gas and made a successful landing at the Russell Islands, from which he later brought his plane safely back. The damage to the cooling system of Barber's left motor prevented him from pulling more than 30 inches of mercury at low levels and 25 inches at 4/5,000 feet but despite this limitation to his speed and rate of climb he also brought his plane in safely to base.

The success of this extraordinary mission—a 435-mile interception by land planes largely over water—was due in large measure to Major Mitchell. On the eve of the flight, the mission was thoroughly explained to each pilot—there were no generalities. Each minute detail was discussed, with nothing taken for granted: take-off procedure, flight altitude, exactly when and how to drop belly tanks, radio silence, the tremendous importance of precise timing and position of covering elements, until Major Mitchell was sure that each of his pilots knew both his part and that of each other pilot from take-off to return.[25]

The report was identified as having been prepared by Capt. William Morrison and Lt. Joseph E. McGuigan, the army and navy intelligence officers who had helped Mitchell when he was laying out the course. Neither Mitchell nor Barber were consulted during the preparation of the report.

On April 24, a weekly action summary report was sent from Admiral Fitch's headquarters to Nimitz, with an information copy to Admiral King in Washington:

THIS IS ULTRA.
HIGHLIGHTS OF REPORT MAILED ON BUIN ACTION
OF 18TH. 12 P-38S WERE COVER FOR 4 P-38S WHICH ALL

ATTACKING. 33 MILES NORTHWEST KAHILI SIGHTED 2 BOMBERS TOGETHER AT 4500 FEET. 6 ZEROS 1,500–2,000 FEET ABOVE SLIGHTLY TO REAR. BOMBERS PARTED AND DIVED WHILE ZEROS STRUCK AT P-38S. 1 ENEMY BOMBER WAS ATTACKED JUST ABOVE TREE TOPS. WING FLEW OFF AND BOMBER WENT FLAMING TO EARTH. SECOND BOMBER QUOTE TAIL SECTION FLEW OFF BOMBER TURNED ON ITS BACK AND PLUMMETED TO EARTH. A THIRD BOMBER ENCOUNTERED WHEN P-38S WITHDRAWING EXPLODED IN AIR.[26]

Meanwhile, Halsey forwarded the secret combat report in letter form to Nimitz in Hawaii who endorsed it on to Admiral King in Washington:

1. The enclosure to the basic letter covers an operation on a particularly high plane of secrecy carried out under a directive of the Commander, South Pacific Force. In these circumstances no publicity of any kind should be given this action.
2. Major Mitchell and his associated pilots of the U.S. Army Air Force conducted this operation with the utmost gallantry and determination. It is assumed that Commander, South Pacific Force has initiated appropriate awards to the participating pilots.
3. Additional information complementary to this report is available from ULTRA sources. C. W. Nimitz.[27]

Meanwhile, according to an official history, "Admiral Mitscher was so pleased with the results that he requested permission to grant the Navy Medal of Honor to Mitchell and the Navy Cross to all other participants, but the awards were scaled down."[28] The study also cited a confirming letter from Lt. Gen. Millard F. Harmon, commander of the Thirteenth Air Force to Lt. Gen. H. H. Arnold, commander, U.S. Army Air Forces, May 1, 1943.

The report signed by Morrison and McGuigan and the follow-up messages were thus accepted by army and navy commanders as the official version of this epic mission. In the ensuing years, many, but not all, service historians would also give credence to these original reports as to what actually happened that day and accept them at face value. These reports would suggest that Lanphier was totally responsible for Yamamoto's demise. As a result, he would thereafter proclaim himself the only pilot who deserves credit for the shootdown of Japan's top naval leader.

Those who flew with Lanphier on the Yamamoto mission did not believe he could claim the honor since no one at the time knew which bomber the admiral was in. Barber was quite certain that he had shot down a bomber that crashed in the jungle; however, because he had momentarily lost sight of both bombers, he was not absolutely sure the bomber he shot down was the lead bomber.

As Louis Kittel, one of the pilots in the cover flight and an avid hunter, put it, the Yamamoto mission was a "trophy hunt" and, "like all trophy hunts, the one who bags the trophy bird or beast garners honor among his peers. Lanphier was desperate for that honor."[29]

The dispute would continue far into the future.

7
THE OTHER SIDE OF THE STORY

HE WAR HAD GONE BADLY FOR YAMAMOTO after Pearl Harbor when the losses were all added up. The Battle of the Coral Sea on May 7–8, the first naval engagement to be fought by forces that never came in sight of one another and traded blows only by air, was certainly not a clear victory. His biggest loss was, of course, the Battle of Midway. On August 8–9, 1942, his forces barely eked out a victory in the Battle of Savo Island. And he could certainly claim no great honors for the Battle of the Bismarck Sea which began on March 2, 1943, when a B-24 piloted by Lt. Walter Higgins discovered a convoy of fourteen ships heading for Lae, New Guinea. This force was soon joined by eight more for a total of twelve troop transports and ten cruisers and destroyers.

On the first day of the action, March 4, 1943, American planes destroyed eight troop transports with more than five thousand troops on board destined for New Guinea from Rabaul on New Britain Island. Yamamoto's force also lost four of eight destroyers. Sixteen Army Air Force P-38s engaged the defending Zeros at altitude while Boeing B-17s level-bombed and North American B-25s and Douglas A-20s used new low-level skip-bombing techniques to hammer the slow-moving ships below. By late afternoon of the second day, the Japanese had eighty-three planes destroyed or damaged. The air force lost one B-17 and three P-38s in combat. With the opposing planes out of the air, the Americans concentrated on the remaining ships. As darkness fell on March 4, not a single Japanese craft of the original 22 was still afloat. The U.S. Air Force had lost 13 men; the enemy, approximately 12,700.

Emperor Hirohito's displeasure at this latest loss was quickly relayed to Yamamoto, now based at the great fleet base on Truk atoll in the Caroline Islands. Knowing full well that the tide was turning badly against his forces as he had predicted it would before the war began, he made a flight to Rabaul on April 3 to bolster morale and make plans to retake the initiative in the air. On April 7, under the code name Operation I-Go, he launched his pilots on a series of 100-to-200-plane raids against Guadalcanal and American bases in New Guinea.

On four separate days—April 7, 11, 12, and 14—a total of 486 Japanese fighters, 114 carrier-based bombers, and 80 land-based attack planes took part in missions against American forces. Each time aircraft took off from Rabaul, Yamamoto stood beside the runway dressed in dress whites and waved his cap in farewell.

The Japanese claimed that 134 American planes were shot down during those four days; the Americans reported only 25 lost. The Japanese reported that only 42 of their own planes were destroyed in combat, whereas American pilots claimed they had bagged 51 of the enemy.

Late in the day of April 13, when the last Japanese stragglers limped in, the message was sent from Rabaul by Vice Adm. Tomoshiga Samejima, the commander of the Eighth Air Fleet, announcing Yamamoto's intention to visit the forward bases at Bougainville on the eighteenth.

On the seventeenth, Yamamoto had lunch with Lt. Gen. Hitoshi Imamura, commander of the ground forces at Rabaul. Imamura, who had barely escaped death in the air two months earlier on a similar flight to Buin on the southern tip of Bougainville, advised Yamamoto not to go. Rear Adm. Takaji Joshima, a long-time friend of Yamamoto's, flew in to plead with his superior not to expose himself to a possible aerial ambush. He called the trip "madness" and "an open invitation to the enemy" because of the proximity to American air bases. Adm. Jisaburo Ozawa, commander in chief of the Third Fleet, also objected and offered to send a great number of planes to accompany Yamamoto.

Yamamoto was grateful for this expression of concern but would not change his plans. If the weather was good, he would go. Despite glowing reports of the great losses to the Americans and minor losses to his own forces, he realized the power of the Americans to stop his forces was growing stronger each day. His resources were spread too thin. He canceled Operation I-Go, recognizing that he could not sustain the effort any longer. He had lost many experienced pilots in the Battle of Midway and subsequent engagements. The replacement pilots were inexperienced and their morale was sagging. He felt it was his duty to visit the units at Ballale, Buin, and Shortland Island and encourage them to greater valor in the name of the emperor. A personal appearance was necessary to prove to his men that he had confidence in the ultimate outcome.

Yamamoto was a striking figure in his white uniform. He stood out in sharp contrast to the dark green service uniforms worn by his men in combat. However, on April 18, he chose not to wear the white uniform and emerged from his quarters wearing the green. Accompanied by Chief of Staff Matome Ugaki, he went by staff car to the airfield on the east side of Rabaul where two Mitsubishi G4M land-based attack planes of the 705th Naval Air Squadron (Kokutai) were waiting. Yamamoto boarded the first plane—No. 323—with the fleet medical officer, Rear Adm. Rokuro Takada; Comdr. Kurio Toibana, a staff officer; and Comdr. Nonoru Fukusaki, an aide. Fleet Warrant Officer Takeo Kotani was the pilot; Chief Flight Seaman Akiharu Ohsaki, copilot. There were five other crewmen aboard.

Ugaki boarded the second plane—No. 326—with Capt. Motoharu Kitamura, chief paymaster; Comdr. Rinji Tomono, the fleet weather officer; Comdr. Kaoru Imanaka, communications staff officer; and Comdr. Suteji Muroi, a navy–air force staff officer. Flight Petty Officer Hiroshi Hayashi was the pilot; Chief Flight

Seaman Fumikatsu Fujimoto was copilot. There were also five air crewmen aboard No. 326.

The two Mitsubishi G4M attack planes, called "Flying Cigars" by the Japanese and "Bettys" by the Americans, took off precisely at 6:00 A.M. Immediately following were the six Model 32 Zeros of the 204th Naval Air Squadron, led by First Lieutenant Morisaki. The Zeros immediately split up into two Vs of three planes each and took position on each side of the two bombers. The weather was clear, an excellent day for flying.

The bombers climbed to 6,500 feet, the fighters slightly higher. After an hour and a half of uneventful flight, Kotani passed a note to Yamamoto seated behind him: "Expect to arrive at Ballale at 0745."

In the other bomber, Ugaki was dozing. Hayashi noticed that his plane was vibrating slightly because an antenna pole had come loose and was shaking in the windstream. He throttled back and No. 326 began to lag slightly behind Yamamoto's plane. The gap widened to about two and a half miles, according to Ugaki's estimate. When the engines changed their sound, Ugaki awoke suddenly sensing that something was wrong. He recalled:

"Suddenly Hayashi, at the controls, saw a red tracer flash past. Tanimoto [an observer crew member] jabbed Hayashi on the shoulder and shouted, "Enemy aircraft!"[1]

Startled, Hayashi glanced up and saw a P-38 flash by overhead. He jammed the throttles to the stops, pushed the control wheel forward, kicked right rudder, and headed toward the sea. The lead bomber, still flying about two and a half miles to the right, had also nosed down toward the jungle treetops. It slowed down noticeably and began to spurt black smoke and flames. Ugaki shouted to the pilot Hayashi, "Follow plane Number One! Follow plane Number One!"

Hayashi ignored Ugaki's plea. He took violent evasive action and continued downward headed out to sea. The lead plane could no longer be seen. A tall column of black smoke began to rise lazily out of the jungle. Hayashi, now over the ocean, was being pursued by a P-38. He was skimming about 100 feet above the wave tops when he suddenly lost control. Number 326 plunged into the water off Moila Point at the southwestern extremity of Bougainville Island.

Warrant Officer Kenji Yanagiya, pilot of one of the six Zeroes assigned to accompany the two bombers, was honored to be selected to fly cover for the famous admiral. He had been flying combat in the theater since the previous October and had about one hundred missions in his logbook. His plane and the other Zeros were equipped with a 20mm cannon and 7mm machine guns. Like the other Zeros, his had no radio because the pilots had elected to take them out to lighten the aircraft. There was no way they could communicate with the bombers except by hand signals or wing-wagging.

The pilots were not briefed to expect any interception from American fighters. It was to be a routine escort flight and the Zeros were to fly about 1,500 feet above and behind the two Bettys to the destination.

Yanagiya's element of three Zeros was to the right of the bombers. His flight leader belatedly saw the P-38s attacking and immediately dove toward them. They made one pass at a P-38 and zoomed upward to try again. As he climbed, Yanagiya saw Yamamoto's bomber smoking and heading for the jungle. The other was heading for the ocean.

Yanagiya believed that he and the other Zero pilots were delayed in seeing the Americans begin their attack because they were accustomed to looking skyward. They did not think the P-38s would be climbing from a lower altitude. Aircraft flying over the jungle were harder to spot from above.

Yanagiya was separated from his element and flew toward Shortland Island. He stated he saw a P-38 in level flight at about 9,000 feet and attacked. The P-38 did not burn but white vapor, probably gasoline, poured out as his bullets scored. Yanagiya zoomed past the P-38 and did not see it go down. He did not make a second attack and would not say that he deserved credit for a kill. (Yanagiya did not know until 1988 that one P-38, piloted by Lt. Ray Hine, did not return to Guadalcanal.)

Yanagiya turned back toward Buin and made a pass over the field wagging his wings. He fired a few bursts from his guns to signal the encounter to ground personnel. Apparently they already knew; he was the last to land. Of the six Zeros, one made an emergency landing at Shortland Island; its difficulty, whether from battle damage or aircraft malfunction, has never been ascertained. (Yanagiya stated in a 1988 interview that not only were none of the six Zeros shot down but none of the five that landed at Buin had any combat damage. He made no statement about the sixth Zero that landed at Shortland.)[2]

The flight leader made his report to the air base commander at Buin and the five Zeros and, presumably, the one at Shortland were ordered to return to Rabaul about two hours later. The Zero pilots reported three P-38s were shot down; however, no Japanese pilot confirmed the kills of any other pilot.

Yanagiya recalled that the Buin airfield had always been noted for the great clouds of dust that swirled around when aircraft took off and landed. In order to get ready for the expected arrival of the commander in chief, the Buin airfield commander had ordered all hands to participate in a massive cleanup of the runway. Officers and men worked all night. When the Zeros came in to land, the pilots were surprised to see the base's entire garrison standing at attention in spotless dress uniforms along the freshly cleaned runway.

Replying to questions at the Yamamoto Retrospective in 1988, Yanagiya said he was convinced that the Americans knew who was flying in the lead plane and that the attack was deliberate, not an accident. He does not believe any of the Zeros on the ground at Kahili got airborne. However, there is one un-documented report by an American writer that about thirty fighters had departed from Kahili to search for the attacking Americans but were too late. This was later confirmed by Japanese historians.

Unknown to the Americans until many years after the war, there were three survivors of No. 326, the second attack bomber containing staff members, after it smashed into the sea off Moila Point: Vice Adm. Matome Ugaki, chief of staff of the Combined Fleet; Petty Officer Hiroshi Hayashi, chief pilot; and Rear Adm. Motoharu Kitamura, chief paymaster, Combined Fleet. Ugaki kept a diary, later published in Japan under the title *Sensoroku*, in which he recorded his traumatic experience that day. His entry for April 18, written several months later, was extensive, but because Ugaki was still hurting badly when he wrote it, his account is inaccurate and exaggerated:

As soon as I entered the second bomber, both aircraft began their takeoff runs down the field. The lead bomber took to the air first. As our planes passed over the volcano at the bay's end we slid into formation and took a southeast course. Clouds were intermittent and, with excellent visibility, flying conditions were good.

I could see our escort fighters weaving in their protective pattern; three fighters flew off to our far left, three remained high above and behind us, and three others, making nine in all, cruised to the right. Our bombers flew a tight formation, their wings almost touching, and my plane remained slightly behind and to the left of the lead ship. We flew at approximately five thousand feet. We could clearly see the admiral in the pilot's seat of the other bomber, and the passengers moving within the airplane.

We reached the west side of Bougainville Island, flying at 2,200 feet directly over the jungle. A crew member handed me a note reading: "Our time of arrival at Ballale is 0745 hours [Tokyo time]." I remember looking at my wristwatch, and noting that the time was exactly 0730. In 15 minutes we would arrive at our first stop.

Without warning, the motors roared and the bomber plunged toward the jungle, close behind the lead airplane, leveling off at less than two hundred feet. Nobody knew what had happened, and we scanned the sky anxiously for the enemy fighter planes we felt certain were diving to the attack. The crew chief, a flight warrant officer, answered our queries from his position in the narrow aisle. "It looks as if we made a mistake, sir. We shouldn't have dived." He certainly was right, for our pilots should never have left our original altitude.

Our fighter planes had sighted a group of at least 24 enemy planes approaching from the south. They began to dive toward the bombers to warn them of the approaching enemy planes. Simultaneously, however, our bomber pilots also sighted the enemy force and, without orders, raced for low altitude. Not until we had leveled off did our crewmen take their battle positions. Screaming wind and noise assailed our ears as the men unlimbered the machine guns.

Even as we pulled out above the jungle, our escort fighters turned into the attacking planes, now identifiable as the big Lockheed P-38s. The numerically superior enemy force broke through the Zeros and plunged after our two bombers. My own plane swung sharply into a 90-degree turn. I watched the crew chief lean forward and tap the pilot on the shoulder, warning him that the enemy fighters were fast closing in.

Our plane separated from the lead bomber. For a few moments I lost sight of Yamamoto's plane and finally located the Betty far to the right. I was horrified to see the airplane flying slowly just above the jungle, headed to the south, with bright orange flames rapidly enveloping the wings and fuselage. About four miles away from us, the bomber trailed thick, black smoke, dropping lower and lower.

Sudden fear for the admiral's life gripped me. I tried to call to Commander Muroi, standing immediately behind me, but could not speak. I grasped him by the shoulder and pulled him to the window, pointing to the admiral's burning plane. I caught a last glimpse myself, an eternal farewell to this beloved officer, before our plane swung sharply over in a steep turn. Tracers flashed by our wings, and the pilot desperately maneuvered to evade the pursuing fighter plane. I waited impatiently for the airplane to return to horizontal position, so that I could observe the admiral's bomber. Although I hoped for the best, I knew only too well what the fate of the airplane would be. Yamamoto's plane was no longer in sight. Black smoke boiled from the dense jungle into the air.

Alas! It was hopeless now!

Even as I stared at the funeral pyre of the crashed bomber, our own plane straightened out from its frantic maneuvering and at full speed raced toward Moila Point. Shortly we were over the open sea. We noticed the concentration of dogfighting planes in the area where Yamamoto's bomber had plunged into the jungle; other fighters were separating from the group and turning toward us now. I stared hopelessly as a silver H-shaped P-38 half-rolled in a screaming zoom, then turned steeply, and closed rapidly toward our plane. Our gunners were firing desperately at the big enemy fighter, but to no avail.

The bomber's 7.7mm machine guns could not reach the approaching P-38. Taking advantage of his superior speed, the enemy pilot closed in rapidly and, still beyond the range of our defensive guns, opened fire. I watched the P-38's nose seem to burst into twinkling flame, and suddenly the bomber shook from the impact of the enemy's machine gun bullets and cannon shells. The P-38 pilot was an excellent gunner, for his first fusilade of bullets and shells crashed into the right side of the airplane, then into the left. The drumming sounds vibrated through the airplane which rocked from the impact of the enemy fire. We knew we were now completely helpless, and waited for our end to come. The P-38 hung grimly to our tail, pouring in his deadly fire.

One by one our answering machine guns fell silent. Abruptly our crew chief, who had been shouting orders to his men, fell from our view. Several of the crew were already dead, as the bullets screamed through the airplane. Commander Muroi sprawled over the chair and table in the fuselage compartment, his hands thrown out before him, his head rolling lifelessly back and forth as the plane shuddered.

Another cannon shell suddenly tore open the right wing. The chief pilot, directly in front of me, pushed the control column forward. Our only chance of survival was to make a crash landing in the sea. I did not realize it at the time, but a Zero pilot above us in the futile attack against the grimly pursuing P-38, reported heavy smoke pouring from our bomber. Almost into the water, the pilot pulled back on the controls to bring the airplane out of the dive, but he could no longer control the aircraft. Enemy bullets had shattered the cables. Desperately the pilot killed our power, but again it was too late. At full speed the bomber smashed into the water; the left wing crumpled and the [plane] rolled sharply over to the left.

[We] prepared for an emergency landing. I do not recall being injured in the crash. Apparently the shock of the plane's meeting the water at such high speed numbed my senses, for when I was hurled into the aisle from my seat my body was bruised and cut.

The impact of the crash momentarily stunned me, and everything turned black. I felt the crushing force of salt water pouring into the fuselage and almost immediately we were below the surface. I was completely helpless. Convinced this was my end, I said a requiem to myself. Naturally it was difficult to remember coherently everything which happened in those incredible moments, but I vaguely recall that I felt as if life had come to its end; I could not bring myself to move and could only lie perfectly still. I do not believe I was actually knocked unconscious. I did not swallow any sea water.

Ugaki's diary described what the search parties had found at the lead bomber's crash site and noted that "even in death dignity did not leave the great naval officer. To us, Admiral Yamamoto virtually was a god." Ugaki then related what he learned later: "As to the wreckage of my own plane, divers went to 67 feet below the water's surface, but found only the wheels, engine, propellers, machine guns, and one officer's sword. The following day the bodies of two crewmen were washed up on shore.[3]

Between Ugaki's diary entry for April 18 and later testimony by the pilot Hayashi, Yamamoto biographer Agawa reconstructed what he believed happened. Following is a paraphrased version:

The plane was burning when it struck the water. Ugaki and Hayashi were thrown out of the plane, through the canopy over the cockpit. Ugaki and Hayashi began swimming to shore and were fired on by army lookouts stationed along the coast. Hayashi shouted and the firing stopped. The two were hauled ashore and given first aid. Ugaki was seriously injured but Hayashi had only a few bruises and a cut on his mouth. Kitamura, meanwhile, was also injured and was dazedly swimming alone. He was rescued by a navy seaplane and brought ashore. He had a hole in his throat and could not speak.

Hayashi was flown out next day to Rabaul and promptly isolated in the hospital. He was questioned and cautioned by intelligence officers not to tell what had happened. He returned to flying two months later.

Ugaki was hospitalized for several months after his rescue and blamed himself for the loss of the two bombers and their passengers. He noted in his diary: "Although death is an everyday occurrence in war, I feel that I am to be blamed for this incident." He repeated over and over that it was all his fault. His brother officers feared he might commit suicide.

According to a Japanese history of this time period, Ugaki, Yamamoto's chief of staff, had wanted to visit the Shortland area for some time,

to heighten the morale of the first-line officers and men and then to fly to the 17th Army Headquarters in Bougainville to thank them for their services rendered by the army since the Guadalcanal operation.

Although necessitated by the naval operation, the chief of staff felt a moral responsibility for the severe battle fought by the 17th Army after the opposite side started to recoup Guadalcanal which was occupied under the initiative of the navy. He would personally persuade the 17th Army to evacuate if it refused. Even after the evacuation was fortunately complete, the chief of staff was uneasy lest the army headquarters might take the blame in one form or another and it was only after hearing of its safe arrival in Shortland that the vice admiral was relieved.

Even so, the chief of staff still felt obliged to visit the 17th Army, as he knew the misery suffered by the army over the past half year.

On his way to the billet in the late afternoon of the 4th of April, Admiral Yamamoto told the chief of staff who shared the car with him that he would go to Shortland, too. The commander in chief made known his wish of visiting the first line for the first time that day.

The C-in-C later asked his staff to make a concrete plan of visiting Shortland, while the chief of staff was being treated for dengue fever in a field hospital, hinting that he would go alone. if the chief of staff could not go with him.

Be that as it may, the C-in-C's plan of visiting the first line was finalized around the 13th of April, with details of the plan cabled to . . . the commanders of the South East Fleet and the 8th Fleet after having been approved by the C-in-C.[4]

(On August 15, 1945, the last day of World War II, Ugaki, then commander in chief of the Fifth Fleet, led eleven bombers under his command on a final suicide mission against targets on Okinawa from which he did not return. At his side he wore a short sword that had been presented to him by Yamamoto. Curiously, there is no record of any attack by Japanese aircraft on that date.)

It was about noon on April 18 when the first news of the downing of the two bombers reached Rabaul from Buin. An "Official Secret" message was sent from Rabaul to the navy minister and the chief of the naval general staff in Tokyo. That night a steady stream of top naval leaders began to arrive at the ministry. There was hope that Yamamoto had survived.

In Rabaul, Yasuji Watanabe, Yamamoto's administrative chief of staff and close friend, arranged to fly to Buin, but a sudden afternoon squall delayed his departure until the next day. Arriving at Buin early the next morning, he went directly to the hospital to see Ugaki, who had suffered a compound fracture of his right arm and a severed artery. When Watanabe entered the hospital room, Ugaki burst into tears and pleaded for Watanabe to get to the crash site quickly because their chief might still be alive.

Watanabe commandeered a seaplane and flew over the area, which was easy to locate from the scorched trees around the wreckage. Watanabe had brought some rubber balls with him which he slit open. He inserted a message in each: "This is Watanabe. Please wave your handkerchiefs." He dropped the balls in long net bags as close to the site as he could. There was no sign of life below.

Watanabe ordered the pilot to land beside a waiting minesweeper that had a ground party aboard. He took command and the group went ashore near the mouth of a small river. All that day the searchers chopped their way through the jungle until Watanabe called a halt at midnight. Meanwhile, another group had set out on land from Buin and they, too, could not reach the spot before dark. An army road construction gang, led by Sub. Lt. Mitsuyoshi Hamasuna, was closer to the scene. They had seen the dogfight and an airplane go down. They had cheered because they thought the black smoke coming out of the jungle was from an American P-38.

Hamasuna received orders by radio to form a search party and proceed to the wreckage. They set out immediately on the afternoon of April 18 but had to give up when darkness came. The following day they tried again and found the wreckage of the lead bomber. From an extensive report filed by Hamasuna afterward, Agawa describes the scene:

The wings and propellers had survived, but the massive fuselage had broken just in front of the Rising Sun mark, and the section extending from there to the cockpit was a burned-out hulk. Dead bodies were lying about the wreckage. Among them was a high-ranking officer. He sat as though abstracted, still strapped into his seat, amidst the trees. He had medal ribbons on his chest, and wore white gloves. His left grasped his sword, and his right hand rested lightly on it. His head lolled forward as though he was sunk in thought, but he was dead. This officer was the only one who had been thrown out of the plane in his seat.[5]

Hamasuna realized that this was Yamamoto. He searched through the corpse's pockets and found a diary and copies of some poems. In a letter sent to Japanese historian Shingo Suzuki in 1986, Hamasuna provided a sketch of the positions of the bodies and added:

"I found Admiral dead outside fuselage sitting on the cabin seat (seats belt on) as if he still alive. Holding sword straight between his thigh and jaw. Held the hilt of the sword firmly with his head a little drooped (eyes closed). After forty years, my recollections become somewhat faint, but I can say with confidence about how each body was. I always talk truth as I trust this is the way to repay the spirit of Admiral Yamamoto."[6]

"What seems to have impressed itself most strongly on Hamasuna and his men," Agawa reports, "was the thick wad of white toilet paper and the clean white handkerchief that emerged from Yamamoto's pockets. The rank and file at the time suffered from an extreme shortage of, among other things, toilet paper. As one of the search party said, 'You get to use good paper when you get to be C. in C.' "[7]

Suzuki also reported that Hamasuna found no machine guns in or around the lead bomber's fuselage; normally three guns were installed. Flight Petty Officer Hiroshi Hayashi, the pilot of the second bomber, told Suzuki that because his plane would be overweight on the flight to Buin, he left the extra ammunition drums at the base in Rabaul to lighten the load. Consequently, if there was any ammunition on board, there was probably only one ammunition drum for each gun. "After that [is used up]," Hayashi said, "only thing we can do is just escape." If that is true, Suzuki wrote Barber, "they had only little ammunitions [sic] for their guns and this is the reason why they could not/did not fire against you."[8] Kenji Yanagiya, in a 1988 interview in Tokyo, stated that he believed the two Betty bombers carried the standard crew which included a tail gunner and two side gunners.

Hamasuna's men set up camp around the wreckage and made a temporary shelter for the eleven bodies. On April 20, the bodies were carried out to the coast where Watanabe met the group and had Chief Medical Officer Okubo reportedly make a preliminary examination. The bodies were transported to Buin where autopsies were performed on only five of the bodies, including Yamamoto, by Lt. Comdr. Gisaburo Tabuchi, chief medical officer at the Buin air base. Presumably, the other bodies were too badly burned to be autopsied. Tabuchi's autopsy report on Yamamoto stated:

"1. Almost center part of left shoulder blade, there was a wound the size of the tip of a little finger. The wound towards inside and up.

"2. A shot hole at left side of lower jaw. Outlet of upper part of right eye, size fingerprint by thumb."[9]

After the autopsies were completed at Buin, the bodies were placed in pits and cremated at the Sasebo Sixth Special Land Unit's farm outside of Buin. Yamamoto's body was cremated in a special pit and his ashes were retrieved by Watanabe, who placed them in a wooden box lined with papaya leaves. The ashes of the others were also collected and earth mounds were erected over the pits. Two papaya trees were planted beside Yamamoto's mound.

Watanabe returned to Rabaul on April 22 with the ashes of all the men in the lead bomber. Yamamoto's death was kept a secret even from the units at Rabaul; his ashes were flown to Truk and placed aboard his flagship, the *Musahi*.

Just as the mission was to become controversial among the American pilots, so did the time of death for Yamamoto among Japanese historians. If he survived the crash for even a few hours, the blame for not making a greater effort to get to the scene of the crash would be laid on the units at Buin. To add to the controversy, an autopsy was reportedly made by Capt. Chikahiro Ninagawa, another medical officer, before Tabuchi saw the body. In a book entitled *The Last Moment of Isoroku Yamamoto* by his brother, Chikamasa Ninagawa, the postmortem examination on Yamamoto indicated little bleeding, and no maggots were observed on the body when Hamasuna's party reached the crash site on the 19th. In the jungle, maggots appear and multiply rapidly after a person has suffered cuts; the average breeding time is from four to seven hours. Therefore, it is possible that Yamamoto survived the crash and was pulled or crawled from the wreckage. He then may have died the next day, April 19.

This theory was enhanced when it was found that Chief Surgeon Takata's body also had no maggots. There were marks on the ground that indicated he might have crawled a few feet on the ground toward Yamamoto. It was speculated that Takata may have placed Yamamoto, still alive, in the seat and then died. Takata's body was found spread-eagle, face up, about fifteen feet from Yamamoto.

Biographer Agawa comments, based on Hamasuna's report:

None of the bodies was magotty yet, but their faces were all swollen and puffy, except Yamamoto's, which was relatively presentable. Odd though this may seem, it is apparently the truth; it was to give rise to all kinds of speculative legends in later days—that Yamamoto had looked as though he was still alive; that he had in fact been alive, but had committed suicide after leaving the plane; that his eyes were wide open and staring; that he was in such-and-such a posture. These spread still further and took still more elaborate forms after the war. Some American writers have suggested that, on the contrary, a man in a plane that had been shot down could hardly have looked so presentable, and that the Japanese had fabricated the story in order to make a god of Yamamoto.[10]

Historian Shingo Suzuki believes that if Yamamoto were alive for twenty-four hours after the crash, the fact was kept hidden for fear of "big trouble" for the Japanese navy, army, and air force personnel who should have made greater efforts to get to the scene. As Suzuki states, "To avoid such troubles, I think somebody ask to the Inspector to make report to show Admiral died on his Betty."[11]

The first details the Japanese transmitted about the loss of the two attack bombers were contained in a "Highest Priority, Confidential" message from the commandant, Sixth Air Force to the commandant, Eleventh Air Fleet:

1. TWO RIKKO CARRYING C-IN-C, COMBINED FLEET AND HIS PARTY ENGAGED IN AERIAL COMBAT WITH OVER 10 P-38s AT ABOUT 0740. SECOND PLANE FORCED DOWN INTO THE SEA OFF MOILA POINT. CHIEF STAFF, CHIEF PAYMASTER (BOTH WOUNDED) ONE PILOT RESCUED. FIRST PLANE IN FLAMES SEEMED TO HAVE PLUNGED AT A SLIGHT ANGLE INTO THE JUNGLE ABOUT 11 MILES WEST OF RXP [Buin]. SEARCHING UNDERWAY.
2. TWO DIRECT-ESCORTING PLANES SHOT DOWN SIX HOSTILE PLANES (OF WHICH THREE PLANES WAS FORCED LANDING; CERTAIN). NO DAMAGE TO OUR SIDE. Tele. 181109. Top Secret Ro-3 Code. April 18, 1943.[12]

Yamamoto's death was officially confirmed to the Navy Ministry on April 20. The immediate requirement for the top naval leaders was to find a replacement for Yamamoto. Adm. Mineichi Koga was an obvious choice and arrived aboard the *Musahi* at Truk to take over his new command on April 25. Since Yamamoto's death was still a state secret, Koga was said to be on an inspection tour.

An envelope was found in Yamamoto's safe aboard the *Musahi* when its contents were cleaned out. It contained a poem written by Yamamoto in the Japanese poetic style—alternating five- and seven-syllable lines. Its message was later paraphrased as follows:

Since the war began, tens of thousands of officers and men of matchless loyalty and courage have done battle at the risk of their lives, and have died to become guardian gods of our land.

Ah, how can I ever enter the imperial presence again? With what words can I possibly report to the parents and brothers of my dead comrades?

The body is frail, yet with a firm mind with unshakable resolve I will drive deep into the enemy's positions and let him see the blood of a Japanese man.

Wait but a while, young men!—one last battle, fought gallantly to the death, and I will be joining you![13]

On May 7, the *Musahi* sailed from Truk carrying the ashes of Yamamoto and the others who had died with him. It arrived in Tokyo Bay on May 21, its secret still kept from most of the crew. That afternoon, a Tokyo radio announcer interrupted the regular program and announced: "In April this year, Admiral Yamamoto Isoroku, commander in chief of the Combined Fleet, met a gallant death on board his plane in an encounter with the enemy in the course of directing overall operations at the front line." The announcer broke down in tears and could not continue.

The next day, a plain text message was sent to all units of the Japanese navy which said in part:

. . . THE STATEMENT REGARDING THE DEATH IN ACTION OF THE COMMANDER IN CHIEF IS IN NO WAY AT VARIANCE WITH THE TRUE FACTS. THE POLICY WILL BE TO ISSUE NO FURTHER STATEMENT HEREAFTER, OTHER THAN THE ABOVE, SINCE SUCH MIGHT BE OF BENEFIT TO THE ENEMY.[14]

On May 22, it was announced that Emperor Hirohito had promoted Yamamoto posthumously to Fleet Admiral and awarded him the Grand Order of the Chrysanthemum, comparable to the Medal of Honor awarded by the Congress of the United States to Americans for heroism "above and beyond the call of duty." The emperor also decreed that Yamamoto was to be accorded a formal state funeral, a rare tribute that had been given to only eleven others in the nation's entire history. The only other admiral ever so honored was the man Yamamoto had served under and admired most: Adm. Heihachiro Togo.

Meanwhile, the news of Yamamoto's death had been con-

veyed officially to the family and unofficially to his favorite
geisha, Chiyoko Kawai, on May 18.

On May 23, Yamamoto's ashes were transferred to the destroyer *Yugumo* and taken to Yokosuka and then by train to
Tokyo where members of the family, Japanese royalty, and top
military personnel waited. A procession then escorted the ashes
to the Navy Club at Shiba where they were placed on a Buddhist
altar; a private ceremony was held there with only family and
close friends in attendance. A few days later, the ashes were
divided and placed in two boxes; one was to be placed in Tama
Cemetery, the other taken to a Buddhist cemetery in Nagaoka,
Yamamoto's home town.

(It has been rumored that ashes were placed in a third box and
given secretly to Chiyoko Kawai, his mistress. This has not been
substantiated.)

Yamamoto's state funeral was held on June 5, 1943. That
morning, the ashes for the Tama interment were placed in a
small coffin draped with a white cloth and placed on a black
artillery caisson. The procession, led by a naval band playing
Chopin's Funeral March, proceeded slowly to Hibiya Park near
the Imperial Palace in the center of Tokyo. The roads were lined
with mourners and an estimated three million Japanese crowded
into the area near the cemetery to pay their last respects to a
national hero. When the funeral was over, the small coffin was
taken to Tama Cemetery and the urn was placed in a grave next
to Admiral Togo, Yamamoto's hero and superior officer during
his early navy service.

The other half of the ashes were taken to Nagaoka and buried
near the grave of his adopted father on the grounds of a Zen
temple. A stone was inscribed with his adopted name and the
words: "Killed in action in the South Pacific, April 1943."

In December 1943, a full-length statue of Yamamoto was
erected at the Kasumigaura Flying School where he had been
stationed as deputy commander and learned to fly. After the
Japanese surrendered in 1945, General MacArthur ordered all
military statues destroyed throughout Japan. Yamamoto's statue
was cut in half and dumped into a nearby lake. In 1955, a scrap

dealer, searching for metal, recovered the top half of the statue and sold it to friends of Yamamoto. Funds were raised and it was placed on a stone pedestal in the middle of a small memorial park in Nagaoka. The other memorial in Tokyo was carefully polished every day for years by Yamamoto's old friend Yasuji Watanabe.

8
"BULL" HALSEY RAGES

EITHER LANPHIER NOR BARBER FLEW ANY more missions from Guadalcanal after April 18. Both returned to the 339th headquarters at Noumea a few days later and were immediately given ten days' rest leave. They flew to Auckland, New Zealand, with Brig. Gen. Dean C. Strother, operations officer for the XIII Fighter Command. The three, joined by J. Norman Lodge, senior Associated Press war correspondent in the theater, played golf almost every day. To Barber's surprise, Lodge seemed to know most of the particulars about the mission and kept asking if he and Lanphier would verify certain details that he presented to them. Barber does not know where he got the basic information. It was possible that he had first heard about it on Guadalcanal or at other air bases he had visited in the South Pacific.

"As we played," Barber recalled, "he would talk about the mission, give us some fact, then ask, 'Is that about right?' We would agree or if he was incorrect on details, we would correct him. He knew generally about every detail of the mission.

"I believe that enough information was known so that any reporter could have found out the general details from anyone on Guadalcanal. Lodge would have had no problem gaining information from many sources."[1]

While on the golf course, Barber talked to Strother and Lanphier when Lodge wasn't listening and said, "I've been wondering how they ever got a mission report together to send to higher headquarters."

Barber said Lanphier replied, "Don't worry about it, Rex. I went over to the Ops tent that evening and wrote the report. I also helped write our citations for the Medal of Honor."[2] (General Strother verified this statement by Lanphier in a conversation with Mitchell and Barber at a squadron reunion in Colorado Springs in 1986.)

Barber was stunned. He and Lanphier were good friends and had helped each other out of aerial scrapes several times in the months they had flown together. Barber knew that Lanphier was very ambitious and anxious to make a name for himself. He recalled how on Fiji in the summer of 1942, Lanphier said he had talked his way onto a B-17 bombing raid against Truk as a waist gunner. Lanphier said he shot down a Zero. It was learned later that the crew of the B-17 refused to confirm this kill. However, Lanphier claimed it as his first victory over a Zero.

Lt. Col. Henry Vicellio, the squadron commander at the time, was furious at Lanphier for risking his life on a mission at a bomber crew position that a corporal would normally occupy. He censured Lanphier severely for risking his neck when the government had spent much time and money on his training.

"A couple of nights later, Tom and I were sitting in front of our quarters having a drink," Barber said.

I asked him why he risked his life and his value to the Air Force for a mission like that. He laughed and said, "Rex, you're here because you're patriotic. Well, I'm here because I'm patriotic, too, but I have another reason. I want to be President of the United States and I'm going to stake my life on a war record that will allow me the opportunity to do just that. If my attempt for this record costs me my life, so be it."

I looked at him and could see he was dead serious. "Don't laugh at me," he said. "Look how many people have already done this." He cited Presidents Grant and Teddy Roosevelt as examples and said, "I'm going to do the same thing."

Admiral Isoroku Yamamoto, Japan's naval hero who planned the surprise attack on Pearl Harbor. His first name is "Fifty-six" because that was the age his father was when Isoroku was born. (National Archives photo)

Admiral Yamamoto (front row, fourth from the left), Commander in Chief, Japanese Combined Fleet, poses with staff on board his flagship *Musahi*. (Photo courtesy estate of John Brannon, counsel with the International Military Tribunal for the Far East)

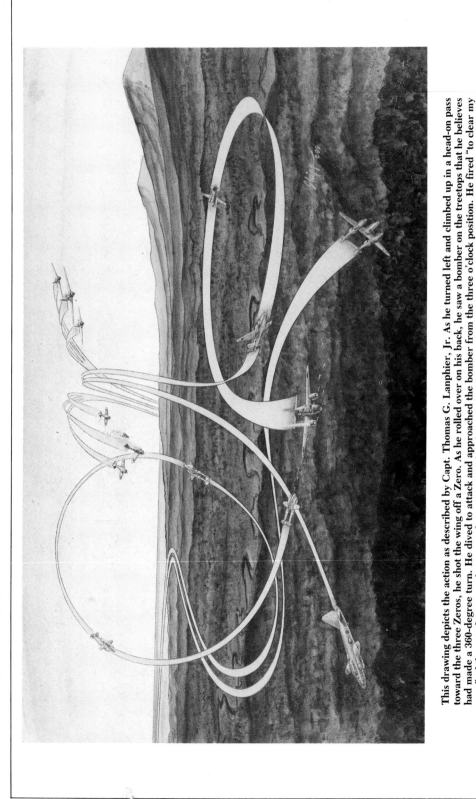

This drawing depicts the action as described by Capt. Thomas G. Lanphier, Jr. As he turned left and climbed up in a head-on pass toward the three Zeros, he shot the wing off a Zero. As he rolled over on his back, he saw a bomber on the treetops that he believes had made a 360-degree turn. He dived to attack and approached the bomber from the three o'clock position. He fired "to clear my guns" while out of range and expressed amazement when he saw the right engine of the bomber burst into flames and the right wing separate from the bomber. He reported steady fire from the tail gun position of the bomber, which then plunged into the jungle. He

This drawing depicts the action as described by Lt. Rex T. Barber, the wingman for Capt. Thomas G. Lanphier, Jr. Barber has stated that after Lanphier turned 90 degrees to the left and climbed up into three escorting Zeros, he continued toward the two Betty Bombers. As he rolled out of a right turn onto the bombers, he lost sight of both of them momentarily, then saw one ahead. He began firing from the six o'clock position for about twenty to thirty seconds and directed his fire into the fuselage and engines of the bomber as it dived toward the treetops. He saw smoke and flames from the bomber as it suddenly rolled left and slowed abruptly. Barber turned right quickly to avoid a collision. As he looked back, he saw smoke coming up out of the jungle. (Illustration by Wayne Shipp)

Above
Aerial view of Henderson Field, Guadalcanal, taken in August 1944. (Air force photo)

Below
Air force fighter pilots lived in tents on Guadalcanal. Creature comforts were few and far between. After the Japanese were driven off the island, one of the major enemies was the mosquito. (Air force photo)

bove

Capt. Thomas G. Lanphier, Jr., Lt. Besby F. Holmes, and Lt. Rex T. Barber, three of the four "killer flight" pilots, pose before one of the 339th Squadron P-38s the day after their famous mission. The fourth member of the flight, Lt. Raymond K. Hine, did not return from the mission and was never found. (Air force photo)

elow

The surviving pilots who flew on the Yamamoto mission are shown posing on Guadalcanal by one of their P-38s after the mission. Front row, left to right: Lt. William E. Smith, Lt. Douglas S. Canning, Lt. Besby F. Holmes, Lt. Rex T. Barber, Maj. John W. Mitchell, Maj. Louis R. Kittel, Lt. Gordon Whittaker. Rear row, left to right: Lt. Roger J. Ames, Lt. Lawrence A. Graebner, Capt. Thomas G. Lanphier, Jr., Lt. Delton C. Goerke, Lt. Julius Jacobson, Lt. Eldon E. Stratton, Lt. Albert R. Long, Lt. Everett H. Anglin. Not shown: Lt. Raymond K. Hine, who was missing and presumed dead. (Photo courtesy of Douglas S. Canning)

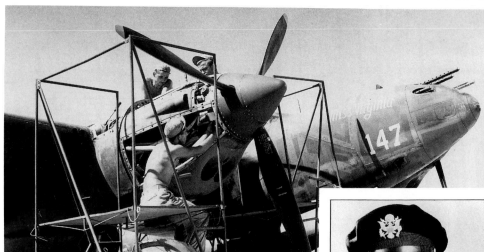

Above

Miss Virginia, the aircraft flown by Lt. Rex Barber on the Yamamoto interception, receiving maintenance on Guadalcanal. This aircraft received 104 hits from Japanese Zeros after he shot down the admiral's Betty bomber. (National Archives photo)

Right

Lt. (later Lt. Col.) Rex T. Barber was Lt. Thomas G. Lanphier's wingman on April 18, 1943. According to the author, Barber deserves full credit for the destruction of the Betty bomber in which Admiral Yamamoto was a passenger. (Air force photo)

Below

Capt. Thomas G. Lanphier (kneeling, right) chats with his ground crew on Guadalcanal. (Photo courtesy of Douglas S. Canning)

Capt. Thomas G. Lanphier, Jr., toured United States Air Force training bases after completing his combat tour in the South Pacific. He claimed 7 enemy aircraft shot down, one of them while flying as a passenger on a bombing mission. He is now officially credited with only 4½ enemy aircraft after air force historians researched his claims. (Air force photo)

At the Yamamoto Retrospective, Fredericksburg, Texas, April 1988, from left, flight leader John W. Mitchell, Rex T. Barber, Besby F. Holmes, Makato Shinagawa (interpreter), and Kenji Yanagiya, the sole surviving Japanese escort pilot. (Admiral Nimitz Museum photo)

Col. John Mitchell, leader of the epic interception, briefs the audience at the Yamamoto Retrospective. Mitchell is credited with eleven victories over Japanese aircraft during World War II and four during the Korean War. (Admiral Nimitz Museum photo)

Japanese visitors to the Yamamoto crash site on Bougainville Island erected this plaque in his memory after World War II. (Photo by Terry Gwynn-Jones)

Shinto shrine erected in memory of Admiral Yamamoto at the crash site of Betty bomber No. 323 shortly after being shot down on April 18, 1943. The site, visited over the years by many Japanese who served under Yamamoto, has been disturbed and vandalized. (Photo courtesy estate of John Brannon, counsel with the International Military Tribunal for the Far East)

Of the twenty-two American and Japanese pilots who flew on the Yamamoto mission, only nine are alive today. They are shown at the Yamamoto Mission Retrospective, April 1988. Left to right: Roger Ames, Rex Barber, Douglas Canning, Kenji Yanagiya (Japanese Zero pilot), Delton Goerke, Julius Jacobson, Besby Holmes, John Mitchell, and Louis Kittel. (Admiral Nimitz Museum photo)

The fuselage of the Betty bomber looking aft. Bullet holes were found indicating shots had come from the rear as Barber has always claimed. (Photo by Terry Gwynn-Jones)

Later on Guadalcanal, Tom flew every mission he could. At that stage of the war we didn't encounter many enemy aircraft so that none of us could run up a lot of aerial victories. Most of our targets were on ground support missions—bombing enemy troops dug in on Guadalcanal, freighters and supply ships, interspersed with a few reconnaissance missions. Tom flew every mission he could get on. Make no mistake, he was a good pilot. The Yamamoto mission was a "must" for Tom if he were to get a record that would get him national notice.[3]

Barber's suspicions about Lanphier's motivations were magnified after the revelation about writing the intelligence report and he wondered what the report said. He never saw it until the late 1950s when many World War II records were declassified. "If I had known then what I know now," he told the author, "I would have objected strenuously, especially after Tom told me he had helped write the report."[4]

Lodge, a veteran reporter, knew a story when he had one. On May 11, he datelined it from an "advanced Pacific base" and submitted it to navy censors. If approved, it was to be sent collect to his office in San Francisco. He reported in the terse, pithy newswire style of that era:

japanese admiral who boasted he would make peace in the white house has been shot down in a bomber plane nearing kahili, according to information believed to be correct paragraph

the magnificently executed maneuver took place april eighteen with captain thomas g lanphier or lieut rex t barber culver ore getting in the shot that sent the plane down in flames paragraph

lanphier son of colonel thomas g lanphier lists detroit as home and barber been recommended for congressional medal of honor for exploit which one most daring raids made this war paragraph

intelligence had trailed Yamamoto for five days finally sending information two bombing planes would take off from certain field kahili-bound stop lanphier barber with escort led by major johnw mitchell enidmiss left on 410 mile allwater route to point interception which exactly at time place. paragraph quote we flew entire distance about ten to thirty feet above water unquote lanphier said requote barber and myself were going in to attack while major mitchell others gave us protecting umbrella stop we spied enemy with six zero escorts about three miles from kahili stop immediately started getting altitude came in on them at 4500 feet stop we ran parallel to enemy then swung right through to the attack paragraph

requote one bomber nosed down other took upward course both in acrobatic set maneuvers with diving turns stop zeroes dropped belly tanks came after us stop eye saw eye could not get bomber on initial run so turned my plane up into zeroes stop first plane exploded other badly hurt as eye fired bursts in passing stop reaching 6000 feet eye nosed over and caught bomber at treetop height stop eye fired long burst and wing bomber flew off burst into flames fell into trees stop by now zeroes were frantically chasing me stop eye had disadvantage being lower altitude so hedgehopped over trees kicking rudders slipping skidding with tracers flying all angles past my plane paragraph

requote eye finally outran them but caught two seven point seven slugs in horizontal stabilizer stop barber went for other bomber but overshot it on his initial dive stop whipping back with plenty of zeroes on his tail he caught the bomber in his second run and destroyed it stop it too fell in flames stop sky now veritable hell of zeroes which had taken off from kahili paragraph

requote as barber shot bomber it exploded right in his face and piece destroyed bomber flew off and went right through his left wing knocking out the left inner cooler stop other chunks of plane left paint streaks all along his wing so close was his attack driven home paragraph

requote while slipping sliding attempting get away from pursuers eye flew over kahili airdrome at about five feet thoroughly messing up traffic pattern stop japs were scurrying about all over place as eye followed others enroute home unquote paragraph

but the day was not ended for the twinfuselaged fighters stop enroute home group spied bomber doing lazy eights near kahili stop barber with zeroes still pouring bullets into tail kicked over his rudder and went after the unsuspecting bomber blowing it up with one burst stop terrific dogfight ensued and not one of protecting escort swerved from previously arranged cover stop twas barber and lanphier with two other attack planes against the world paragraph

col dean strother winfield kansas group leader of thirteenth explained extremely evasive tactics lanphier barber had use to successfully escape tactics which japs found not to liking for before clear skies ahead three zeroes were blown to bits paragraph

quote we have every reason believe twas yamamoto in one of bomber unquote colonel strother said requote certainly it was some bigwig and as we had been tracking yamamoto right into truk and had known where he was every minute of those five days there is little doubt but that he was in one of the planes stop either lanphier or barber shot him down and certainly no one of the personnel aboard either plane is alive unquote paragraph

strother said lanphier barber had been told their mission was practically sure death yet each of the fighter pilots expressed their willingness and eagerness to take the chance stop quote they are magnificent fellows unquote strother said requote and each of them is an excellent flier stop lanphier already had seven zeroes to his credit and barber had five stop each had been decorated and redecorated for other exploits stop in my opinion both should get the congressional medal and each has been recommended for it unquote paragraph

arriving back at their own station lanphier barber found telegrams exnimitz awaiting them paragraph

quote congratulations unquote it said requote have every reason believe one your quail was peacock unquote

and if twas yamamoto who downshot twas peacock indeed

lodge[5]

Halsey was furious when he read Lodge's article and immediately "bottled up the story," as he noted in his memoirs. Noted for venting his wrath when aroused, he frequently embarrassed the Navy Department and the government for his off-the-cuff remarks and irascible behavior. In short, he often raged like a bull in a china shop.

After Strother, Barber, and Lanphier returned to Nouméa from rest leave, there was a message telling them to report to

Admiral Halsey aboard his flagship anchored in the harbor. They were taken to the ship by motor launch and immediately shown to the admiral's cabin on the main deck by a stern-faced aide.

The three officers entered the cabin and stood at attention in front of Halsey's desk. They saluted and held their salutes, expecting Halsey to return them.

"He just stared at us," Barber recalled.

He finally said, "Hands down" but left us at attention. I was scared to death. He kept staring at us and we didn't know what to do.

Then he started in on a tirade of profanity the like of which I had never heard before. He accused us of everything he could think of from being traitors to our country to being so stupid that we had no right to wear the American uniform. He said we were horrible examples of pilots of the Army Air Force, that we should be court-martialed, reduced to privates, and jailed for talking to Lodge about the Yamamoto mission. He raved on about security and officer responsibility about security matters.

He paced back and forth while he shouted profanely, waving his fists and declaring that we were the sorriest trio of Americans he had ever seen. I knew he had been nicknamed "Bull" Halsey by the press and now I understood why. He asked no questions and would not give any of us the opportunity to say a word or answer his charges. It was the worst "chewing out" I ever received.

When Halsey's rage tapered off, he turned to a large oak table nearby and fingered through five pieces of paper on his desk.

"Know what these are?" he asked rhetorically. "These are recommendations for Mitchell, Lanphier, Barber, Holmes, and Hine to get the Medal of Honor. As far as I'm concerned, none of you deserve even the Air Medal for what you did. You ought to face a court-martial, but because of the importance of the mission, I'm reducing these citations to the Navy Cross."

With a curt wave of his hand toward the door, we all saluted but, again, he did not return the courtesy. We about-faced and left. We were shocked by this encounter and really didn't know what to make of it. We had been tried and judged guilty.

The three of us went back to our base; shortly afterward, Lanphier and I received orders to return to the States. Lanphier was ordered to Washington and I was sent to Westover Field, Massachusetts, as a gunnery and dive bombing instructor. I received the Navy Cross there from some navy captain at an award ceremony. The other four received their Navy Crosses elsewhere. All other pilots on the mission received the Distinguished Flying Cross.

I have felt bad about this episode ever since. Not for myself or Lanphier because we should not have talked to Lodge at all, even though he had all or most of the information. I feel sorry for John Mitchell who did such a superb job of planning and leading the mission and had nothing to do with the Lodge episode. *He* should have received the Medal of Honor, just as Jimmy Doolittle did for leading his famous raid on Japan. I wish I could do something about this injustice.[6]

When Lodge's story reached Nimitz's CINCPAC headquarters in Hawaii from Halsey in mid-May, intelligence officers were aghast at what Lodge had reported. The story was immediately classified top secret because of the mention of Yamamoto and especially that "intelligence had trailed Yamamoto for five days."

Nimitz ordered an immediate investigation. If the capability to decode the Japanese fleet's top secret messages became known through the release of Lodge's story, the Japanese would immediately change their code drastically and it would set back communications decoding efforts many months. Information about enemy strategy, tactics, and fleet movements would be denied to the serious disadvantage of all Allied forces in the Pacific.

Although the loss of Yamamoto was a tremendous blow to the Japanese, the cryptographers were apprehensive from the start that the Japanese would realize their communications were insecure. W. J. Holmes, in his book *Double-Edged Secrets*, states that "The apprehension of the cryptographers was justified because security for handling Ultra information on Guadalcanal was woefully inadequate."[7]

On May 24, Nimitz sent a top secret "eyes only" message to Halsey:

FOR ADMIRAL HALSEY ONLY X ATTENTION LODGE'S
ARTICLE FORWARDED BY YOUR SERIAL 00848 OF 16
MAY X SECURE AND SEAL IN SAFE ALL COPIES AND
NOTES PREPARED BY LODGE X CINCPAC WILL RETAIN 2
COPIES NOW IN HIS POSSESSION X WARN LODGE AND
ALL OTHERS HAVING INFORMATION THIS MATTER TO
MAINTAIN COMPLETE SILENCE SEE MY 160039 APRIL
AND MY PERSONAL LETTER 15 MAY X CONDUCT IM-
MEDIATE INVESTIGATION MAINTAINING AS FAR AS
PRACTICABLE PERSONAL SUPERVISION THEREOF X
THIS SHOWS WIDESPREAD AND FLAGRANT DISREGARD
OF SECURITY ULTRA INFORMATION X INITIATE IM-
MEDIATE CORRECTIVE MEASURES AND TAKE DISCI-
PLINARY ACTION AS WARRANTED X SUBMIT REPORT
ALL ACTION TAKEN[8]

The order to investigate the breach of security was forwarded
from Halsey to the lower echelons of navy and Army Air Force
commands in the South Pacific. Comdr. William Read recalled:

We soon heard that Admiral King regarded this as an extremely serious breach of security and was very annoyed. In
fact, we had the inspector general of the navy visiting our
camp, in short order, questioning various officers, including
all of us and Admiral Mitscher himself. Of course, in our camp
the word spread like wildfire, whether from the pilots involved or how, I don't know. Everybody in the place knew
about the mission in a few hours and the effect on morale was
simply miraculous. This was the first time we had any success
of major proportions against an enemy force. . . . What this
did for all the poor mechanics and enlisted men who had been
stranded there from various sunken ships and had not been
relieved truly had to be seen to be believed.[9]

On May 30, Admiral Mitscher reported the results of his
investigation in a "Most Secret" letter to Admiral Fitch, his
immediate superior. Mitscher reviewed the events of April 17
including the briefing of Mitchell, Lanphier, and his staff on the
original Yamamoto itinerary message that launched the operation.

"No mention whatsoever was made of the source of informa-

tion contained in the dispatch," Mitscher wrote. However, he acknowledged that Yamamoto's name had been mentioned during Mitchell's briefing of his pilots. After the mission, Mitscher reported:
"The officers returning were briefed in a routine manner with only Lt. Col. E. L. Pugh, USMC, Lt. Col. H. Vicellio, AAF, Major J. P. Condon, USMC, and Capt. W. Morrison, AAF, a USAFISPA representative, present. According to Capt. Morrison, the only reference made concerning the enemy naval officer concerned was a remark, believed to have come from Capt. Lanphier, that, 'That son-of-a-bitch won't dictate any peace terms in the White House.' "
Mitscher then assured his superiors that the action report treated the strike as "a routine fighter sweep." He added, "No evidence has been unearthed which would indicate that any information concerning this strike was passed to newspapermen directly or indirectly."[10]

It is interesting to note that of all the fifteen surviving pilots on the mission, the only one who ever said he was debriefed by anyone was Lanphier. He said later that he had reported his actions on the mission to Vicellio, McGuigan, Morrison, Pugh, and Condon. None of the other pilots, including Mitchell, Barber, or Holmes, was ever asked for their input. This was confirmed in a "Most Secret" letter from Adm. Aubrey W. Fitch to Halsey. Fitch acknowledged that the action "became generally known throughout the greater part of the South Pacific Area. While Yamamoto's name was mentioned in the briefing of the pilots, no mention was made of the source of the information. In view of the stake of this mission it is considered that mentioning of this name to the participants of the strike was to insure its fulfilment."
He explained further:

The leakage of information to other military personnel was due to the overexuberance and abandonment of secrecy of the personnel who participated in this flight due to their intoxication with its apparent huge success. This is considered normal reaction coupled with any outstanding achievement and in the major theater of operations where personnel are relatively isolated it is very difficult to suppress. The results of this strike were therefore generally known in military circles. Enclosure C discloses that only one member of the strike force [Lanphier] was interviewed, the remaining members were not available. While it is not known whether interviewing the other members of the strike force would disclose any additional specific information, it is the opinion of Commander Aircraft, South Pacific that collectively, the pilots on this mission were indirectly responsible for the knowledge of this information being widely disseminated. Subject to the foregoing, every effort was made by persons of responsibility to withhold the military information under discussion from unauthorized personnel, and that there is no evidence brought forth to show that any military personnel gave direct information or notes to any members of the press or those closely associated with the press, nor knowingly discussed the action with the knowledge or expectation that it would reach the press.[11]

Col. H. J. Mitchell, commander of the Fleet Marine Force on Guadalcanal, was required to submit a report. He said that none of his personnel knew about the strike beforehand. However, "immediately after the strike it was common gossip and common knowledge that an important mission had been successfully accomplished and it was commonly rumored that important Japanese personnel had been shot down. It was common gossip after the strike that the mission had been accomplished as a result of an intercepted Japanese message." He denied that any of his pilots had discussed the matter with the press but listed the names and ranks of seventy-six pilots who had heard about the mission.[12]

Lt. Gen. Millard F. Harmon, commanding all air force units in the South Pacific, reported to both Fitch and Halsey that he had called in all officers assigned to the mission who were then still available on New Caledonia.

These officers were as a group and individually admonished by me for having in unauthorized manner discussed phases of this operation subsequent to its accomplishment. They were thoroughly enjoined to exercise due care in the future in regard to safeguarding military information. No inquiry was conducted by me as to the transgression of any particular individual and they were informed that for the purpose of this talk they were all considered guilty.

I subsequently had a similar talk with Brigadier General Dean C. Strother and directed him to contact all those officers remaining in the area whom I had not myself personally contacted and see that they received similar admonitions and instructions.[13]

Maj. Gen. Nathan F. Twining, commander of the Thirteenth Air Force, also had to report the results of his investigation of Army Air Force personnel still in the area who might have known of the mission and revealed it to unauthorized persons. His report was also negative. However, "Colonel Vicellio stated that after landing, on return from the mission, the participants were congratulated by a large number of personnel who apparently had knowledge of the purpose of this mission."[14]

Twining added that the mission had been discussed "quite openly" at a subordinate base "by a large number of people and that the action was common knowledge there."

Brig. Gen. Dean C. Strother was also requested to make a written statement. He acknowledged that in Auckland he had met Norman Lodge, who "was already in possession of the salient facts as far as I knew them and I discussed the mission with him. Mr. Lodge wanted to get the story released by COMSOPAC, and I explained to him that this mission was not a story and probably would not be released for security reasons. I gave him no authority to quote any member of my command or myself and no authority to submit the results of our discussion as an interview."[15]

It was July 9 before Admiral Nimitz received all the reports from his subordinate commanders. There is no record of his reaction. Meanwhile, however, the communications intelligence community expected the worst. Although the reports played down the possibility of leaks, it was apparent that there could be literally hundreds of Army Air Force, navy, and marine personnel in the South Pacific who had some knowledge, however slight or erroneous, of the Yamamoto shootdown. Some were already returning to the States with tales of their experiences. Although the word spread that the mission was not to be discussed by anyone, too many officers and enlisted men never got the word or were already transferred elsewhere, unaware of the damage their knowledge, no matter how meager, could do to American forces in the Pacific if revealed.

Naval communications security personnel were instructed to check all intercepted messages for any evidence that the Japanese realized their codes had been compromised. Military investigators and FBI personnel in the United States were instructed to scan American newspapers and magazines to see if any security leaks had developed.

While the American investigation was going on, the Japanese people were devastated by the loss of their beloved naval leader. His death was a severe blow to national morale—a blow as cruel to their psyche as the Doolittle raid on Tokyo had been a year before.

When the word flashed to the world that Yamamoto had died, *Time* magazine put its staff to work on a story about his demise. At least one *Time* magazine reporter was on Guadalcanal when the mission returned who "wrote up a lot of information after talking to us," according to Doug Canning, one of the members of the top cover flight. The presence of a *Time* reporter on Guadalcanal was confirmed by Lt. Comdr. Read, Mitscher's administrative officer, in Read's oral history statement. Stateside *Time* reporters checked out the rumors about the shootdown that persisted in Washington and elsewhere to verify the report from the correspondent in the South Pacific.

The May 31, 1943, issue of *Time* displayed a caricature of Yamamoto and reported his death. The story inside, on page 28, said that a meeting of the Imperial Rule Assistance Association in Tokyo had adoped a resolution:

"We, the 100,000,000 people of Japan, have simultaneously expressed our deepest condolence and we are burning with a greater spirit to fight against our enemy, America and Britain. Let us march in line in one united body . . . so that the spirit of the late Fleet Admiral may be kept alive."

Rear Adm. Hideo Yano, chief of the Japanese navy's press

section, was quoted: "The Japanese Navy will stride forward with the profound will to destroy the enemy. The war is to be prolonged and I, with you, to make the spirit of the Fleet Admiral live, must preserve and fulfill his will. . . ."

The magazine ended the story with these words: "When the name of the man who killed Admiral Yamamoto is released, the U.S. will have a new hero. Said one veteran of Pacific service: 'The only better news would be a bullet through Hitler.' "

It can be assumed that Time's reporters knew who the "hero" was and the details of the mission. On page 66 of the same issue, there was a large photo of Lanphier, captioned: "High man in a brother act." Under the title "Heroes," was this story:

To military theorists the South Pacific was still a static battle area. But in the day-to-day run of patrols and minor battles, new heroes were born, new air tactics proved by flyers grown skillful and canny in the school of war.

Out from a Solomons base streaked 16 twin-tailed Army Lightning fighters, feathering their own wind-blown wakes as they hugged the water to stay out of the beams of Jap radiodetectors. Near the enemy base at Kahili, twelve of the pilots horsed back on their wheels, ripped skyward with whining turbosuperchargers to give top cover. The four near the water bored on, found unexpected game; three Jap bombers waddling home with a heavy cover of Zeros.

The bombers lurched frantically for the cover of their own anti-aircraft. The Zeros piled into the Lightnings and both top covers swirled in a thundering dogfight. Down below, Lieut. Rex T. Barber whipped into a bomber, sawed off its tail with a burst of fire, knocked off a second as he pulled out of the attack.

The squadron commander, lean, black-eyed Captain Thomas G. Lanphier, tangled with a low-flying Zero, shot it down. He swung away, picked a bomber, shot it down, too. Up above the top-cover fight had broken off. A mission had been completed. The squadron whisked back to the Solomons base, wondered if it had nailed some Jap bigwig in the bombers.

The article noted that Lanphier's younger brother Charles, a marine pilot, had recently arrived in the Solomons and had participated in a battle over Russell Island flying a Vought Corsair at the same time his brother Tom was engaged in a dogfight at a higher altitude in a P-38. "The coincidence made that day's combat reports remarkably fine reading for their father, L. Col. Thomas G. Lanphier, Sr., a West Pointer who won his pilot's wings in World War I, later resigned to survey commercial air routes and is now on duty again with the General Staff in Washington."

To the casual reader, the two items in the same issue of *Time* would seem unrelated but in light of subsequent revelations about the Yamamoto shootdown, it is obvious that *Time* reporters had learned the details from a knowledgeable source.

There was great apprehension within the intelligence community that the extensive codebreaking capability of the Americans would at last become known to the Japanese. Apparently, that issue of *Time* did not reach the enemy's intelligence experts. If it did, they did not tie the two news items together; besides, their code experts still believed their code was unbreakable.

Before Mitchell left the South Pacific, Lt. Gen. Millard F. Harmon asked him to hand-carry a personal letter to Lt. Gen. H. H. "Hap" Arnold, commander of the Army Air Forces. On Nouméa, Admiral Halsey had asked General Harmon to let the navy make presentations of medals and Harmon had agreed. When he gave Mitchell the letter, Harmon told him that if Halsey didn't give Mitchell the Medal of Honor for his outstanding leadership, he would. This conversation took place after General Harmon had reprimanded Mitchell and several of his pilots verbally as he had stated in his letter to Nimitz.

The letter Mitchell carried to Arnold explained his role in planning and leading the mission. Since Harmon had agreed that the navy should make the awards to Mitchell and his men, it was Harmon's way of assuring that the top-ranking general of their own service would know how Harmon personally felt about Mitchell's planning and leadership ability. It was also to assure that future air force historians would know who deserved recognition for the mission's success in case the navy downplayed its significance or chose not to acknowledge that the participants were Army Air Force pilots.

Harmon's letter noted that "This was a beautifully conceived mission and executed from start to finish with high determination and consummate skill. All the officers participating are to be highly commended and for this action the Navy requested and we acceded to their request to bestow decorations upon them.

"The Navy's insistence on secrecy in connection with this mission I am sure you will appreciate as public knowledge of all the facts involved would adversely affect the intelligence sources that made the accomplishment of this particular mission possible."[16]

Harmon also wrote a letter of commendation to Mitchell:

There have been few if any missions in the history of our Air Force in which such outstanding victory has been achieved in the face of seemingly insuperable difficulties. You and your squadron have demonstrated that the combination of sound planning, a trained organization, superior equipment and perfect execution under outstanding leadership can accomplish the impossible. The excellent results obtained in combat at extremely low altitudes when enemy equipment enjoyed every advantage in performance and maneuverability reflect the soundness of your fighting technique and the excellence of your indoctrination and air discipline. The splendid performance of equipment is a triumph for the officers and men of your organization responsible for its maintenance and servicing and we all pay tribute to their superior work.

In a final paragraph, Harmon stated: "This letter is in no manner to be considered in lieu of any combat award, but rather as the expression of appreciation of the Army Forces in the South Pacific by the Commander thereof."[17]

On May 26, 1943, Mitchell, Lanphier, Barber, Canning, Goerke, Holmes, and Jacobson received orders transferring them back to the States. Mitchell and Lanphier were ordered to Washington where they were interrogated by army and navy intelligence and operations officers. They made many recommendations concerning fighter operations which were published in the classified Army Air Force's *Command Informational Intelligence Series*. No mention was made of the Yamamoto shootdown in the secret report disseminated to intelligence officers in the field.

Always seeking to report good news, the War Department's Bureau of Public Relations issued a press release on June 17, 1943, quoting Mitchell and Lanphier's favorable opinions about the Lockheed P-38 Lightning and their experiences fighting in the South Pacific. Mitchell was credited with downing eight Japanese planes; Lanphier with seven. There was no direct mention of the Yamamoto shootdown. The release stated:

> Captain Lanphier brought down two Japanese bombers on April 18 while participating in a sweep led by Major Mitchell. While the Major climbed with 12 Lightnings to furnish high cover, Captain Lanphier's flight of four started the attack, and brought down a total of six enemy planes.
>
> . . . The first fighter plane this fighter pilot shot down was while he was on an intelligence mission in a B-17, last August. Twelve Zeros attacked the bomber and three other B-17s in the flight. Captain Lanphier seized a waist gun and knocked down one of the attackers. All of the Japanese planes were destroyed."[18]

Despite the concerns of the naval communications intelligence experts, this release, actually prepared by the Army Air Force's public information personnel, might also have given the Japanese a clue about how the Americans had learned of the admiral's itinerary. Again, no evidence has ever been found that the Japanese had any inkling that Lanphier was the American "hero" who was believed to have caused the admiral's demise or that their naval code had been compromised.

The official War Department news release also gave affirmation to Lanphier's claim that he had shot down a Zero while acting as a gunner on a bombing mission, thus crediting him with the first of seven victories, even though no one witnessed this "kill" and no one on the B-17 crew ever confirmed Lanphier's "victory." No other fighter pilots before or since were ever given credit for kills while acting as gunners on a bomber.

But Lanphier was in Washington and had access to the War Department news release writers; the anonymous B-17 crew did not. The War Department release also stated:

"Fighter pilots account as confirmed victories only those enemy planes which they see burn, explode, fall apart, crash, or from which the pilot bails out. No others are accredited victories, regardless of how many rounds a pilot may be sure he has pumped into the enemy plane or pilot—if the enemy is not visibly destroyed, he does not count on the record as a victory."

Mitchell, Lanphier, Barber, and Holmes received their Navy Crosses in separate ceremonies at bases where they were later assigned. The citation for Lanphier reads:

For extraordinary heroism while attached to a Marine Fighter Command in action against enemy Japanese forces in the Solomon Islands on April 18, 1943. Leading a division of fighter planes at dangerously low altitude in the longest planned interception mission ever attempted, Captain Lanphier contacted the assigned objective, consisting of two enemy bombers and six escort fighters, with complete tactical surprise and launched a fierce, determined attack. In the ensuing engagement he operated with such daring courage and excellent marksmanship that he sent the leading bomber crashing in flames, and subsequently shot down one of the hostile fighters when it furiously attacked his plane.

Barber's citation states:

"Participating in a dangerously long interception flight, First Lieutenant Barber contacted a formation of two enemy bombers escorted by six fighters in a complete surprise approach. Quickly engaging the enemy, he pressed his tactical advantage and struck fiercely, destroying one Japanese bomber at such close range that fragments from the explosion lodged in the wings of his plane, and shooting down the escorting enemy fighter plane which had been attempting to divert the attack."

Lanphier had told Barber that he had written these citations for the Medal of Honor and those for Mitchell, Holmes, and Hine, which Halsey had downgraded to the Navy Cross.

The assignment to the Pentagon was to Lanphier's liking. His father had been assigned there when called to active duty as a lieutenant colonel after war had been declared. Both Lanphiers had ready access to public information personnel who were always on the lookout for good battle news and heroes who could be exploited for public relations purposes. The elder Lanphier, extremely proud of his son, had known Gen. Henry H. "Hap" Arnold, chief of the Army Air Forces, and other generals since World War I days. He had easy access to his old friends now serving in high air force positions.

A short time after arriving in Washington, the younger Lanphier and Mitchell were sent on a tour of air force basic flying training bases to talk with student pilots and reassure those who were apprehensive about volunteering to fly fighter planes. The author, while a flying instructor at Enid Army Flying School, Enid, Oklahoma, met Lanphier in late summer of 1943. He buzzed the field with his Lightning to proclaim his arrival and was introduced to the instructors and students as a recently returned fighter ace. With his "fifty mission crush" cap pushed back on his head, he entertained the students with combat tales of the South Pacific. He was the embodiment of the devil-may-care fighter pilot whose self-confidence was exceeded only by his ability to colorfully describe aerial encounters with the enemy.

The story submitted by J. Norman Lodge for security clearance, based largely on Lanphier's input, had killed any chance of Mitchell getting the Medal of Honor.

"The Navy tracked me down when I got to Washington," Mitchell recalled.

I was told that Admiral King wanted to see me. I went to King's office, but rather than see me, I was shunted off to some three-star admiral. He told me King was disturbed about the leakage of information concerning the Yamamoto mission and he asked me to fill him in on what I knew about the security [on Guadalcanal] or lack thereof.

Figuring that they might be trying to make a scapegoat out of me, I told them I had plenty to say. I asked them to give me a secretary and I would tell it all, the way I saw it. After some two hours of dictation, during which I told them of the lack of security on the island, that there were many people in the dugout at our briefing who had nothing to do with the mission, that the ground crews, having to hang the larger external tanks, knew it was a long mission, and when the mission was over there was much elation (uncontained) by the pilots, and that Lanphier stated loud and clear that he had shot down Admiral Yamamoto, etc. etc.

That was the last I heard of anything about that matter. But when Lanphier and I went to Lockheed a couple of weeks later to pick up two P-38s to use to visit all of the basic flying schools in the U.S., we were treated with much deference and courtesy. I am convinced they had word on the Yamamoto mission and had probably been informed by Lanphier because they all knew we had been awarded Navy Crosses.[19]

On August 28, 1943, Lt. Charles C. Lanphier, Tom Lanphier's younger brother, a marine Corsair pilot, was shot down over Russell Island and was captured by the Japanese. He was imprisoned at Rabaul, New Britain. When the news was received in Washington, it gave the navy another reason why no information about the Yamamoto shootdown should be released. In Admiral Halsey's memoirs, explaining why he was so upset about the possible leak of the story to Lodge, the Associated Press reporter, he said he was also concerned for Lanphier's sake:

"His brother was a prisoner of war, and if the Japs had learned who had shot down Yamamoto, what they might have done to the brother is something I prefer not to think about. I have in mind the nurses they caught on Guadalcanal and raped for 48 hours before cutting their throats; and the two Marines whom they vivisected; and the young girl on New Guinea whom they forced to watch her parents being beheaded; and the Marine pilot in a parachute, whose feet were chopped off by the propellers of a Zeke."[20] (Lt. Charles C. Lanphier died of malnutrition on Rabaul while a prisoner of war on April 29, 1944. His death was not known until after the Japanese surrender.)

The concern about the possibility of the Japanese discovering that their codes had been broken was widely felt. In January 1944, General MacArthur sent a classified letter to his commanders:

"Revelations of the Yamamoto incident by the returnees from the Pacific theater are developing into a serious situation. It is directed that before they return to the United States, you order all those concerned under your command not to reveal such information to friends, relatives, or news media. Further revelation of information will ultimately lead to compromising the information source."[21]

With the continuing concern about the Japanese finding that their top secret naval codes had been compromised, and Lanphier's brother's capture always in mind, the air force would not reassign Lanphier to the Pacific; instead, he was assigned to the Pentagon and given some unspecified duties. In addition to his flights around the country, he made a trip to England and observed fighter operations there. He was promoted to major and later to lieutenant colonel just before the war ended in mid-1945.

Lanphier had long before resolved he was going to write his version of the Yamamoto shootdown and his exploits as a fighter pilot and have them cleared for release. He submitted two stories for security review in 1944. They were finally cleared for public consumption, along with a War Department news release, on September 11, 1945. The bylined stories appeared in the *New York Times* and a slightly different version, syndicated by the North American Newspaper Alliance, was widely published in other U.S. newspapers. Lanphier appeared to have won his objective to receive national acclaim for the most noted aerial ambush in history.

9

THE AFTERMATH

THE FORMAL SURRENDER OF THE JAPANESE took place on the deck of the USS *Missouri* on September 2, 1945. It was a welcome relief from the long months of tension. However, there were still serious concerns among members of the communications intelligence community about revealing any information concerning breaking the Japanese codes. James Forrestal, who had become Secretary of the Navy in May 1944, wrote in his diary about an interesting exchange of "Urgent, Top Secret" messages that took place among the U.S. Navy codebreakers a few days after the surrender:

In the enthusiasm of victory someone let out the story of how in 1943, Admiral Isoroku Yamamoto, the Japanese naval commander in chief and architect of the Pearl Harbor attack, had been intercepted and shot down in flames as a result of the American ability to read the Japanese codes. It was the first public revelation of the work of the cryptoanalysis divisions, and it brought an anguished cable from the intelligence unit already engaged at Yokohama in the interrogation of Japanese naval officers: "Yamamoto story in this morning's paper has placed our activities in very difficult position. Having meticulously concealed our special knowledge we now become ridiculous." They were even then questioning the Japanese officer who had been responsible for those codes, and he has been hinting that in the face of this disclosure, he would have to commit suicide. The cable continued: "This officer is giving us valuable information on Japanese crypto systems and channels and we do not want him or any other promising prospects to commit suicide until after next week when we expect to have milked them dry. . . ."

Washington answered with an "Operational Priority: Top Secret" dispatch: "Your lineal position on the list of those who are embarrassed by the Yamamoto story is five thousand six hundred ninety two. All of the people over whose dead bodies the story was going to have been published have been buried. All possible schemes to localize the damage have been considered but none appears workable. Suggest that only course for you is to deny knowledge of the story and say you do not understand how such fantastic tale could have been invented. This might keep your friend happy until suicide time next week, which is about all that can be expected. . . ."[1]

Tom Lanphier and the other participants in the Yamamoto mission had been forbidden to tell their versions of the shootdown publicly until after the war. Lanphier had actually written his account in 1944 but it was withheld on security grounds. When Lanphier's stories were published after the Japanese surrendered and the War Department published a news release giving Lanphier full credit for Yamamoto's demise, the surviving pilots were astonished. Each wondered how Lanphier could claim credit so blatantly in syndicated stories that were published nationwide in hundreds of newspapers. The official reports of the mission claimed three Betty bombers and three Zeros had been shot down. All of the surviving members of the Yamamoto mission accepted those figures as fact. However, in 1945, it was not yet confirmed by the Japanese that Yamamoto was aboard the bomber that had gone down in the jungle. And no one had ascertained that there were only two Betty bombers instead of three. No one but Japanese personnel and local natives had visited the wreckage during the war. No Japanese had yet published any eyewitness accounts of the events surrounding the mission.

As soon as Rex Barber read Lanphier's account in a California newspaper, he telephoned Lanphier, still assigned to the Pentagon. Barber was then squadron commander of the 27th Fighter Squadron at March Field, California. In the presence of Col. David Lee "Tex" Hill, famous Flying Tiger ace and Barber's group commander, Barber lambasted Lanphier for making a claim he knew was not true. Lanphier, taken aback by Barber's uncharacteristic fury, replied with a telegram. Lanphier implied that the story would be changed and "you will be included in everything as you certainly deserve." He added, "Meanwhile, say nothing repeat nothing."²

After Barber's phone call, Lanphier also wrote Barber a letter:

Enclosed is a copy of the story I sold the *New York Times*. It was released the day after the War Department put out its story. Also released at that time were stories on the same subject by J. Norman Lodge who got his dope from Strother, by Bors who got his story from Admiral Mitscher, and by Mahan who got his story from Mitchell at Nouméa. All of the stories mentioned all three of us—you, Mitch and me— equally. The story you read, which left you both out, must have been pretty short not to have included you.

. . . The War Department release, while mentioning every-one, gave me the best of it—why, I don't know. They had all the facts at hand—Mahan's, Lodge's, Bors, and my stories— all written at different times. They also had all the intelligence reports and citations for reference.

They broke the story, apparently because the Navy did first. Also seems all Jap prison camps have been taken over as well as their radio and press facilities. . . .

As you know, and as you will note, I mention in my story I am very much indebted to you—for my neck as well as other things. I don't know what I can do to remedy the situation— but I certainly am not happy that you felt you got shafted. I am stationed here in the Pentagon for a month or two, as of today—and will be glad to do whatever I can. I talked to the PRO [Public Relations Office] people this morning and asked them why they didn't reissue all the Navy Cross citations in an effort to further clarify the fact that credit is due a lot of people for that mission. They are going to. Would have thought they'd do that in the first place.[3]

Barber was furious at Lanphier's reaction to his phone call and tried to report his own version of the Yamamoto mission through official channels, rather than through the press as Lanphier had done. Unfortunately, no one in Barber's chain of command paid any attention to his request for a review of the mission. He never received replies to his letters. He enlisted the help of intelligence officers he knew and asked them to see what they could do to check the official classified records. One of those who tried to assist Barber in having his claim acknowledged about shooting the lead bomber down was Col. Luther Kissick, then serving with Barber as an intelligence officer at Kweilin, China.

"I was shocked at that time after talking with Barber," Kissick said, "that there was no intensive, detailed debriefing of this mission, as important as it was. . . . The intelligence information on the location of the top Japanese leader was very precise and accurate. Where was the accurate intelligence follow-through on the mission flown to tidy up the operation?"[4]

Unfortunately, since the action had taken place in another theater, Kissick was unable to help Barber tell his side of the story.

The official report, which Lanphier had told Barber he had written, remained classified secret for many years. Barber was not able to see a copy for over a decade after the mission.

Barber's claim rested on a single premise. If Yamamoto was in the lead bomber, Barber was certain he had shot it down. Lanphier had reported that the two Betty bombers had separated when he and Barber were trying to close in.

"The Bettys definitely did not split at that time," Barber asserts. "They were still together and on their original course when I caught up with them, and after Lanphier had turned toward the Zeros. This is a key error in the official report. Had the lead bomber turned left when Lanphier said it had, it would have rammed right into the bomber flying on its left wing because they were flying close together."[5]

In a history of the Thirteenth Air Force, historians noted: "Both Lanphier and Barber destroyed a Betty which the Zeros tried desperately to protect, but Barber's Betty disintegrated at 5,000 to 6,000 feet. A subsequent report by the Japanese states that Yamamoto was found dead in the wrecked plane, which would indicate that he was a victim of Lanphier. The Japs claimed likewise that he was shot down by 30 or 40 fighters." This information was based solely on an interview with Lanphier in Washington on September 10, 1945.[6]

John Mitchell, a colonel at the end of the war, was also furious at Lanphier's persistent and continuous play for the national limelight. Regarding the NANA story in which Lanphier said Mitchell had verified over the radio that he saw a bomber burning in the jungle, Mitchell states emphatically, that "I did *not* reply on the radio that I saw a bomber burning. In no way could I confirm that he had shot down a bomber. I saw smoke rising out of the jungle and nothing more from where I was at about 16,000 feet. Lanphier claimed from Day One that he shot the admiral down, and defied anyone to say he didn't."[7]

At the same time that Lanphier was getting extensive newspaper coverage through his stories (which he claimed he had copyrighted but are not recorded in the U.S. Copyright Office), the *Washington Post* carried a gossip column by Leonard Lyons that gave further credibility to Lanphier's claim to fame:

Lt. Col. Tom Lanphier, Jr., the Army flier who shot down the plane in which Admiral Yamamoto was a passenger, almost ran out of gas on his flight back to Guadalcanal. He thought he'd have to land on the Russell Islands, 50 miles away, but finally decided to go on. He radioed to the Guadalcanal airfield, asking that the field be cleared for his landing because he didn't have enough gas to circle it. Then he added the news that Yamamoto would be unable to dictate any peace in the White House. . . . The puzzled radio operator at Guadalcanal asked him to explain, but Lanphier remained silent. But by the time the pilot landed, all personnel on Guadalcanal had heard the rumor that Yamamoto had joined his ancestors.

Colonel Lanphier's commanding officer ordered him retired from combat flying for two reasons: The possibility that he'd be shot down and captured and perhaps tortured into revealing that the Americans had broken the Japanese code. Furthermore, Lanphier's brother was a prisoner of war. . . . The colonel finally persuaded his commanding officer to allow him to visit England for two weeks, promising not to do any flying. Lanphier arrived in England with a bag in which there were only a toothbrush and four bottles of liquor. One bottle was for Ira Wolfert, the war correspondent. The other three were for bribing Thunderbolt and Lightning squadrons to allow him to fly. Colonel Lanphier flew in all those planes before he came home.[8]

When Lanphier received so much publicity after his stories were published nationwide, Mitchell decided that he would not stand by without objecting to Lanphier's blatant claim to fame. In a speech at a luncheon in San Antonio on January 8, 1946, Mitchell said that positive credit could not be given to Lanphier because no one knew at that time which bomber the admiral was in. "I rather resent the credit being given to Captain Lanphier and the ignoring of Captain Barber. When details of the death of Yamamoto were finally announced, I felt that an injustice had been done to Captain Barber. I would simply like to put the record straight."[9]

Shortly thereafter, a story appeared in *Army Times,* a service newspaper, which Mitchell said "contained the same old stuff" about Lanphier getting the credit for not only the shootdown but planning and leading the mission. The article stated:

> Another big triumph of the 13th Air Force occurred on April 18, 1943, when Lt. Col. Thomas G. Lanphier, Jr., then a captain, intercepted and shot down the plane of Admiral Isoroku Yamamoto, who was credited by the Japanese with the boast that he would dictate peace terms from the White House.
>
> Acting on information relayed to commands in the Southwest Pacific by the Secretary of the Navy, Lanphier and a group of 13th Air Force fliers in P-38s departed Guadalcanal for their rendezvous with Yamamoto, who was accompanied by his entire high command. Admiral Yamamoto later was officially announced by the Japanese to have been killed in combat with the enemy, and Colonel Lanphier was awarded the Navy Cross for the success of his mission.[10]

Mitchell was furious. Once more Lanphier's story had been given credibility. One of the youngest colonels in the air force at the end of the war, Mitchell had served overseas three times during the war and had eleven enemy aircraft to his credit. He was flying missions over Japan when the war ended.

When he read this article, he had had enough of Lanphier's continual demand for credit. A colonel stationed at Maxwell Field, Alabama, at the time, he decided to write to Gen. Carl Spaatz, commanding general of the Army Air Forces. In the letter he said:

First, Lanphier did not lead this mission. It was led by the undersigned. Secondly, no one knows who shot down the bomber in which Yamamoto was riding. Lanphier was leading the attack flight of four planes. When my wingman spotted Yamamoto's plane, he called in *two* bombers, which was correct. They were flying side by side, identical in every respect. As Lanphier and his flight made a pass at the bombers, they were intercepted by six Zeros who were escorting. They were forced to pull up and the bombers headed for the treetops. In the next few seconds the bombers were lost to view. Later, Lanphier and his wingman, Major Rex T. Barber, then a 1st Lieutenant, after becoming separated from each other, each shot down a bomber in widely separated spots. Therefore, there was no way of knowing which bomber was the lead bomber nor of knowing in which airplane Yamamoto was riding.

I have read many accounts of this in the past with Lanphier claiming credit completely, and I consider it an injustice to his wingman, Major Rex Barber, who just as likely destroyed the Japanese admiral, and to the other men in the flight who were all responsible in making the mission a success by carrying out to the letter the exact instructions given them the night before.

It is my opinion that the records should be set straight and that some kind of public announcement be made to credit Barber with his share of this achievement, and to emphasize that it is just as likely that he made the kill as Lanphier.[11]

Mitchell received a cryptic, noncommital reply; the Army Air Forces, then in the throes of planning to detach itself from the army and become a separate service under the Department of Defense, took no action.

Meanwhile, Lanphier decided that there was no future for him in uniform and quickly separated from active duty as a lieutenant colonel in October 1945. He went to Boise, Idaho, where he became managing editor of the *Idaho Daily Statesman,* the state's largest newspaper, reportedly owned by a close friend of the Lanphier family. He joined the Idaho National Guard as "senior air officer" of the 190th Fighter Squadron.

In February 1946, he was "selected" as third vice president of the newly formed Air Force Association. He was to serve until general elections could be held the following year. In announcing his selection, *Air Force,* the association's magazine, reported that he participated in more than one hundred combat missions in the South Pacific. "Among his outstanding exploits was the shooting down of the plane carrying Admiral Yamamoto."[12]

Lanphier became the first elected president of the association in 1947 and, again, the magazine credited him with Yamamoto's demise. In his inaugural address at the association's convention, he said he was going "to visit every state that has a wing at least once, and I may be able to borrow a P-51 to swing it." He traveled extensively around the country speaking about the virtues of American airpower and making many political contacts. Sponsors always billed him as "the man who shot down Yamamoto."

An article in *Air Force,* described the election and other activities of the convention and again gave him credit for the kill:

> Tom was in the flight of fighters assigned to intercept that trip. His personal mission: to take care of the Admiral. Intelligence had reported the exact minute Yamamoto was due to arrive at Bougainville. The Admiral was punctual. So was Tom. He dove in and got the Admiral's bomber and with it the man who was reported to have boasted that the Japs would dictate peace terms in the White House. In the same pass, Lt. Rex Barber dove in and knocked off the second bomber in the Jap party. Tom and Barber were jumped by the Admiral's fighter escort of six Zeros, got three of the six in the getaway.[13]

In January 1949, Lanphier was given the Air Force Association's Exceptional Civilian Award for "outstanding journalistic endeavor in support of airpower and his dynamic leadership of the AFA." The award was made by W. Stuart Symington, the first secretary of the air force. In the ensuing months, Lanphier loudly and publicly advocated merging the Air National Guard and the Air Force Reserve forces. He ran into fierce opposition on this and other national defense issues, not only from members of the two reserve components of the newly established air force but from the active duty hierarchy and many members of Congress as well.

Air force historians released a seven-volume history of World War II in 1950 which was published by the University of Chicago Press. The account, obviously derived from the original official action report signed by Capt. William Morrison and Lt. Joseph McGuigan, stated:

> Two hours and nine minutes after takeoff at 0725, as sixteen P-38s flew in toward the coast of Bougainville barely clearing the water, there ahead appeared the enemy almost as if the entire affair had been prearranged by mutual consent. Two Bettys turned to escape, while their six Zero escorts tried in vain to cut off Lanphier's attack section. Lanphier exploded one fighter, then dived on one bomber, sending it flaming into the jungle, while Barber disintegrated the other Betty. Escape of the P-38s was doubtful, since now the advantage of altitude lay with the Zeros, but by hedgehopping, skidding, and sideslipping, the attackers pulled away under a heavy counter-attack. Only Lt. Raymond K. Hine failed to return from this flawlessly executed mission which had cost the Japanese their highest ranking officer, victim apparently of Captain Lanphier's guns and Major Mitchell's flawless timing of the flight.[14]

In the chapter notes, the historians said that the information was based on an interview with Captain Lanphier and a summary of "Enemy Aircraft Destroyed by Army Fighter Pilots in the Solomon Area Covering Period from August 22, 1942 to June 30, 1943." Neither Mitchell, Barber, Holmes, nor any other survivor of the mission was interviewed. The chapter note also stated:

Much secrecy surrounded this exploit, since its success rested on U.S. ability to understand the Japanese codes. Not one of the original intelligence reports examined ever gave any indication that Yamamoto was involved. Some difficulty arises in fixing responsibility for shooting down the victim's plane. Both Barber and Lanphier destroyed a bomber, and so did Holmes over Moila Point. But this last one fell in the water, Barber's disintegrated in the air at 5,000 to 6,000 feet, while Lanphier's crashed into the trees. A subsequent report by the Japanese stated that Yamamoto was found dead in his wrecked plane, which would indicate that it was Lanphier's work.[15]

When Rex Barber read this, he wrote to the Office of Air Force History saying that he did not intercept the bomber at 5,000 to 6,000 feet and explained the significance of this error. The bombers were at low level when he went after the lead bomber. He received a reply to his letter thanking him for his input and stating that the corrected information would "be included in any revised edition of our Volume IV." Volume IV has never been revised.

Barber decided to remain in the air force and received a regular commission. Not a glory-seeker, he quietly went about his subsequent air force assignments, all the time seething at Lanphier's claim. He had served in China as a squadron commander with the Fourteenth Air Force after his tour on Guadalcanal and flew twenty-eight combat missions there. He was shot down in enemy territory; although seriously injured, he evaded capture.

Barber continued to fly fighters after the war was over. He participated in initial test work with the Lockheed P-80 Shooting Star, the air force's first jet fighter, and commanded the first squadron in the air force to be equipped with jet fighter aircraft. He also participated in the 1946 Bendix Trophy Race, the first time a jet aircraft competed.

In 1950, Barber was sent to Korea on a special assignment

during which he flew three combat missions. Subsequent assignments included duty with the Air Defense Command and as air attaché in Colombia and Ecuador. He retired as a full colonel in 1961 after twenty-one years of active duty.

After Lanphier left office as AFA's president, he was named to its board of directors. Still wanting to stay in the Washington limelight, he volunteered in 1949 to fly around the world on commercial airlines to dramatize and publicize the progress aviation had made in the forty-six years since the Wright brothers' historic first flights at Kitty Hawk. The flight had potential news value because Lanphier vowed he was going to break the record for round-the-world passenger travel set in 1948 by Edward Eagan, chairman of the New York State Boxing Commission. Eagan's record was six days, three hours, forty minutes.

Lanphier left New York on December 2, 1949, and returned in four days, twenty-three hours, fifty minutes.

After Lanphier returned to Washington, he told friends about his night arrival at Tokyo's International Airport. He also related this story later to one writer and reportedly later included it in his unpublished memoirs. He said he was met there by a representative of the American embassy who told him there was a group of Japanese who wanted to see him.

Lanphier left the plane and said he was greeted by Mrs. Isoroku Yamamoto. Lanphier said she spoke through an interpreter and presented him with a bouquet of flowers.

Lanphier said she spoke quietly and seemingly without resentment as they exchanged pleasantries. She mentioned that her son was then a student at Harvard University and liked America. Lanphier was flustered by the meeting and mumbled his appreciation for the flowers. She smiled wanly and disappeared.[16]

Lanphier said he walked to the terminal where local newsmen confronted him with extensive questions about what he thought of Admiral Yamamoto and requested details about the shootdown of their revered naval hero. He said he answered them candidly and then continued on his record-breaking flight.

There is no verification for this story, other than Lanphier's statement to colleagues and a book writer. Its retelling, however, enabled him to restate and further his claim that he was the pilot who deserved full credit for Yamamoto's demise. The encounter received no press coverage and the extensive story Lanphier wrote describing his trip for a January 1950 article in *Air Force* magazine carried no mention of the meeting. No evidence has been found confirming that the meeting with Mrs. Yamamoto actually took place.

Lanphier left Idaho in late 1949 for Washington, where he had made many political contacts and where he thought his future lay. He had become an outspoken critic of the nation's military policies, and any time his name was mentioned, he was referred to as the man who had shot down Yamamoto.

In 1950, he was appointed to the staff of Air Force Secretary W. Stuart Symington with the title of "special assistant." A historian on Symington's staff recalled that staff members resented Lanphier being hailed around the country as the man who shot down Yamamoto. This source added: "This alleged achievement vaulted Lanphier into a number of key assignments. No doubt Lanphier had a lot of ability, but there is also no doubt that his questionable claim to sole credit for the shootdown did not hurt his advancement."[17]

Lanphier continued to serve with Symington when the latter was appointed chairman of the National Security Resources Board. In 1951, Lanphier moved to San Diego to become vice president of the Convair Division of General Dynamics Corporation and continued to gain public attention for his vocal commentaries on military affairs.

On January 26, 1960, syndicated columnist Joseph Alsop wrote an article that appeared in the *Washington Post* and other newspapers saying that he and Rex Barber had met in China in 1944 after Barber, then flying with Chennault's famous Flying Tigers, had been shot down by Japanese fighters but not captured.

"He had been too badly injured to walk," Alsop wrote. "He had been carried several hundred miles on the backs of Chinese guerrillas. He had several hairbreadth escapes from Japanese patrols."

According to Alsop, "after a good many 'kan peis' of the local white mule," Barber allegedly told him "the man who got the admiral was Tom Lanphier. I was his wing man. He led the attack. We each got a bomber, but he took the first one, and the first one had Yamamoto on board."

Alsop wrote there was a good reason for bringing up "this snapshot of the forgotten past out of memory's album. This same Tom Lanphier, whom the Major [Barber] talked about for much of the rest of that happy, long-ago evening, is again being talked about here in Washington. But this time Lanphier is being discussed in very different language, by men on the highest level of the American government."

Alsop stated that Lanphier was a center of attention in the nation's capital because he "is a worried man, and because he has attacked the thing that worries him with the same devil-may-care, go-for-the-lead-bomber determination that he showed when Yamamoto met his end."

At the time, Lanphier, as a vice president of Convair, was in charge of the Atlas intercontinental ballistic missile program. Since he had served as a special assistant to Senator W. Stuart Symington (Democrat, Missouri) when Symington became the first secretary of the air force, Alsop said he was Symington's close friend, "and in the last months Symington and Lanphier, with Lanphier feverishly spurring Symington on, have desperately pressed for a cold, hard new look at the changes in the military balance between the United States and the Soviet Union."

In a meeting with Symington and CIA Director Allen W. Dulles, Alsop reported that Lanphier "all but broke up the party by declaring that his own manufacturing experience proved the dangerous overoptimism of the official estimates of Soviet missile output."

Alsop pointed out that Lanphier "has an obvious interest in bigger Atlas orders from the air force. Thus a good many men on the higher governmental level are smugly saying that Tom Lanphier has just been 'selling a bill of goods with his furious, worried talk about the missile gap.' "[18]

Once more, Barber's anger mounted over Lanphier's renewed public claim for the Yamamoto shootdown. He recalled having had a conversation with Alsop in China but certainly did not give credit to Lanphier for the Yamamoto shootdown. He immediately called Alsop's office.

"I told his receptionist who I was," he recalled. "She put me on hold, and returned shortly to say that Mr. Alsop could not talk to me then. I asked that he call me back. He never returned that call, or any of a number of follow-up calls I made during the following two weeks. Finally, the receptionist told me it was useless for me to continue calling, as Mr. Alsop had told her he was 'not in' as far as I was concerned."[19]

In 1984, while preparing a manuscript for his memoirs, Lanphier wrote to Alsop requesting permission to quote from his 1960 column. Alsop gave permission and added, "But do you really want to in view of your controversy with Barber?

"If the column is printed with its date, as it ought to be, any reader will be able to see that I was recalling an episode in China a good many years earlier than the date of the column. And China, moreover, is not the right context for the destruction of Yamamoto.

"Hence the astute reader will not, and indeed should not, take this column as evidence in the dispute between Barber and you."[20]

In addition to getting renewed public attention as "the man who shot down Yamamoto," Lanphier continued to expound his views about the so-called "missile gap." He appeared on the "Today" show twice in early 1960 castigating the shortsightedness of the Eisenhower administration concerning the Soviet Union's growing missile capabilities.

Barber's blood pressure rose every time he heard of Lanphier's invoking the Yamamoto shootdown to further his own publicity-grabbing interests. In June 1960, Barber was Wing Materiel Officer for the 363d Fighter Wing at Myrtle Beach Air Force Base, South Carolina. The air force asked his wing to conduct cold-weather tests on the F-100 jet fighter in the climatic hangar at Eglin Air Force Base, Florida. His duties required him to monitor these tests. Many aircraft manufacturers and high-level government officials were invited to look at the results of the tests under simulated arctic conditions pertaining to oils, lubricants, guns, armament, etc.

As the visitors, including Lanphier, arrived for an official briefing, Barber was the official greeter. He talked with Lanphier and asked him why he had been on the "Today" show a few weeks before attacking President Eisenhower and his administration's defense policies. Barber knew Lanphier was a Republican and was surprised that Lanphier would criticize the president so stridently on national television.

Lanphier took Barber aside. "What you don't understand," Lanphier said, disdainfully, "is what's going on in Washington these days. Senator Symington and I are very close. We are going to the Democratic National Convention this summer. We believe the convention will be deadlocked between Senators Johnson and Kennedy and the delegates will finally have to settle for a dark-horse candidate. Senator Symington is the one most likely to be nominated as a compromise candidate for the presidency. Symington is going to take the unprecedented step of naming me his vice presidential running mate. By doing this, we can split the Republican vote and win."[21]

Barber could not believe what he was hearing. Lanphier had always been clever, articulate, and fast-thinking. He had such a convincing way about him that Barber didn't know how to respond. On the way back to his base, Barber recalled those days in the South Pacific when he and Lanphier had been close friends and had flown on many missions together, each helping the other out of scrapes against enemy planes. He remembered Tom saying that he had great ambitions for a political career after the war and that he was going to establish an outstanding war record so he would become nationally known.

Barber also remembered that Lanphier had told him not to worry about the details in the intelligence report on the Yamamoto mission because he had written it. Lanphier also said he had helped write the citations for the Medal of Honor for Mitchell and the four "shooters."

The brief 1960 encounter with Lanphier suddenly brought the controversy over the shootdown into sharp focus once again for Barber. Lanphier had been deadly serious about coming out of the war a hero whose name would be so well known that he would be able to travel in the highest government and industry circles and be listened to because of his fame as "the man who shot down Yamamoto." It all fitted together and summed up the personality of a man who seemed to be driven by a deep psychological need for admiration, fame, and power.

W. Stuart Symington had served as the first secretary of the air force from September 1947 until he resigned in 1951 in protest over cuts in the air force budget. He won election to the Senate in 1952 and, in 1960, was unsuccessful in his bid for the Democratic presidential nomination. After John F. Kennedy was nominated, Symington was mentioned prominently as a vice presidential candidate before that offer went to Lyndon B. Johnson of Texas. The name of Thomas G. Lanphier, Jr., never surfaced. The convention was not deadlocked, so Symington had no opportunity to name a vice president.

In 1967, an unnamed air force officer investigated the original 1943 report signed by Capt. William Morrison and Lt. Joseph McGuigan and wrote: "The Report is enough to make one weep. It reads like a fiction tale and the facts appear to be intertwined like Medusa's locks."[22]

In 1973, Kit C. Carter and Robert Mueller, air force historians, prepared a "Combat Chronology" for the Air University and the Office of Air Force History. Under the chronology of events for 1943, they summarized the Yamamoto mission for April 18, 1943 and tersely concluded: "In the air battle, Capt. Lanphier and 1st Lt. Rex T. Barber shoot down the bmr carrying Yamamoto."[23] The air force had thus concluded in a review of all victory credits of World War II pilots that Lanphier and Barber should share credit for the Yamamoto shootdown.[24]

In May 1983, at a reunion of the American Fighter Aces Association, Lanphier learned, apparently for the first time, that the air force had officially split the victory credits between him and Barber. It was the first time that Mitchell, Barber, and Lanphier had been together since World War II. The story about the division of credit by Barrett Tillman ran in the *Arizona Republic*.

"When Tom saw the article, he came unglued," Tillman told the author. "He was irate and took offense, saying that his integrity had been assailed. The official nature of USAF Study

85, the overall revision of USAAF credits (not claims, just credits) did little or nothing to alleviate Tom's rancor."[25]

On April 11, 1985, Lanphier was invited to appear at the Smithsonian's National Air and Space Museum in Washington, D.C., to talk about his life and, especially, the Yamamoto shootdown. It was the first of at least three talks he planned to give during that spring. The talk at the Smithsonian was one of a continuing series of presentations by men and women in aviation who have participated in aerospace events of historical interest. The lectures are always well attended by aerospace enthusiasts.

Introduced as the man who had caused the admiral's demise, Lanphier proved to be an engaging speaker. He regaled the audience with tales of his life, illustrated with slides. He told of his early years as the son of a man who had made his own contributions to the history of the air force. His father was a West Point graduate, a World War I fighter pilot, and former commanding officer of the First Pursuit Squadron. The elder Lanphier's friends included the famous military aviation names of the day—"Billy" Mitchell, Charles Lindbergh, Jimmy Doolittle, "Hap" Arnold, Ira Eaker, Carl Spaatz, famous racing pilots, and others. Born in 1915, Tom, one of three sons, had grown up at various Army Air Corps bases where his father was assigned.

The Yamamoto shootdown was the main thrust of Lanphier's talk. He said his brother Charles had told a fellow prisoner the night before he died in prison camp, "My brother is the guy who shot down Yamamoto." Lanphier did not say how he learned about his brother's deathbed revelation.

Lanphier, well aware that the audience knew of the continuing controversy about the shootdown, called Barber "one of the most decorated, one of the most aggressive, effective fighter pilots in the Solomon Islands." He added quickly, "He got the staff bomber on the Yamamoto mission. I got the lead bomber."

Lanphier claimed that Secretary of the Navy Frank Knox, when told of the Yamamoto itinerary, called Gen. "Hap" Arnold to ask if they should go after the admiral. Lanphier said Arnold replied, "Yes, kill the S.O.B."

Lanphier then stated that when President Roosevelt was contacted by Captain (later Admiral) Zacharias, a naval aide, and told of Yamamoto's planned trip, President Roosevelt said, "If Knox doesn't approve it by noon tomorrow, tell him 'I told him to do it.' "

Again, Lanphier offered no substantiation for his unusual statements.

Lanphier next quoted the alleged message that has never been found:

SQUADRONS OF P-39s AND P-38s MUST AT ALL COSTS REACH AND DESTROY. PRESIDENT ATTACHES EX-TREME IMPORTANCE THIS OPERATION. KNOX.

Lanphier gave much praise to Marine Maj. Gen. John Condon, who was in the audience. Condon had been a major on Admiral Mitscher's staff at the time of the mission and Lanphier credited him with the detailed flight plan for the successful interception. He gave no credit to Mitchell for planning the mission.

Lanphier then described the mission from the moment the two Betty bombers and six Zeros were spotted:

At this point I started to turn parallel to climb and fire-walled it. For a couple of minutes they didn't see us down there. Mitchell was on his way up to his altitude. At this point I also lost my number three and four men. They couldn't get their wing tanks off so they went off down the coast. So it was just Barber and myself against the six Zeros when we got up parallel with them.

When they saw us, they dropped their belly tanks and dove on us. Three of them came between me and the lead bomber. The lead bomber dived down and away. The wing bomber came over and at us [toward] the sea—with the staff in it. I pulled up into the lead fighter of the first three because I couldn't get at the bomber there in between them. He caught fire and went under me and I went between the other two. I flipped over on my back and looked down and there was this bomber back down on the treetops heading again toward Kahili and Ballale.

I then dove down from an altitude wherever I was—about 6,000 feet—to get ahead of him and cut across on him. I got going so fast—I ran on him for about two minutes—maybe ten miles at some 300 miles an hour. I turned into him and leveled out. I had dropped my flaps to slow down. I figured I was at the point to check my guns. I checked my guns. They had worked up above but I squeezed. I cleared the guns and when I did, the right engine [of the lead bomber] started to burn. I was at about 70 degrees, which is an impossible angle to hit anything. I kept on a curve of pursuit and his right wing began to burn also. Just as I went behind him with his cannon shooting out the rear end, the wing came off and he belly-whopped into the jungle and I went on past.

I came down through a cloud of dust and the Zeros were making a dust storm back over here [Kahili] where he was burning. I got out safely. Barber, meanwhile, followed the wing bomber out here [toward the ocean] and shot it down in the water. . . .

Lanphier showed photos of the Betty's wreckage in the jungle and said, "Yamamoto was obviously sitting in the cabin facing backwards, strapped in his seat when he was thrown out. He had his left hand on his sword.

"When I killed him, I hated him," Lanphier continued. "He was the only personalized killing I've been involved in. Naturally, I became interested and learned a great deal about him. He was a gambler, a poet, a calligrapher, master strategist, planner, courageous man, cared for his men, didn't give a damn for his superiors, the ones who didn't agree with him. Altogether a truly great man whom I admire and respect and if I had the chance to kill him again, I'd do it in a minute."

Lanphier showed a slide of the page from the 1943 issue of *Time* "which says I'm a hero." He said that *Time* "knew full well it was jeopardizing the Magic system" by running the article.

Lanphier's talk created no press coverage. During the spring of 1985, he formed a corporation called The Flight Group to produce a series for television on the history of flight. He solicited the support of a number of persons he believed could provide financial backing, research the archives, and write the scripts. He asked the author to assist by writing and researching for the series and insisted that one of the episodes "must be on the Yamamoto shootdown because it's one of the epic missions of all time." The only work ever completed was an interview he partially conducted with Gen. James H. "Jimmy" Doolittle using questions furnished by the author. He also had a segment filmed on himself describing how he shot the admiral down. The filmed interview with Doolittle was eventually included in a 1989 PBS television special entitled "Jimmy Doolittle: An American Hero." The interview about the Yamamoto mission was included in a video tape entitled "Wings over Water." Both were produced by Varied Directions, Inc., Camden, Maine.

In October 1985, Mitchell, Barber, and several other former members of the 339th Fighter Squadron attended a squadron reunion in San Antonio, Texas. They decided to visit the Admiral Nimitz State Historical Park at Fredericksburg, Texas, birthplace of Nimitz. The park includes a Museum of the Pacific War which features an exhibit about the Yamamoto shootdown.

The visit was a turning point in the shootdown story, as far as Mitchell and Barber are concerned. Included in the exhibit was a filmed interview with Kenji Yanagiya, the only surviving pilot of the six Zeros that escorted the admiral. The interview by Hideo Otomo was conducted for the benefit of the museum and was entirely in Japanese. It took place in the studios of the Sony Corporation in Tokyo, Japan, on June 13, 1975, and was paraphrased in English for the exhibit by Frank Turner.

In the interview, Yanagiya confirmed that there were only *two* Betty bombers, not three, in the air over Bougainville that day in April 1943. He also stated that after the first pass of the Zeros trying to ward off the attacking P-38s, he saw a P-38 "firing from *the rear of the lead bomber* [italics furnished] into the tail of the lead bomber. Admiral Yamamoto's bomber began to leak gasoline. This was followed by a stream of black smoke, and soon flames enveloped the lead bomber and it fell into the jungle where it continued to burn."[26]

Yanagiya told the interviewer that he then flew at a low altitude around Buin airfield, firing his guns, to alert personnel on the ground that something abnormal had occurred.

After the film was shown, Mitchell and Barber looked at each other. Here was testimony from one of the Japanese Zero pilots who actually saw the attack on the lead bomber *from the rear!* Yanagiya knew nothing about a P-38 attacking from the right side, as Lanphier had claimed.

Yanagiya had no reason to lie. This was an interview conducted in 1975 by an interviewer who had no stake in the outcome of the controversy among Americans. Mitchell told the author, "From that moment on, there was no doubt in my mind, whatsoever, that Rex Barber deserves *full* credit for shooting down the lead bomber."[27]

At a talk he gave at the reunion, Mitchell told his former squadron mates what they had learned at Fredericksburg and determined that from that time on, he would do his best to give credit where credit was due—to Rex Barber and not Tom Lanphier. No matter what "official" 1943 reports Lanphier would always cite as his defense for his claim, this testimony by a surviving enemy pilot, who had no ax to grind, was the proof that Mitchell had been looking for. Barber was pleased, of course, but no more so than Mitchell.

Thomas G. Lanphier, Jr., died in the San Diego Veterans Administration Hospital on Thanksgiving Day 1987. He was 71. Obituaries were carried in a number of newspapers, each mentioning the April 18, 1943, mission "in which he shot down the plane carrying Japanese Adm. Isoroku Yamamoto." However, the (Portland, Oregon) *Oregonian* reported in the Lanphier obituary that Barber "has sought to prove that it was he, rather than Lanphier, who should have been given credit for shooting down Yamamoto."[28]

The controversy did not end with Lanphier's death. Air force historians have long been dubious about Lanphier's claim. In 1959, the first attempt to compile a preliminary list of fighter aces was completed under the code name Project Ace. In 1968, five reserve officers assigned as historians to the United States Air Force Historical Research Center began to prepare a final list. These awards were later published in 1978 as an official listing entitled "USAF Credits for the Destruction of Enemy Aircraft, World War II." The listing was based on available records and was an attempt by the Office of Air Force History to settle for all time disputes about victories over enemy aircraft claimed by air force pilots in all the theaters of war.

The historians assigned to the victory credit team judged that the destruction of Admiral Yamamoto's Betty bomber resulted from the gunfire of the two P-38s piloted by Lanphier and Barber. At the same time, the board gave credit to Barber and Lt. Besby Holmes for destroying the other Betty bomber. The board discounted the report that there was a third Betty bomber shot down as claimed by Holmes.

On March 22, 1985, a six-member Victory Credit Board of Review was convened in response to a request from Brig. Gen. Michael J. Jackson, USAF (Ret), executive vice president of the American Fighter Aces Association to Dr. Richard H. Kohn, chief of the Office of Air Force History. Disturbed that the dispute between Lanphier and Barber had become public knowledge through an article in the Phoenix *Arizona Republic* during a reunion of the association in May 1984, Jackson had requested "a formal board of inquiry" be convened to settle "this vital question."

"As a major source of embarrassment to the American Fighter Aces Association and the U.S. Air Force," Jackson wrote, "the extent of damage over this controversy is not yet totally clear but it has potentially severe adverse implications. Of major concern is the question of integrity."[29]

The board deliberated for several hours and prepared a report:

Verifying this particular victory was made more difficult because of the scarcity of primary source materials, the conflicting accounts of the engagement in a key source, and the large amount of publicity that occurred in the years following the mission. For the purposes of this review and determination, the board considered only primary sources: The mission planning documents, the post-engagement intelligence debriefing, and the eyewitness account of a Japanese survivor, Vice Admiral Matome Ugaki, Chief of Staff of the Combined Fleet, who recorded an account of the engagement in his diary. Secondary sources such as newspaper articles, citations for awards, and the personal recollections of the participants forty-two years later were excluded from consideration.

Because of the security surrounding this particular World War II mission, XIII Fighter Command did not assay claims and issue general orders officially confirming these singular victory credits. Historians are thus left with only two primary sources: The eyewitness account of a Japanese survivor, and the post-mission intelligence debriefing that appears to have helped generate the dispute in question.

The crux of the dispute hinges on the true number of Betty bombers involved in the engagement. Were there only two bombers, a determination made by the original victory credit team, or actually three bombers, as implied in the narrative of the Army intelligence debriefing after the mission?

The three-page Army intelligence debriefing of 18 April 1943 is flawed on two counts: First, it did not identify statements contained in the narrative with any particular pilot (though identification can be inferred), and second, it presented conflicting evidence regarding the number of bombers involved. In the excitement and elation of the moment, what appears as an obvious discrepancy was not identified and addressed, at least not until many years later. Meantime, the debriefing precipitated disparate accounts of the engagement in Air Force histories and the open literature.

The board arrived at the following conclusions:

1. Clearly, only two Betty bombers were involved in this six-to-ten-minute engagement, not three as at first supposed by Army intelligence.

2. Capt. Lanphier and 1st Lt. Barber therefore did not destroy one bomber each over the jungle.

3. The evidence points to 1st Lt. Barber as the first to fire on Admiral Yamamoto's bomber, setting it afire and causing a portion of the tail empennage to fly off. But the burning bomber, in the words of Admiral Ugaki, continued to fly under power just above the jungle, losing altitude. Barber's wingman [sic], Capt. Lanphier, once disengaged from the Zeros, next struck Yamamoto's bomber broadside, severing a wing. The bomber turned over on its back and plummeted to earth. Barber, on looking back after his pass, saw the airplane fall and understandably presumed it to be the result of his attack.

4. During the heat of the ensuing dogfights, 1st Lieutenant Holmes observed Admiral Ugaki's Betty proceeding southeasterly near Moila Point. Holmes attacked the second bomber, setting it smoking in the left engine. Barber "polished it off," pieces of the bomber exploding outward from the impact of the 20mm cannon shells, some of them striking his fighter. Admiral Ugaki's bomber, however, did not explode in the air as Barber supposed, but rather dove out of control into the sea.

5. Based on the guidelines established by XIII Fighter Command for the awarding of victory credits, credit for the destruction of both bombers is properly shared; the findings of the original USAF Historical Division victory credit team are judged to be accurate and confirmed; the official USAF shared credits will remain unaltered for this engagement.

The board's report added the following comment:

Having considered and debated the evidence, members of the Board agreed unanimously in these findings and conclusions. It was noted that *any speculation* about the ability of Admiral Yamamoto's crippled bomber to continue another ten minutes in flight just above the jungle to its destination on Ballale, if Lanphier had not attacked, had no bearing whatsoever on these deliberations and must remain always— speculation.

Members of the Board expressed the hope that these findings and conclusions would settle permanently any debate over the victory credits assigned in this action, and help allay any acrimony that may have developed among members of the team that intercepted Yamamoto's flight on 18 April 1943. Surely, all of those who flew on this mission can share credit for what was demonstrably one of the most momentous and remarkable army air forces episodes of World War II.[30]

The report was signed by the recorder, R. Cargill Hall, Chief, Research Division of the United States Air Force Historical Research Center, and Lt. Col. Frederick E. Zoes, board chairman.

The board's reconsideration of the Yamamoto shootdown and confirming the previous award to Lanphier and Barber of a shared victory did not satisfy either Lanphier or Barber. Lanphier died still claiming that he deserved sole credit; Barber contends that he did the shooting that brought the admiral to a flaming death in the Bougainville jungle.

What kind of a man was Thomas G. Lanphier, Jr.? Julius "Jack" Jacobson, Mitchell's wingman on the mission, may have known him better than any of their squadron mates. He was a classmate of Lanphier's in flying school and shared a tent with him on Guadalcanal and Fiji. They both resided in San Diego. Jacobson describes Lanphier as

a very self-assured individual. Socially gregarious, which tended to irritate me on occasion. He was the world's greatest "name dropper." He appeared to enjoy life with little worry about the future. He was expected by his buddies to eventually make a "name" for himself, either in the political or business world. He was a "climber." In spite of his braggadocio, he was well liked by his associates and friends. He was a terrible poker player, but took his losses good-naturedly. He was promoted to Captain ahead of others from his same flying school class with lower serial numbers. Many thought his promotion was a result of his close relationship with the squadron C.O. Tom's father was the C.O. of the 1st Pursuit Group, and a graduate of West Point. I'm sure that had an influence on his status with the C.O.[31]

And so, this fighter pilot died still contending that only his name should be inscribed in the air force's history books for the outcome of this epic mission. He was well aware that few of his contemporaries believed all of the stories about his exploits. He had sent drafts of his memoirs to nearly a hundred people, including Senator Symington, Gen. Jimmy Doolittle, and other "name" personalities he had known. Many replied with extensive letters, some praising him and others, especially his contemporaries, disputing his facts and claims about the Yamamoto mission.

His manuscript was sent to a number of publishers, all of whom turned it down. When the author requested access to the manuscript and permission to use its contents in order to report

Lanphier's final statement about the Yamamoto mission here, the Lanphier family refused, asking that he "rely on official war records and documents in the public domain for his side of the story. The family chooses to allow the official records and our faith in our husband and father to stand as our public statement at this time."[32]

The controversy would continue after Lanphier's death.

10
THE YAMAMOTO RETROSPECTIVE

O N THE SECOND FLOOR OF THE ADMIRAL Nimitz State Museum of the Pacific War in Fredericksburg, Texas, is a section devoted to the Yamamoto shootdown. In addition to a display, there is a continuous showing of a 1975 interview with Kenji Yanagiya, the only surviving Zero pilot on the Yamamoto flight. As a follow-up to the museum's display about the Yamamoto shootdown, the Nimitz Museum Foundation invited survivors of the mission to Fredericksburg to participate in a "Yamamoto Retrospective" on April 16–17, 1988. It was the first symposium attempted by the museum and was made possible by a grant from the Texas Committee for the Humanities, a state program of the National Endowment for the Humanities. This assured participation from the academic community and assistance with the exhibit.

According to Helen B. Springall, curator of exhibits and programs, "the major turning point [in organizing the retrospective] came in late November 1987, when Dr. Jerry Kelley [a San Antonio surgeon] visited the museum and expressed an interest in supporting a special project. The time was ideal and it assured us the financial stability that meant we could invite our Japanese participant, Mr. Yanagiya."[1]

Over 250 people gathered in the high school auditorium. More than 500 others who could not be accommodated in the auditorium were seated in a school room equipped with TV monitors. The sessions were also broadcast on local cable television.

The all-day session was divided into two parts. The first part of the meeting consisted of presentations by a panel on the ethics and morality of war, with emphasis on the shootdown of Yamamoto. The panel consisted of Professors Joseph Dawson, Roger H. Beaumont, and Manuel Davenport of Texas A&M University; Paul Woodruff of the University of Texas; and Capt. Roger Pineau, USN (Ret), noted naval historian. The panel moderator was Dr. Dean Allard, head of the Naval History Office.

The second part was a review of the Yamamoto mission by all eight of the American survivors of the mission and Kenji Yanagiya, the only surviving Zero pilot. Hiroshi Hayashi, pilot of the second bomber, is the only other living Japanese survivor. He declined to participate. This panel was moderated by R. Cargill Hall, Chief, Research Division, United States Air Force Historical Research Center.

Dr. Dawson began his discussion by stating that "Military officers have always understood that being in the service of their country eventually could place them in personal danger. . . . Trying to figure how or *if* the loss of a top army or fleet commander affected or might have affected the outcome of a battle, campaign, or war has been one of the perennial subjects of discussion among students of history." He reviewed a list of Civil War generals on both sides who either died in battle or had close calls: Jeb Stuart, Joseph E. Johnston, Stonewall Jackson, and A. P. Hill of the Confederate Army; John Reynolds, James B. McPherson, and John Sedgwick on the Union side. In the Indian wars, George Custer and Edward Canby were cited as leaders who paid the supreme price in combat.

But of these many examples there is a sharp contrast with the death of Admiral Yamamoto in 1943. None of the examples, perhaps with the exception of Canby, show direct deliberate singling out of the officers mentioned. The deaths came about through happenstance or pressures of the moment.

Naval officers, like army officers, understood and accepted the dangers of warfare. In the 1700s and 1800s, marine sharpshooters could take a terrible toll of enemy officers on the opposite decks as ships closed in for final broadsides. Obviously, those shots were deliberately made with careful aim. A sharpshooter's bullet took the life of Admiral Horatio Nelson at Trafalgar in 1805.

We know some commanders concluded that the chance dangers of combat and service life were enough without intentionally directing fire against enemy commanders. The story of the Duke of Wellington at Waterloo is perhaps the most famous example of *not* firing on an enemy commander, even when the opportunity seemed right. Across the field stood Napoleon Bonaparte with his staff. An alert English artilleryman called out to the Duke:

"There's Bonaparte, Sir. I think I can reach him. May I fire?"

The Duke was aghast.

"No, no. Generals commanding armies have something else to do than shoot at one another."[2]

Was not firing on Napoleon only a matter of what Wellington, and some other 19th century commanders, may have considered "sporting" or "fair"—or something that "was just not done" to a brother general? It was universally admitted that any officer, no matter how high his rank, might die coincidental to combat or campaigning, but here is the prime 19th century example of one senior officer who would not order disciplined troops to fire upon the known location of a senior enemy soldier while simultaneously all-out efforts were made to kill or cripple thousands of other enemy soldiers on the same battlefield.

Some points of contrast suggest themselves between Wellington's order not to fire in 1815 and the direct orders to bring down Admiral Yamamoto in 1943. First, by 1943 the outlook of "total war," developed over nearly a century from the American Civil War, had changed the attitudes of military men and their civilian superiors. By the 1940s, almost any action would be taken *if* it *might* lead to ultimate victory, or might contribute to that victory, even in a minor way.

A second point of contrast is the difference in technology. By 1943, the sophistication of military technology—and Americans have always been fascinated with technology—had made possible actions and attacks, including direct forms of attack, that were unavailable in the combat of earlier eras. In other words, the Americans, caught up in the technology available to them, combined their knowledge of Yamamoto's whereabouts (gained through high technology intelligence methods) and the capability of striking against this particular hated enemy commander across hundreds of miles (using the high technology fighter aircraft of the day) with the logic of total war. It was both an opportunity and a challenge in the use of technology.

Unlike Wellington in 1815, the Americans in 1943 seized the chance to bring down an enemy commander."[3]

Professor Beaumont followed with an overview of World War II and:

a consideration of the [Yamamoto] mission from the standpoint of what has come to be called "special operations."

In April 1943, the war was no longer in that grim early "too little, too late" phase . . . that grim interval in which defeat after defeat was suffered by the Allies, from December 1941 to mid-1942. But in spite of some successes—Coral Sea, Midway, Alamein, Stalingrad, Hill 609—the outcome of the war was not yet certain in April 1943, but was at the point that Winston Churchill referred to as the "hinge of fate," and major problems faced the Allies at every turn.

German U-boat sinkings were approaching a peak in the Battle of the Atlantic of almost a million tons a month. The Anglo-American alliance had no foothold on the continent of Europe; Rommel was building the West Wall as part of Festung Europe. The Second Front, a major landing in northwest Europe, postponed in 1942, was being postponed again. In the air war, both U.S. Army Air Force bombers and the Royal Air Force were facing serious problems with bombing accuracy. They were also beginning to feel the effects of the "fighter escort gap" as B-17 and B-24 bombers began to attack targets inside the Third Reich, where Albert Speer was about to begin the substantial renovation of the Nazi war machine that vastly increased its productivity. The one bright spot for the

Western Allies was North Africa, where American, British, and French forces tightened a fatal noose on German and Italian armies in Tunisia.

The Nazis still held the strategic advantage on the Eastern Front, in spite of their setback at Stalingrad. They were massing tanks near Kursk for the biggest armor battle until the 1973 October war. Their defeat was not seen as certain, and the Soviets conducted secret talks in Stockholm with Nazi representatives until after that battle, even though the Western Allies had issued the "unconditional surrender" proclamation at Casablanca in January 1943.

Atrocities abounded in almost all theaters of war. The Gestapo was at work in occupied Europe. In 1942, the village of Lidice in Czechoslovakia had been obliterated in retaliation for the assassination of Himmler's henchman, Reynard Heydrich. All across Europe, the trains of the Holocaust were rolling to the death camps, day and night, carrying out the policy of extermination laid down a year earlier at the Wannsee Conference.

Farther east, the pattern was similarly grim. Japanese armies massed on the borders of India, and the British who then held India as an imperial possession faced the peril of uprising, having jailed many prominent leaders of the Congress Party, including Gandhi, in 1942. Again, the Guadalcanal campaign had become a battle of attrition, a grinding away by both sides on the land, in the air, and at sea, and would not be clearly resolved until late 1943.

The campaign in New Guinea was still a matter of slogging, small gains and high casualties, as MacArthur and his air commander, George Kenney, worked out the by-pass strategy that would soon accelerate progress in the area. In the north Pacific, Japanese forces held Attu and Kiska in the Aleutians. The marines had not yet made the first of the series of their major amphibious landings that marked the rungs of a bloody climb up the Central Pacific. The effectiveness of the navy's submarine force had been blunted by major defects in the fuses of its torpedoes and the problem was not yet fully solved. The only clear-cut American strategic naval success had been at Midway almost a year before.

The war in the Pacific had also become a savage one in the true sense, beyond the grimy, marginal living conditions. Charles Lindbergh, working as a Lockheed "tech rep," noted this sorrowfully in his diary, describing the use of Japanese skulls as drinking cups. The ferocity ran both ways, as John Dower has noted in his study, *War Without Mercy*. Reports of the torture and execution of U.S. fliers from the Doolittle Raid downed in China had come back through intelligence channels. Fury in America over the apparent sneak attack at Pearl Harbor ran unabated until after the war, when more details were released. It was reported, perhaps apocryphally, that Mrs. Roosevelt, while visiting her son James, executive officer of Carlson's Raiders (who were far from being Eagle Scouts), had been so shocked at what she saw that she recommended six months quarantine before returning to polite society.

To turn to the Yamamoto mission as a special operation, it had the basic characteristics of "special ops"—speed, accuracy, and a linkage to technical intelligence systems and psychological warfare. It was not the only special operation carried out by standard forces. There were the Hammelburg Raid in Europe, and the Cabanatuan and Los Banos raids which rescued prisoners of war in the Philippines, all in 1944.

As for the matter of precedent, when the British commandos had earlier tried to kill Rommel, unsuccessfully, the Germans treated the prisoners rather straightforwardly, considering Hitler's fury over earlier commando operations. Dr. Dawson has pointed out previous practices and values. The view on targeting enemy commanders, however, changed in the twentieth century, partly due to dispersal of armies and fleets in space and time, controlled by webs of communications radiating out from central headquarters. The sense of the vulnerabilities of such systems led J. F. C. Fuller, the British military theorist and armored warfare pioneer, to suggest in the First World War that the object of war was not to kill off a foe's privates one by one, but to surprise the enemy generals at the breakfast table. Thus, while headquarters chateaux above division level were generally not targeted deliberately by artillery or air in the Great War, by 1940, French general headquarters used no radios for fear that what is now called in command-and-control parlance an electromagnetic "signature" would attract enemy air attack.

Although deliberate attacks on enemy commanders were relatively rare, they did occur, and extensive camouflage was deployed to mask headquarters. The Royal Air Force purportedly tried to "take out" Hitler in Munich on one occasion and their low-level raids against German headquarters demonstrated a new dimension of "surgical" aerial special operations. Both Hitler and Churchill spent much time in underground headquarters.

On a more personal level, German officers plotted to kill Hitler at various times, and German intelligence infiltrated at least one agent to try to kill Stalin, who lived in conditions of very tight security. Ukranian nationalist partisans behind Soviet lines ambushed a Red Army commander, Marshal Vatutin, in 1944. And in the Battle of the Bulge, a false estimate that Nazi special operations maestro, Otto Skorzeny, was trying to kill principal Allied commanders led to major security measures that bottled up the high command for several days.

The matter of assassination of hostile leaders reemerged in the 1975 Church Committee hearings which examined intelligence policy in the wake of Vietnam and Watergate, and other cases. A special subhearing led to legislation which outlawed assassination in the conduct of American foreign policy. The collapse of restraint regarding the targeting of commanders and headquarters is recognized in both Soviet and British command-and-control networks, which are designed to operate on the basis of surviving nodes, irrespective of rank.[4]

Retired navy Capt. Roger Pineau followed with his presentation on the codebreaking capabilities of the U.S. Navy at the time of the Yamamoto mission. His talk was covered in chapter two, "The Codebreakers."

Dr. Paul Woodruff and Dr. Manuel Davenport explored the ethics of targeting an enemy commander. Woodruff addressed the question: Was it right to try to kill Yamamoto?:

1. I want first to anticipate the objection that ethical considerations do not apply to warfare.

At this point you might want to say that I'm on the wrong track. There is nothing unusual about killing in wartime. After all, war routinely involves acts of violence against persons and property—acts that would be considered unethical in peacetime. Nevertheless, we do not condemn normal acts of warfare on ethical grounds. We accept, as ethically permissible, acts of violence in wartime that we would otherwise condemn. The reasons for this are controversial, and I will not go into them here. The point I want to make initially is this: Not all acts of violence in wartime are ethically permissible. Sad to say there are such things as war crimes, ethically speaking. We must not be misled by the fact that some cases of war crimes are hard to distinguish from permissible acts of war. History abounds with clear cases of unethical acts of war: the senseless torture of prisoners, for example, or the mass killing of innocents, or even the attempted massacre of an entire race. I do not want to invite comparison with these atrocities; I mention them only to make my point that however hellish warfare may be, there are still ethical and unethical ways to go about it.

2. The Yamamoto mission was unusual in being directed at a person.

Conventional military targets are forces, or weapons, or installations. The mission we are discussing, however, was directed specifically at Isoroku Yamamoto and no one else. As we have heard, he was the builder of Japanese naval air power and the designer of the attack on Pearl Harbor. He was, also, a brilliant chief of staff of the Imperial Japanese Navy, which depended heavily on his devoted and intelligent leadership.

I have said that part of evaluating an action ethically is examining the intention behind it. Intentions are not blind. They aim at specific things understood in different ways. To say that the intention behind our mission was to kill Yamamoto is far too simple. As ethicists, we should want to know more: was this intended as an act of punishment? . . . or revenge? . . . or as part of a plan to reduce the effectiveness of the Japanese Imperial Navy? This is closely linked to another question: Under what description was Yamamoto considered as the target for the operation of April 18, 1943? Was the admiral responsible for Japanese success in the war? As the criminal who committed the sneak attack at Pearl Harbor? Or as an enemy officer who was expected to continue inflicting great losses on U.S. forces? Yamamoto was all of those things, and more.

3. The motive of punishment may have played a part.

This is unusual in the context of active warfare. Although we have many reasons for being angry at enemy troops, we rarely think of them as personally guilty of crimes for which they deserve to be punished. Simply carrying a rifle in an enemy army, and shooting it at our troops in battle, is not a crime. If it were, we would treat prisoners of war as criminals. But we do not do this. When we do think of an enemy as a war criminal, we hope to bring him to public trial and punishment, after the war is over, as an example to the world.

It is a fact peculiar to Yamamoto (and a few others) that as a military man he was considered to be a criminal by many on the Allied side of the war, and during the war itself. Moreover, he was someone we could not wait to punish.

Now that a generation has passed, I think we all recognize that whatever else he was, Yamamoto was not a scoundrel. Arguably, he shared responsibility for a criminal act, owing to his prominent role in the attack on Pearl Harbor. I am inclined to doubt that this attack was a war crime in the proper sense. But that should not concern us here. Our question is this: Supposing the Allies considered him a criminal, would it be permissible for them to punish him in mid-war, without trial? The question answers itself. *No act of war is justified on the grounds that it punishes a guilty individual.* Those killed in war are rarely thought guilty of any crime; and those who are thought guilty are, when possible, held for trial. So, if the intention were to *punish* Yamamoto, it would not pass the usual ethical tests.

4. The case of revenge is more complicated.

The desire for revenge against an enemy plays a part in the motivations of troops at all levels, from commanders to grunts in the field; and anyone who has been in action has some cause for vengeance against the enemy. Yamamoto, as the most prominent and dangerous of the enemy, was naturally a lightning rod for the American revenge against Japan. The U.S. had suffered so much in this unsought war, and in so many ways, that it would have been superhuman not to want vengeance. The many Americans who wanted revenge on Yamamoto were not superhuman.

Still, the case is worrying, mainly because anger at what a nation had done was directed against one individual person. The revenge motive that operates in familiar military situations is impersonal. It does not matter who, in particular, occupies the enemy foxhole. They are the enemy, and the enemy killed your buddies . . . and so you act. But the case of

Yamamoto seems to have been intensely personal. And that raises both practical and ethical questions. The thirst for personal revenge does not make for good soldiering on the whole, and it even led to atrocities against helpless enemy prisoners and even against innocent civilians.

There are precedents for personal revenge, of course, in military history and myth alike. The most famous is the oldest: sulky Achilles was brought back into the war of Greeks against Trojans when his buddy Patroclus was killed by Hector. The story of Achilles' terrible revenge is the centerpiece of Homer's *Iliad*, which begins with the word "wrath." . . . But we soon learn that Achilles' proclivity for anger was not entirely a good thing. The anger of that first line was Achilles' anger *at his general*, over a skewed division of the spoils of battle. True, it is the same trait that brings Achilles storming back onto the battlefield, intending to kill the enemy's top spearman and drag his body by the heels through the dust.

"Here is the man," Achilles says when he first spies Hector, "who beyond all others has troubled my anger, who slaughtered my beloved companion." Achilles has become a "man with no sweetness in his heart," and when he loses Hector in the mist, he launches into a merciless assault on every Trojan he can catch. When at last Hector is cornered by Achilles, and sees that his time is up, he begs Achilles to return his body to Troy for proper burial. But Achilles is too angry to have any respect for the gentle and heroic Hector.

It is interesting that Achilles does not [return the body]. When his fury is spent, and Hector's elderly father comes by night to beg for the body, the two men sit down and grieve together over their losses, the young man and the old. And then Achilles, reminded of his own father, relents, and restores Hector's body to Troy.

I tell this old story because I think it helps to clarify the issues, as myths often do. Achilles' great intention is personal vengeance, moved by anger. That makes him an awesome soldier, but not a particularly good one, since his anger moves as readily against his commander as it does against his enemies. No commanding officer would want an Achilles as his subordinate. Personal revenge is not a reliable intention in warfare (or anywhere else for that matter). But that is not yet precisely an ethical consideration, merely a practical one.

Is it wrong to kill enemies in war out of a desire for revenge? In itself, there is nothing wrong with Achilles' killing

Hector. He would have been right to do that even if he was not personally angry at Hector, for Hector was the most prominent and dangerous officer in the enemy's forces. There is something ethically wrong, however, when Achilles storms into battle with his mind totally clouded by his lust for revenge. The results are terrible for the Trojans, who sustain great losses. More serious in its ethical significance is the fact that Achilles' perception of his enemy is warped. Hector, whom we have just seen as a loyal son, a kind husband, and a gentle father—Hector, who never wanted this war, but fights it bravely only for the sake of his father and his country—this Hector comes to Achilles' eyes to look like a beast who deserves to have his flesh eaten raw and bleeding from his bones. This attitude extends to all of the Trojans in Achilles' mind, and that no doubt explains why Achilles in his anger slaughters prisoners of war when there is no military need for this.

The ethical problem about revenge in war is mainly this, that it leads to an attitude of blind anger towards the enemy, an attitude that can lead to all sorts of atrocities.

So far I have not spoken directly about Yamamoto in the context of revenge, but I hope you have already noticed the analogy: a good man, basically, like Hector, a reluctant but noble warrior, a man moved by exemplary loyalty to his country—Yamamoto becomes the focus of a personal, vitriolic anger, this time of a whole nation, not just of an Achilles.

The intention to get revenge brings with it a distortion of the facts, and that distortion may, in the long run, and in all its ramifications, have terrible consequences. The happier side of this story is that anger passes in time, and we are able to see Yamamoto more generously and even to sit down together with his countrymen to grieve over our respective losses. So much for revenge.

5. Could the Yamamoto mission have been a legitimate act of war?

The evidence I have seen suggests that the primary intention of the U.S. decision-makers was not punishment or revenge, but the elimination of an exceptional threat to U.S. interests in the war.

While punishment and revenge look backwards to what has been done in the past, legitimate military intentions look forward, towards what can be prevented, or towards what can be gained. Ethical intentions in war look mainly forward, towards bringing war to an end. I do not mean to say that ending the war is all that matters ethically speaking; I do mean to say that backward-looking aims like punishment and revenge are strictly irrelevant to proper military decisions, and can lead in unethical directions.

Those who decided to get Yamamoto were probably looking more forward than back—more to the devastating effect on Japan of the loss of their great admiral than to what that admiral had done in the past. U.S. decision-makers thought that the Japanese had no one to replace Yamamoto. Nevertheless, they took great pains about ethical issues, consulting the highest secular and moral authorities before deciding to get Yamamoto. This, too, does them credit. [As has been noted earlier, there is no proof that Admiral Nimitz or anyone else sought "the highest secular and moral authorities" before ordering the interception.]

6. The mission was not an assassination.

Assassination raises special ethical problems because it takes place outside the theaters of war. Nonuniformed personnel behind the lines gain access by stealth to an enemy leader (who may also be nonuniformed), and kill him. I have nothing to say about this except that it is very unlike the Yamamoto mission. Yamamoto was in uniform in a military plane, and he was attacked openly by U.S. military aircraft. This is like what happens when snipers aim at officers, or when soldiers throw grenades towards radios, knowing that officers are marked by radios nearby. Officers in action, if they are identifiable, have always been especially vulnerable. Everyone knows that the loss of top officers can paralyze an army.

What raises suspicions in this case is that Yamamoto was not identified in a conventional way, but through the decoding of a secret message intercepted by radio. But the use of such devices to detect enemy movements and dispositions has never seriously been in question.

7. Conclusion: The action against Yamamoto was ethically permissible precisely to the extent that it was not intended as revenge or punishment.[5]

Professor Manuel Davenport was the final panel speaker:

To begin, I want to summarize, as carefully and accurately as I can, Professor Woodruff's arguments because I believe he raises the correct and necessary conceptual, factual, and ethical questions.

He points out that the killing of Yamamoto was not, by definition, an assassination. He then argues that on the basis of available evidence it was not intended primarily as an act of punishment or revenge, but was intended primarily as the elimination of an exceptional leader whose continued existence would have prolonged the war.

In considering the ethical questions, Professor Woodruff argues that the killing of Yamamoto could not be justified ethically as an act of punishment or revenge, but could be justified ethically if intended as the elimination of a military threat. Because he believes the intention was, primarily, to eliminate a military threat, he concludes that the killing of Yamamoto was ethically permissible.

I have tried to reconstruct Professor Woodruff's argument with care because I find myself in a most curious position. I agree with everything he says except his conclusion. In other words, I think that while the killing of Yamamoto was intended, primarily, as the elimination of an exceptional military threat, this was not sufficient to make it an ethically permissible action. It is quite plausible to argue, I will contend, that it was ethically wrong.

Not only is it possible that the way in which we killed Yamamoto created a bad precedent, in that it limits our own present and future military effectiveness, it is also possible that it increased the will to resist on the part of Japanese military leaders who respected him.

I am more concerned, however, with the possibility that our long-range military objectives, including winning the peace, would have been better served by not killing Yamamoto at all. We carefully avoided in the war with Japan putting the emperor's life in danger because we believed that to win the peace with Japan we needed his cooperation and leadership. It is just as plausible to believe that Yamamoto's cooperation and leadership would have contributed to preserving the values for which they fought. Yamamoto never wanted the war with the United States in the first place; he urged throughout the war that Japan seek a negotiated peace. He fought not out of hatred for the United States, a nation he knew and admired, but out of love of home and loyalty to his emperor.

When I think of Admiral Isoroku Yamamoto, I think of another reluctant but brilliant warrior, who fought a war he never sought against those he knew and admired. I think of General Robert E. Lee. And I ask myself, suppose Lee had been killed during the war by a special strike aimed specifically at him while visiting his troops behind his lines, what would have been the consequences? Would normal relations with the South have been even more difficult to establish?

It may be objected, of course, that given the bombing of Hiroshima and Nagasaki whether the killing of Yamamoto immediately increased the difficulties of winning the war or establishing the peace is irrelevant. In the long run, it may be argued, given our atomic power, the Japanese had no choice but to surrender and accept peace on our terms. But, I would counter, if the killing of Yamamoto, in terms of our long-range military and political objectives was of no consequence, then it has no ethical justification at all.

To summarize, I have argued that our nation, as well as all others, should agree in the conduct of war to adopt rules of war which promote our long-range interests. It follows that we should not adopt rules of war which prevent us from winning, but it does not follow that we cannot show respect for our enemies as fellow human beings. Quite often, even in war, a failure to show such respect for our enemies creates precedents which restrict our own future ability to wage war effectively. In my opinion, the manner in which we killed Yamamoto reinforced, if it did not create, such a precedent.

While we should not adopt rules of war which prevent us from winning wars, it does not follow that we should kill each and every enemy combatant whenever we have the opportunity. Quite often, it is the case that certain individual enemies should be spared because their survival after the war would contribute more to establishing normal relations than their extinction during the war would contribute to ending hostilities. In my opinion, if Admiral Yamamoto had survived the war, his continued life would have served our interests better than did his death during the war.[6]

The participants of the second session were all the surviving P-38 pilots of the Yamamoto mission: John Mitchell, Rex Barber, Doug Canning, Julius Jacobson, Besby Holmes, Louis Kittel, Delton Goerke, and Roger Ames. Kenji Yanagiya, the surviving

Zero pilot, was accompanied by Makato Shinagawa, an interpreter. The moderator was R. Cargill Hall.

Moderator Hall led off the session by introducing John Mitchell, who described in detail his planning for the mission and what he did until Doug Canning called, "Bogeys! Eleven o'clock high!"

Rex Barber told of his part from that moment until he departed Bougainville for the return flight to Guadalcanal. His narration was unfailingly similar to what he had told other audiences and as described herein.

Besby Holmes followed and stated, possibly for the first time, that he saw Rex Barber shoot down the lead bomber. He stated there is no doubt in his mind that Barber, not Lanphier, shot the admiral out of the sky. However, his recollection of going after the second bomber does not agree with Barber's. Holmes said he shot the bomber down and that he and Hine shook Zeros off Barber's tail before Holmes downed one of the attackers.

Kenji Yanagiya did not give a prepared talk but answered questions from the audience through Makoto Shinagawa, the interpreter. He confirmed that the Zeros had no radios or self-sealing gas tanks in them and that none of the planes in his flight were shot down. He believes he fired on and damaged one P-38 which may have been Lt. Ray Hine's. However, he did not claim it as a victory. He said he always wondered what became of that P-38.

Yanagiya was followed by a few remarks by Lou Kittel, Julius Jacobson, Del Goerke, and Doug Canning. Canning, who served as a fighter pilot in all three wars—World War II, Korea, and Vietnam—described his attempt to get on a Zero's tail when his windshield fogged up. He said he thought there were more than six Zeros in the air at the time. This has now been confirmed by Japanese sources. Several pilots described the dust that rose from Kahili from aircraft that were apparently taking off to intercept the P-38s. Barber also believes that several Zeros, other than the six escorts, were in the air by the time he went after the second bomber.[7]

Roger Ames was the last to speak and told of how disturbed he was that Tom Lanphier shouted over the radio that he had gotten Yamamoto and, "That S.O.B. won't dictate terms in the

White House now." Ames said he logged five hours, thirty minutes on the flight.

Ames told of returning to San Francisco shortly after returning to the States in May 1943 and while he and a friend were getting a meal in a small restaurant, a young woman sat next to them and struck up a conversation. Ames said he and his buddy "were yellow as Chinamen" from the Atabrine they had been taking for months in the South Pacific to ward off malaria. She said "I hear Yamamoto got shot down." Ames asked the audience rhetorically, "Now how did that information get out?"[8]

This remark proved how difficult it was to keep the Yamamoto shootdown a secret. He added that he and several other pilots had received two cases of whiskey for their mission sent to them by Admiral Mitscher.

R. Cargill Hall concluded the presentations and then took questions from the audience.

The Yamamoto Retrospective was termed a success. It brought together all the American survivors of this epic mission and the lone Zero pilot survivor. The number of people who attended the two-day affair proved that there is much public interest in World War II events, especially one that was significant in its outcome, as this mission was. Admiral Nimitz would have been proud that his museum sponsored such a public discussion even if the event it memorialized remains controversial.

11

WHO *REALLY* SHOT DOWN YAMAMOTO?

IT IS DIFFICULT, SOME WILL SAY IMPOSSIBLE, to reconstruct accurately a five-minute aerial combat encounter that occurred nearly a half century ago. The P-38s on Guadalcanal did not have gun cameras installed at this time. Neither Tom Lanphier nor Rex Barber officially reported seeing each other after Lanphier made his turn toward the fighters. However, Lanphier, in his North American Newspaper Alliance account, implied that he did. He stated that Barber "bulled his way back through [the fire of the pursuing Zeros] and latched onto the bomber again. This time he drove his attack perfectly home blasting off the entire tail section of the Mitsubishi, which rolled over on its back and plummeted to the earth below. No one jumped out of it."[1]

Barber has vehemently denied this statement since 1945 when he first read Lanphier's story. Barber has been consistent in his statement that as his line of fire passed through the tail section while firing at the right engine, only bits of the rudder came off. Never has he said that the Betty rolled over on its back and plummeted to earth.

No other American pilots were involved in the shootdown of

the lead bomber. Therefore, an analysis must begin with the statements of Lanphier and Barber. First, Lanphier's account as carried in the *New York Times:*

LANPHIER: *"Barber and I got to a point two miles to Yamamoto's right and about a mile in front of him before his Zero cover saw us. They must have screamed the warning into their radios because we saw their belly tanks drop—a sign they were clearing for action—and they nosed over in a group to dive on us, on Rex and me."*

COMMENT: According to Kenji Yanagiya, the surviving Zero pilot, the Zeros had no radios. Barber disagrees that all six Zeros started down immediately. He says only the three Zeros on the near (right) side of the formation started down at first; the other three started down a short time later.

LANPHIER: *"I was afraid we'd never get to the bomber that Admiral Yamamoto rode before the Zeros got us. I horsed back on my wheel to get my guns to bear on the lead Zero diving toward me."*

COMMENT: Barber says Lanphier banked quickly and turned about 90 degrees left and up into the diving Zeros, which was the proper thing to do at that moment. Julius Jacobson, Mitchell's wingman, believes this could mean that Lanphier is the real hero of the episode for taking this action, thus allowing Barber to go after the two bombers without interruption.

LANPHIER: *"Buck fever started me firing before I had my Lightning's nose pointed in his direction. I saw the gray smoke from his wing guns and wondered with stupid detachment if the bullets would get me before I could work my guns into his face."*

COMMENT: This confirms that Lanphier made a left turn into the descending Zeros and proceeded 180 degrees away from the flight path of the bombers.

LANPHIER: *"He [the Zero pilot] was a worse shot than I was, and he died. My machine guns and cannon ripped one of his wings away. He twisted under me, all flame and smoke."*

COMMENT: Yanagiya stated none of the six Zeros were shot down. No other downed aircraft were ever found.

LANPHIER: *"I kicked my ship over on its back and looked down for the lead Japanese bomber. It had dived inland. As I hung in the sky I got an impression, off to the east, of a swirl of aircraft against the blue—a single Lightning silhouetted against the light in a swarm of Zeros. That was Barber, having himself a time."*

COMMENT: According to Barber and Yanagiya, the lead bomber did not dive inland. It proceeded straight ahead. Although Barber overshot the two bombers briefly, he did not fly east of the lead bomber and was not yet pursued by "a swarm of Zeros."

Lanphier says that he spotted a shadow below moving across the treetops and declared that "It was Yamamoto's bomber," although he did not know for certain which bomber the admiral was in. He says he dived toward the bomber while two Zeros chased him.

LANPHIER: *"The two Zeros that had overshot me showed up again, diving toward Yamamoto's bomber from an angle slightly off to my right. They meant to get me before I got the bomber. It looked from where I sat as if the bomber, the Zeros, and I might all get to the same place at the same time.*

"We very nearly did. The next three or four seconds spelled life or death. I remember getting suddenly very stubborn about making the most of the one good shot I had coming up. I fired a long steady burst across the bomber's course of flight, from approximately right angles."

COMMENT: This is the most difficult angle from which to fire at another aircraft. A fighter pilot must "lead" or fire well ahead of his target if he is approaching at right angles. This is the reason fighter pilots were required to practice shooting at towed targets and shoot skeet during their flight training. If the enemy aircraft were directly at right angles to Lanphier when he fired, his bullets would not have scored a hit because of the speed of the bomber. Kenji Yanagiya, a Zero pilot, said in a 1975 interview that he saw a P-38 firing on the lead bomber *from the rear* (italics added) but not from the right side.

LANPHIER: *"The bomber's right engine, then its right wing burst into flame. . . . The two onrushing Zeros saw it, too. They* *screamed past overhead, unwilling to chance a jungle crash to get me. In that second I realized my impetus would carry me directly behind the Mitsubishi's tail cannon."*

COMMENT: No tail guns were ever recovered from this bomber. Japanese sources state they may have been removed to save weight. Kenji Yanagiya said the Betty bombers had a full complement of air crewmen aboard, including three gunners. He believed guns were installed in both bombers, even though they were on a transport mission.

LANPHIER: *"Just as I moved into range of Yamamoto's bomber and its cannon, the bomber's wing tore off. The bomber plunged into the jungle. It exploded. That was the end of Admiral Isoroku Yamamoto."*

COMMENT: If the wing had torn off, it would have been found some distance from the rest of the bomber's wreckage. The bomber would also have begun twisting wildly in flight if a wing were detached because there would be lift on one side of the aircraft and none on the other. According to the report of several who visited the wreckage, the right wing is only a few feet away from the right side of the fuselage.

LANPHIER: *"Everyone in top cover had seen the two bombers crash in the jungle in flames. There was no doubt of their complete destruction."*

COMMENT: No pilots in the top cover saw *any* aircraft crash in the jungle and only one was ever found there. The second bomber crashed in the water off Moila Point. There never was a third bomber, which all believed to be the case at the time since Lanphier, Barber, and Holmes each claimed one upon their return to Guadalcanal.

In the North American Newspaper Alliance syndicated story, Lanphier said that after the two Zeros swooped across the top of his canopy, he had trouble from another source: *"Out of [the bomber's] tail was puffing a steady series of shots from the cannon lodged back there."*

COMMENT: Again, no guns or ammunition were reportedly found in the wreckage of this bomber, which was apparently modified to carry passengers.

LANPHIER: *"For the first time that day, I pushed my microphone button and called Mitchell. I asked him to send down anybody who was not busy at the moment to help me out. I called him once again [to] ask him to verify the burning bomber. He replied that he could see it."*

COMMENT: Mitchell vehemently denies that he saw the bomber burning and told Lanphier that he couldn't see what was burning. Mitchell saw only a column of black smoke coming out of the jungle which probably was a downed aircraft but he didn't know whether it was a Betty bomber, a Zero, or one of his P-38 fighters.

Barber, flying on Lanphier's right wing, saw the Bettys start their letdown while the two of them were still climbing to get at the bomber's altitude. The three Zeros, lagging a considerable distance behind and on the left side of the bomber formation, evidently saw the P-38s first. According to Barber, they nosed down steeply and dropped their tanks. Moments later, the other three on the right side began a steep descent.

BARBER: *"It became apparent that the three Zeros closest to the Bettys on the right side would catch up with the Bettys about the same time as we would turn in on our firing pass and we would be a perfect target.*

"Just before the time we would break right to fall in behind the Bettys, Lanphier suddenly broke about 90 degrees to the left and started a head-on pass up and into the oncoming Zeros. This was a wise maneuver on his part as it allowed me the opportunity to attack the bombers without the Zeros on my tail. I banked sharply right to fall in behind the Bettys and, in so doing, my left engine and wing briefly blocked out my view of both bombers. As I rolled back, there was only one Betty in front of me."

COMMENT: At this point, Barber did not know whether the bomber in front of him was the lead bomber or not. However, the diary of Admiral Ugaki, a passenger in the second bomber, notes that by the time the crew in his plane saw a P-38's tracers, the lead bomber was already low over the jungle and "spurting black smoke and flames." Ugaki's pilots lost sight of the lead plane and turned sharply right out to sea. Barber told the author, "I really didn't know positively whether I had shot down the lead bomber or not until about 1980 when I read the account of my attack [by Admiral Ugaki] in *The Reluctant Admiral*."[2] Yanagiya stated that he saw one P-38 attack the lead bomber from the rear.

BARBER: (After lining up behind the Betty) *"I opened fire, aiming over the fuselage at the right engine. I could see bits of engine cowling coming off. As I slid over to get directly behind the target, my line of fire passed through the vertical fin of the Betty. Some pieces of the rudder separated."*

COMMENT: Wreckage photos show the vertical fin was intact except for a small section missing at the top. Barber subsequently stated the pieces he saw leave the aircraft were the top of the vertical fin, not the entire tail section.

BARBER: *"By this time I was probably no more than 100 feet behind the Betty and almost level with it. Suddenly, the Betty snapped left. As it rotated, I almost struck the right wing as the Betty had slowed rapidly when it snapped."*

COMMENT: Barber did not see the right wing break off. Visitors to the wreckage state that the right wing lies close to the fuselage. This is in direct opposition to Lanphier's statement that the right wing "tore off" as he attacked.

BARBER: *"I looked over my left shoulder as I roared by and saw the bomber with its wing upended vertically and black smoke pouring from the right engine. I believe the Betty crashed into the jungle, although I did not see it crash."*

COMMENT: Holmes stated he saw a Betty "plunge straight down and explode with a terrific flash. In the fracas I couldn't tell who had clobbered it. Since Lanphier had already called for help I thought that it was Rex Barber's guns that knocked the bomber down."

HOLMES: (After seeing three Zeros on Barber's tail) *"I told Ray Hine to take the Zero on Barber's right wing, and I slid over to get the two crowding him from the left."*

COMMENT: Holmes later stated that he could not communicate with anyone by radio since he believed his radio was inoperative at that time.

HOLMES: *"As I slipped in behind the first Zero, I saw the Betty bomber fleeing in front of Barber's P-38. . . . I let the first Zero have a long burst in the tail. The little Japanese fighter, pelted by the deadly, heavy 20mm cannon and .50 caliber bullets, exploded in a sheet of flame. . . . The other Japanese pilot was evidently so intent upon getting Barber that he either didn't see me or was too stubborn to break off the fight. I touched my triggers and watched the bullets nibble at the Zero's tail. Seconds later the airplane flamed and fell off into an inverted dive into the sea."*

COMMENT: Again, according to Kenji Yanagiya, none of the six Zeros accompanying the two bombers were shot down. However, one, with some kind of malfunction, landed at Shortland Island; the other five landed at Buin. However, Japanese sources later stated that at least sixteen Zeros took off from Kahili and may have joined the battle at this point. Holmes and Barber are both credited with one Zero each and share credit for the second Betty bomber.

HOLMES: (After attacking the second bomber) *"Out of the corner of my eye I saw an object streaking down on Barber's tail from the direction of Kahili. Turning quickly, I saw a Zero roaring in for the kill. . . . The enemy pilot saw me, broke off the attack on Barber, and also pulled up. . . . I saw a burst of flame from the Zero as he went out of control."*

COMMENT: Barber vehemently denies that Holmes shot down any aircraft off his tail. However, there is no doubt that Barber was attacked as proven by the 104 bullet holes in his aircraft. After Holmes told his story at a squadron reunion in San Antonio, Barber commented that Holmes must have been describing another mission, certainly not the Yamamoto mission. Other pilots have discounted Holmes's story completely except for the landing episode at Russell Island when he was assisted by Doug Canning. However, Holmes was given credit for one Zero and half of the second bomber. Barber has never disagreed with Holmes receiving one-half credit for the second Betty because he saw him shoot at it and score some hits. Proof that Barber flew into pieces of the Betty as it disintegrated was shown by the fact that Barber's left inner cooler was damaged and other chunks left paint streaks on his canopy and fuselage. Barber has no comment on Holmes's claim of a kill for one Zero but cannot agree that Holmes shot down *three* Zeros. The probability remains that some Zeros did join the action from Kahili.

One of the most revealing statements about the events of April 18, 1943, came from Kenji Yanagiya, the sole surviving Zero pilot. In a 1975 interview in Tokyo, he stated that he saw a P-38 firing on the lead bomber *from the rear* (italics added). He added that the bomber began to leak fuel, which ignited, and fell into the jungle where it continued to burn. However, in a 1988 interview at Fredericksburg, Texas, his interpreter used the plural "P-38s" when describing the attack on the lead bomber. His interpreter was not a pilot. However, this point was clarified later. He confirmed that he saw only one P-38 attack the lead bomber from the rear.

Yanagiya's eyewitness account is a key element in bolstering Barber's claim. Yanagiya, although reluctant to become engaged in the controversy, had no reason to tell anything but what he recalled, although he admitted that his memory is fading. He and the other Zero pilots probably felt guilty about not protecting their leader, but they had no prior information that would lead them to believe they were going to be intercepted.

Unfortunately, the recollections of all who participated in the mission that day are subject to memory failure or mental distortions as time passes. Gen. James H. "Jimmy" Doolittle perhaps expressed this human failing best when he told the author that "as time passes, we tend to remember events and incidents as we wished they had happened, not necessarily as they did. When retelling about events far in the past we have a tendency to shift a few degrees each time from what actually happened—and always in our favor. Human nature, I guess."[3]

Tom Lanphier, especially in the few months before his death, treated everyone who doubted his story with scorn. In response to a 1985 writer's query, he wrote:

I have always felt the simple facts, and the records of them, were enough for me. I have not—nor do I intend—to get into

182

a pointless controversy with people trying to rewrite history from the sidelines decades after the fact. For my part, I do not consider as "official," historical studies written years after the action by men who were not at the scene of the action. I prefer to base the validity of my account of an operational mission on the official debriefing by combat-experienced pilots who were there that day. I'm simply going to cite official records and let it go at that.[4]

Today, the eight American survivors all have slightly different versions of events of April 18, 1943, as they recall them concerning the briefing, the flight to and from Bougainville, their words and actions and those of other pilots, and what happened on the ground after they returned. However, all agree that there was no formal debriefing. Unfortunately, the two intelligence officers—Capt. William Morrison and Lt. Joseph McGuigan—are deceased. And so is Tom Lanphier, who cannot make another effort to prove his contention. Lanphier told several people that he went to the operations tent in the evening after the mission and prepared the mission report for them. He had reportedly written several previous reports. As one of his squadron mates told the author, "Lanphier was a graduate of Stanford University with a bachelor's degree in journalism and was an excellent writer. He could always tell a good yarn and his stories always got better in the retelling."[5]

Unfortunately, this is hearsay evidence. It appears to be Lanphier's story against everyone else's. The air force historians recognize this and remain firm in assigning one-half credit each to Lanphier and Barber for the Yamamoto bomber. "Hard" evidence is needed to change the record.

In retrospect, firm, irrefutable, scientific evidence that will prove beyond any shadow of a doubt whose story we should believe seems elusive. Is it possible that "irrefutable, scientific" proof still lies hidden in the rusted hulk of wreckage amidst the tangles and swampy undergrowth of the Bougainville jungle? Several Americans, Australians, and New Zealanders have visited the site and have sought the needed proof of the direction from which the bullets entered the doomed aircraft. As time passed and each visitor became more aware of the controversy between Lanphier and Barber, the attempts became more determined.

In 1988, a group of World War II pilots and accident investigation experts decided to visit the wreckage to see if they could find the elusive proof that would convince the Air Force Victory Credit Review Board to determine, once and for all, who *really* deserves to be credited with the Yamamoto shootdown.

12
IN SEARCH OF
HISTORY

URING THE YEARS SINCE WORLD WAR II, hundreds of Japanese tourists have visited Bougainville and made their way to the wreckage to pay tribute to their esteemed naval leader. Several English-speaking groups from New Zealand, Australia, and the United States have also visited the area. In 1984, a Japanese newspaper reported that plans were being made to retrieve the wreckage of the Yamamoto bomber and take it to Japan to be displayed on the one hundredth anniversary of Yamamoto's birth. In 1987, a Japanese team flew to the site in a helicopter, removed the left wing, and lifted it to dockside for shipment to Japan. However, the Papua New Guinea government had passed a law that prohibited the removal of any of the war artifacts from the islands, presumably to keep the tourists coming. The group was stopped by agents of the government and ordered to return the wing to the village of the chief who owns the land. The Japanese representative in charge of the group was jailed briefly.

The Japanese were not trying to steal the wing. They had previously negotiated with the chief to build a road to the wreckage site and donate a bus to the village so the natives could maximize their tourist income. The Japanese protested the ruling successfully and the wing was reportedly sent to Japan for display.

D'E. C. "Bunny" Darby, a New Zealand geothermal engineer, has traveled extensively throughout the South Pacific islands searching for World War II aircraft. In 1972, he visited the Yamamoto wreckage with his father and Ken Jacobs, a friend. In 1975, Rex Barber learned of this visit and contacted Darby to see if he could describe the condition of the aircraft and tell from which direction the bullets had entered the fuselage and engines.

Darby replied that the wreckage was difficult to locate but was positive he had found it. "Our local knowledge experts were a Methodist minister who had spent twenty-seven years in the area and a local man named Pia who had visited the crash site years before," Darby wrote:

He was not on the original search party but he knows that the Japs were exceptionally disturbed about this particular crash and the local people quickly realized that someone very important had been killed at the time.

The three of us spent the best part of a week looking for aircraft wrecks in S.W. Bougainville and found only two G4M1 [Betty] bombers, [one of] which had forced-landed on Kahili airfield and obviously was not Yamamoto's aircraft. Several Shinto prayer sticks were in evidence at the [other] crash site indicating recent Japanese pilgrimages to the area. I am reasonably well satisfied therefore that the bomber we found is in fact Yamamoto's aircraft.

The bomber was burning before it hit the ground, evidence being surface fire damage on the fin and to a lesser extent the top of the rear fuselage. Fire damage on the fin was only very minor and there was no fire trace inside the fuselage aft of the entry door.

The aircraft crashed through trees and hit the ground about 40 degrees nose down, wings level, both engines power off and propellers either stopped or were windmilling very slowly. This suggests that at best one of the pilots set the aircraft up as well as possible for impact with the trees, but couldn't control the dive angle. The tailplane and elevators are almost non-existent, but our impression is that they were removed by the trees and did not separate in flight. (Perhaps the elevator control wires were cut by gunfire or burnt through?)

Almost everything forward of the fuselage entry door was destroyed by an intense post-impact fire, the only surviving components being a few feet of the right wing outer panel, both engine/prop assemblies and some of the wing structure. Recognizable parts from the flight deck were about 18" × 18" piece of canopy fairing, part of the main hydraulic junction box and that part of the main instrument panel above the autopilot control unit and extending over to the left vertical speed and turn-and-slip indicator. Everything else was totally destroyed by fire.

I wish that I had received your letter three years ago as I would have made a point of studying bullet entry patterns. As it was we remarked on the lack of gunfire damage in the surviving rear fuselage and tail section and assumed that all the shots went into the wings and forward fuselage. From this it would appear that you did not do much damage to the rear fuselage but the crash angle suggests you would have damaged the elevators.[1]

In a subsequent letter to a friend, Darby said he had

a very strong impression that Rex Barber was the one who shot down the bomber we all know of as Yamamoto's aircraft. The impression comes from my own written and photographic notes of the wreckage, coupled with subsequent (not prior) discussions with interested parties.

Perhaps most telling is the presence of the outer wing panel in the position one would expect to be occupied by the right wing outer panel. In Lanphier's account, the right wing is said to have separated in flight. As I see it, there are only two possible explanations for the anomaly, neither of which I find very convincing:

(1) We are all looking at the wrong aircraft (i.e. not Yamamoto's).

(2) On impact, the left wing flipped over the top of the fuselage and came to rest in exactly the place once occupied by the right wing.

If Lanphier did indeed see something large separate from the bomber in flight, it could only have been one of the ailerons. The reasons are that both of the outer wing panels present were close to the main wreckage, and the elevators and rudder were clearly removed by impact with trees, plus subsequent "souveniring" as the attach fittings and spar remnants were still in place. However, the aircraft appears to have crashed more or less wings level, although at a fairly steep angle, which implies that some degree of roll control remained with the crew right up to impact.

Barber's impression that the bomber seemed to "stop" in the air is also borne out by the propellers, which did not appear to have been feathered. If the engines lost power and lost oil pressure almost simultaneously, the drag of windmilling, unfeatherable blades would have much the same effect as selecting reverse pitch in the air.

Conversely, if the bomber lost a wing (even if only outboard of the engine), it would not slow down suddenly but would be expected to flick to the right into a spin/tumble/cartwheel. The wreckage did not give me the impression of that sort of flight path into the ground.[2]

Al Kauslick, an employee of the Cleveland, Ohio, based Euclid Company, manufacturers of earthmoving equipment, was working at a Bougainville copper mine near Kieta. He made a trip to the crash site in 1978 and returned in September 1986 with co-workers A. J. Craig and J. W. Deschler. His second visit was to ascertain what difficulties would be involved in getting jungle growth cleared away so the wreckage could be more easily inspected. He videotaped the scene extensively on his second trip and documented the relative positions of various pieces of the wreckage by using a theodolite.

In 1981, Terry Gwynn-Jones, an Australian pilot/writer, visited the wreckage, unaware of the controversy in the United States about who downed the admiral. After six torturous hours getting to the site, he and his party were able to remain there only a half hour in order to return during daylight hours. In an article he wrote for *GEO* magazine, he described how a native showed him a relatively undamaged wing "several hundred meters" back in the jungle, which Gwynn-Jones believed to be the right wing of the bomber.

"Bullet holes had punctured the wing in several places," he wrote. "The wing had obviously torn off the aircraft in flight." Gwynn-Jones believed that the fact that the right wing was found virtually complete along the bomber's final flight path some distance from the wreckage gave Lanphier the edge in claiming the victory since he had stated the right wing came off in flight before the aircraft crashed.

"There is no doubt that Barber hit the Betty's tail area," Gwynn-Jones wrote. "Even after 37 years the machine gun damage was still evident on the tail fin of the wreckage. His attack seriously damaged and slowed the fleeing aircraft. With the plane's rudder and part of the fin shot away, the pilot would have been battling for control, especially when Lanphier subsequently shot up the right engine."

Gwynn-Jones concluded: "Barber undoubtedly set the Betty up for his flight leader. But it was still flying and probably would have reached Ballale, or Buin airfield only a few kilometers away. There now appears no doubt, however, that moments later, it was Captain Tom Lanphier who administered the coup de grace."[3]

Gwynn-Jones also wrote an article for *Air Force* magazine in April 1985. Using almost the same words describing his half-hour visit to the wreckage, he concluded that "there was little doubt that the location of the starboard wing was the final evidence needed to settle the controversy."[4]

In September 1988, Gwynn-Jones gave a lecture on the Yamamoto shootdown in Washington as a guest of the Smithsonian Institution's National Air and Space Museum. He revealed that he had made a grave mistake in his writings about the 1981 visit. The wing he had identified behind the wreckage as the starboard wing was actually the port (left) wing. This had been ascertained by experts at the Air Force Museum, located at Wright-Patterson AFB, Ohio who pointed out Gwynn-Jones's error from the photos he brought to the museum. The Japanese red ball roundel he had assumed was on top of the wing was actually on the bottom.

"[The right wing] is at the main wreckage site," he said, "about 15 feet ahead of the fuselage, slightly to the righthand side." This clearly proved to Gwynn-Jones "that the right wing didn't separate in flight but had separated by contact with a tall tree."

He also stated that reports from Japanese witnesses who went into the wreckage site the day after the crash stated there was no rear gun "or any indication of a gun in that position" on the lead bomber. He also said that his research indicated that the radios had been taken out of the bombers, presumably to lighten the aircraft to accommodate the extra passengers.

The native guide who took Gwynn-Jones and his party into the wreckage told him that a shrine had once been left at the site by one of the many groups of Japanese who had visited over the years, most of them men who had served with Yamamoto during the war.

Gwynn-Jones told the audience about the articles he had written for *GEO* and *Air Force*. He said he was unaware of how great the controversy was between Lanphier and Barber when he wrote them. After the latter article was published, he said, "All hell broke loose. I really didn't know what I'd walked into. I found out that there are two very direct schools of thought. There are those that say that Lanphier did it and there are those that say Barber did it. And I don't think anyone is going to convince those people otherwise. Nor could you convince the two pilots otherwise."

Lanphier was one of the many who responded to Gwynn-Jones's article in *Air Force* and stated vehemently that he should not share the credit with Barber. Lanphier called the article "unfair" and sent Gwynn-Jones the chapter of the autobiography he was writing in which he describes his singular version of the mission.

In his concluding remarks, Gwynn-Jones said:

No one, not even Tom Lanphier, contests that Barber had shot down a Betty bomber. There were several witnesses. That is not to say that there are not any witnesses to Tom Lanphier's [shootdown] but I couldn't find any. I don't think that either of those pilots is lying. I think both of them truly think they shot down Yamamoto. Both are entitled to do that. It is my opinion that Barber had a go at the aircraft first and mortally hit that aircraft and it was on its way down.

Lanphier, after going after the Zero, sees an aircraft flying low over the jungle. He begins shooting at a 90-degree angle, the worst possible position for a fighter pilot to be shooting at another aircraft. He starts to shoot early, almost out of range. All of a sudden he sees the [right] wing and engine starting to burn. His report also says that before he got towards the tail and before he got within the angle of fire of the tail gun, the wing came off.

No one could say that Lanphier *didn't* hit the aircraft nor can anyone say that if he hadn't hit the aircraft it would have continued to fly.

Barber says the aircraft was on fire. Lanphier said it was on fire and that the wing came off before the aircraft [went] in. It was right on top of the jungle and Lanphier says he didn't have enough room to go under it. He had to go behind it and he's worried at this stage because he has to go into the firing range of that rear gun. Luckily, the wing comes off before he gets into that precarious position.

From what we've seen of the wreck the left wing came off by hitting a tree. What did Lanphier see come off? Was it the left wing or the right wing striking a tree? Who knows what he believed? There are all sorts of scenarios we could imagine. We could say Lanphier didn't hit it at all. The pilot of the Betty saw the tracers coming and could have decided to put the nose down into the trees. We will never know.

Gwynn-Jones reiterated one more piece of evidence in favor of Barber. The autopsy on Yamamoto revealed that he had been hit with two bullets. One entered the lower left jaw and exited through the right eye. The other entered under the left shoulder blade and went forward and upward. This report was confirmed by the Japanese in 1984. As far as the Japanese are concerned, Yamamoto was killed by bullets fired from behind, not from the right-hand side. It was also confirmed that he had been sitting on the right-hand side of the Betty behind the copilot facing forward.

Gwynn-Jones believes the controversy between Lanphier and Barber "has tarnished the image of a brilliant mission. It was superbly executed and it was a team effort—the top cover pilots, those who broke the code, the ground crews—everybody had a part. If I had to choose one man who was responsible for the success of that mission, I'd put my money on Mitchell. He was the man who got them there on target and on time. He was the leader of that brave band of airmen."[5]

Gwynn-Jones, experienced in aircraft accident investigation, regrets that he could not spend more time at the wreckage site so he could have looked for bullet holes and determined precisely the angle from which the bullets were fired.

Ross Channon, an Australian working for the Goodyear Rubber Company at Arawa, Bougainville, visited the wreckage site on December 1, 1985, and reported what he found:

> There are definite holes on the fuselage top forward of the tail fin which could be bullet holes. Some of these holes are elongated and on an angle of approximately 15 degrees to the right of the fuselage centerline. This would fit with an attack from the rear and above slightly sweeping from right to left.
> The wing, I feel, was torn off because of the crumpled damage on the leading edge, no trace of any bullet holes, only torn metal and the wing's location. The wing is about 150 feet from the main wreckage directly behind. Even at low altitude if the wing had been shot off it would surely be farther away from the wreckage. The position of the wing is more likely to be where the plane first came in contact with the trees.
> One of the guides told us the Japanese still visit the site and perform little ceremonies of respect, leaving bowls of rice, etc. for the spirits (or the rats). I think the latter.
> I did feel a sense of grief for this poor old piece of machinery and hope that somehow it can be preserved for others that are interested, to visit. I don't hold much hope though as back at the landowner's village he was talking of constructing a road down to the plane site. I could see the Kina [local currency] signs in his eyes as he stands at the toll gate collecting K25 fees. The trouble with improving the accessibility to the site means more of the remains will disappear to be used as building materials for bush huts.[6]

Jack P. DeBoer, chairman of Private Jet Expeditions, a Wichita, Kansas, company that will take travelers on "adventure trips," visited the wreckage in June 1988. He took a number of still photographs and made a videotape. After reading an article on the Yamamoto mission by George T. Chandler, he said, "Having been at the site, it appears your apparent conclusion that the wings were intact when the plane went into the jungle is correct."[7]

This observation was later confirmed by Dr. Richard H. Kohn, chief of the Office of Air Force History. He noted that Cargill Hall, Chief, Research Division, received photographs of the wreckage and showed them to an aeronautical engineer attending the Air Command and Staff College. According to Kohn, "The engineer advised that the wing that fell 150 feet behind the aircraft was the outer left wing, damaged on the leading edge on impact with the trees, showing its spars bent backwards. (Had the wing separated in flight, the spars would have been bent upwards.) The right wing outer panel lay where that wing burned with the wreckage; apparently it did not detach in flight."[8]

D'E. C. Darby returned to the site in August 1988 and took closeup photos that show the bullet damage through the bulkheads in the aft section of the fuselage. He reported in a letter to Rex Barber:

The aircraft has deteriorated greatly since I last saw it, largely because the local people allowed a foreign logging company to destroy the rainforest in the area. This caused damage from falling branches and also opened the aircraft to accelerated corrosion. Also, the wreckage has been piled into three or four heaps, leaving only the rear fuselage and engines more or less where they fell. And, with no rainforest cover left, vines and other weeds have covered the piles of wreckage. Sadly, the whole atmosphere of the site has been degraded and cheapened. However, the landowners did have the foresight to leave untouched the two trees that removed the bomber's left and right wings.

I spent several hours at the crash site, and have summarized the results of my findings in the enclosed notes. In summary, there is very little bullet damage of any type on the remaining wreckage, and I could see none at all on the powerplant assemblies, wings, tail or fuselage right side. However, there are bullet tracks and shrapnel damage resulting from bullets that entered through the rear gunner's position and passed directly up the middle of the fuselage, mostly without breaking the aircraft's skin.

In the absence of engine damage, it would appear that the fire you noticed was probably from oil coolers or oil lines on the wing leading edges beside the engines. This could also tie in with my idea that the crew may have had prop feathering problems. The oil cooler was destroyed by post-impact fire, but a really close examination of the crash site may yield some fragments which could provide evidence.

I could find no evidence to substantiate any part of Tom Lanphier's story.[9]

In the formal crash investigation report he wrote on the spot, Darby went into great detail about the damage he observed and the location of various parts of the aircraft. Here are excerpts from that report:

5.1 [Right engine] No bullet damage seen on carburetor, magnetos, starter, generator, prop blades, prop control units, cowlings, cowl flaps or cylinders as visible above ground level.

5.2 [Left engine] No bullet damage visible on cylinders, lower and side cowlings, propeller blades (2 remaining), prop control unit, oil pump or lower surfaces of carburetor and magnetos. (Upper section of engine including accessory casing and accessories is buried in ground). No fire damage.

5.3 [The rear fuselage] is the largest remaining section of the aircraft, and extends back from frame 24, i.e. consists of the rear detachable section of the fuselage, together with the fin and tailplane/elevator stubs.

No trace of bullet or shrapnel damage was seen on the left or right sides of the section (i.e. no gunfire damage from either side). Numerous small holes in the fuselage bulkhead at frame 32 caused by shrapnel traveling directly forwards from rear of fuselage.

In extensive reportage of the bullet damage found on the rear fuselage, Darby stated the following:

(a) bullet entered directly from rear of aircraft through left lower rear tail gunner's window, and traveled forwards through the center webs of frames 37 to 34, directly from rear of aircraft.

(b) bullet traveled through tailplane carry-through spot (at frame 34), directly from rear of aircraft.

(c) bullet jacket or shrapnel traveling forward through fuselage penetrated frames 25 and 24 on right side between stringer 6 and 7.

(d) bullet traveling forward penetrated frame 27 at stringer 6. Possible entry hole at shallow angle from rear in skin immediately adjacent and to rear of frame 27.

No gunfire damage seen on either side or in rear spar of fin. Right tailplane/elevator separated by tree impact, possibly just before ground impact as stub wreckage is bent upwards as well as backwards.

Darby summarized his findings:

All visible gunfire and shrapnel damage was caused by bullets entering from immediately behind the bomber through the tail gunner's position, and traveling forwards through the fuselage. Only one possible bullet entry point was seen in the skin and that was also caused by a bullet traveling forwards.

No gunfire damage was seen on the engines, engine accessories, cowlings or propeller assemblies, although the engines were not turned over to check for damage to the sections now lying against the ground.

No gunfire damage was seen on the left wing, which remains in good condition but is no longer at the crash site, or on any left or right wing sections remaining at the crash site."[10]

George T. Chandler, a World War II ace who flew many missions out of Guadalcanal, had first become interested in the Yamamoto episode in April 1943 when Tom Lanphier and Rex Barber returned to Oua Tom Airfield on New Caledonia where Chandler was checking out in the P-38. He met both pilots just before they left for the States and recalled a discussion he had with Lanphier about fighter tactics.

"I particularly remember Tom saying that the P-38 airplane was so strong in its structure that you didn't need to worry about tearing the airplane apart," Chandler said. "He specifically mentioned that the placarded warning about the maximum speed for extending the maneuvering flaps was very conservative and it was quite effective to extend the maneuvering flaps at a much higher than placarded speed, and the instanteous turn advantage over the Zero would let you get out of a Zero's gunfire in that very first hard turn, and then you would have time to use other evasive tactics."[11]

Through the years, Chandler read everything that came along about the Yamamoto mission, the air war in the Pacific, and World War II in general. "It always fascinated me," he said, "that the controversy which developed between Lanphier and Barber and Besby Holmes seemed to have no means of resolution."

Chandler went into banking after the war but his interest in the air war in the South Pacific never dwindled. He met a number of pilots in the ensuing years who had served there, including the survivors of the Yamamoto mission. His interest in history prompted him to take his recorder along to the annual reunions of the 339th Fighter Squadron and tape their stories.

In 1978, Chandler built a home in Oregon. In 1984, he arranged to meet Barber who had settled in the state after retiring from the air force. The association grew and he reestablished contacts with other pilots who had served on Guadalcanal, including several who had flown on the Yamamoto mission.

"My interest in World War II history prompted me to try to get all of the fellows whom I had known in the Solomons as pilots to give me an oral history," he said. During a reunion in San Antonio in 1985, Chandler visited the Nimitz Museum at Fredericksburg and viewed the 1975 video interview with Kenji Yanagiya that was being shown there. Over a long period of time after that, Chandler had a number of recording sessions with Barber and asked many different questions about the Yamamoto mission. "I was purposely testing Rex to see if through my sort of cross-examination, I could develop any inconsistencies in his versions of what happened," he told the author. "I found none."

Chandler's interest in the controversy deepened the more he researched. He read every book he could find that mentioned the mission and studied Lanphier's accounts written in 1945 and the 1943 mission reports. He attended a talk given by Lanphier at a reunion of the 44th Fighter Squadron and his doubts grew about Lanphier's veracity. "I came to the conclusion that Barber alone had shot down Yamamoto," he said.

However, "I was only about 98% sure. I felt that I could be 100% sure, and the Air Force could be 100% and settle the issue, on the basis of physical evidence examination in the jungle." Chandler thought the controversy could be settled if a thorough, scientific investigation were made of the wreckage and it could be shown that the right wing of the Yamamoto bomber was still attached as it entered the jungle; that there was no bullet damage to the right engine from the three o'clock position; and that all of the bullet damage to any part of the airplane remaining was from the six o'clock position. He noted that Lanphier never waivered from his original story written in 1945 while his memory was still fresh. Lanphier said repeatedly over the years that he fired from the three o'clock position and saw the right wing separate in flight. Barber has stated consistently since the day of the mission that he did all his firing from the six o'clock position.

When Chandler first heard of the Yamamoto Retrospective being planned by the Nimitz museum, he decided that it would be an excellent opportunity to persuade the air force to send an investigating team to the site. However, Chandler met resistance to the idea from R. Cargill Hall, Chief, Research Division at the United States Air Force Historical Research Center at Maxwell AFB, Alabama, who was the moderator on one of the retrospective's two panels.

From correspondence and telephone conversations with Hall before the retrospective, "it appeared to me that Cargill Hall was less than enthusiastic about the Air Force doing any research to determine which pilot shot down Yamamoto—rather I got the very definite feeling that he wanted to leave it exactly like it was—i.e., 50% credit to each pilot, Lanphier and Barber," Chandler told the author.

After the two panel sessions at Fredericksburg, Texas, Chandler asked Hall a direct question: "Assume that an investigation of the wreckage by qualified experts determines that the right wing was still attached to the airplane when it crashed, and there was no bullet damage to the right engine from the three o'clock position, then would you call together a new Victory Credit

Board of Review to examine this new evidence and reconsider the award of half credit to each pilot?" After much hesitation, Hall said, "I'd have to give that question a lot of thought before I could respond."

Hall answered the question by letter to Chandler and reviewed the facts as he saw them:

Available testimony and photographs of the wreckage tell us that the bomber plunged into the jungle at a shallow angle in essentially a normal attitude in roll, with wings attached. The outer port wing separated on contact with the trees and fell behind the aircraft about 150 feet. The propellers of the two engines remained in fine pitch (not feathered) and were not turning at full power. On impact, the forward section of the fuselage and wings burned. Only the two engines, outer wing panels, and about 30 percent of the rear of the fuselage remain intact. Souvenir hunters, I'm told moreover, have been cutting and carrying away pieces of the wreckage for years. According to the P-38 pilots, during the engagement, cannon and machine gun fire were directed at the forward half of the Betty bomber and the inner wings and engines. Except for the engines, however, these parts of the craft burned. So much for the known physical evidence.

The written records agree that Barber first attacked Yamamoto's bomber, and Lanphier followed him. Each originally claimed a bomber destroyed over the jungle; immediately afterwards Barber believed the tail came off, while Lanphier supposed the right wing had separated. [Only Lanphier has ever said the right wing came off and it was so reported in the official Thirteenth Air Force combat report. Hall ignored the Ugaki diary entry which noted a single P-38 firing at the lead bomber.] But only one bomber was shot down and it had lost neither tail nor wing. Air Force historians in the 1960s and 1970s confirmed a shared aerial victory credit between them for one bomber. Based on the evidence available, a Board of Review in 1985 verified these findings and conclusions. More recently, on 15 April 1988, the sole surviving Japanese pilot, Yanagiya, recollected in his interview that P-38s attacked the bombers at the beginning of the engagement.

What might an investigation of the wreckage today add to our knowledge? Some additional physical details can be procured, it seems to me, but the likelihood of producing conclusive evidence that would prove your contention (that Barber alone shot down the bomber) is I think uncertain at best. For example, suppose that the starboard engine shows no damage from gunfire directed at it from the 3 or 4 o'clock position, the position of approach claimed by Lanphier. Does that prove Lanphier did not fire on the bomber? Without the forward fuselage available, it would seem that question simply cannot be answered with certainty.

Many of us may wonder whether Lanphier actually fired on the bomber. But the one person who knew the truth, Lanphier, is gone. Thus, without compelling new evidence, I suspect this case will be debated for years, with the proponents of one side or the other holding strongly to their own views.

At any rate, I wanted you to have my reflections on the proposed crash site investigation. I do not recommend against it, mind you, but I am not confident it will produce the positive evidence you seek.[12]

There was confusion about the translation of Yanagiya's statement at Fredericksburg in which he described the attack on the lead bomber. To clear up this point, Richard Y. Nishiyama, at the request of George Chandler, interviewed Yanagiya in Japan on August 10, 1989. Yanagiya stated:

I saw one P-38 firing into the tail of Admiral Yamamoto's bomber and I saw the admiral's airplane emitting smoke and flames while one P-38 was directly behind it.

I saw the Admiral's airplane descend toward the jungle in an attitude of forced landing within twenty to thirty seconds from when I first saw one P-38 behind the Admiral's airplane firing into it.

From the time that I first sighted any of the P-38s until the Admiral's airplane was down in the jungle was two minutes or less.[13]

Chandler was unpersuaded by Hall's opinion, albeit an important one since he would be the person who would organize and serve on a new Victory Credit Review Board. Chandler refused to give up his quest for the truth, whatever the outcome, and decided to look for irrefutable evidence, one way or the other, on his own. He contacted all the survivors of the mission and many others who might have some knowledge of the events of April 18, 1943, and began to launch his own private investigation.

Chandler reasoned that certain proof of who deserved proper credit for Yamamoto's death obviously lay in the wreckage. He thought that if a properly constituted team of experienced, unbiased accident investigators were to examine the remains of the Betty and determine from which direction the bullets came, their report might produce the new evidence that the air force required before a review board would be formed to reconsider the claim.

In the summer of 1988, Chandler contacted the Veterans of Foreign Wars and pleaded a case for reconsideration of the victory claim. At its annual convention, the VFW passed Resolution No. 302 which urged the chief of the Office of Air Force History "to make all efforts to have the Yamamoto wreckage examined as soon as possible before it is further carried off by souvenir hunters, to determine if the bullet damage to those portions of the plane remaining, and particularly the bullet damage to the right engine, can support or disprove the claims of either Lanphier or Barber."

The resolution also asked that Dr. Richard H. Kohn be urged to convene a Victory Credit Board of Review of exceptionally well-trained crash investigators . . . "to make a determination if the present Victory Credit Award of one-half to Lanphier and one-half to Barber should be changed or confirmed."[14]

In a letter to Howard E. Vander Clute, Jr., adjutant general of the VFW, Dr. Kohn affirmed that a review board would be formed if any new evidence were forthcoming. He said that R. Cargill Hall, Chief, Research Division at Maxwell AFB, Alabama, would oversee a new board "should one become necessary." However, he cautioned that Hall had informed him that "after 45 years the wreckage of the Yamamoto aircraft has been disturbed. If that is the case, analysis of the wreckage will be extremely complicated and must take into account the passage of time and human tampering, if the analysis itself is to be offered as new evidence."[15]

Dr. Kohn defined what he would consider new evidence in a subsequent letter to Chandler. "If careful analysis by a qualified crash investigator shows no bullet damage to the starboard engine or starboard side of the fuselage from the three o'clock position, I would judge that to be credible new evidence."[16]

In the fall of 1988, Chandler founded the Second Yamamoto Mission Association (SYMA), a nonprofit organization made up of air force veterans and people closely associated with the air force. Its purpose was to organize an expedition to the Yamamoto wreckage and search for the truth in a scientific manner. The group would include John Mitchell and Rex Barber, for whom the trip would be a nostalgic return to their fighting grounds. In addition, Chandler invited William H. Allen, an experienced aircraft accident investigator and World War II ace; Gene Monihan, a dedicated World War II historian who has been conducting his own independent investigation of this mission since 1987; Dr. Jerry R. Kelley, a San Antonio heart surgeon, and Marvin Dibben, a skilled video cameraman. All are graduates of The International Group for Historic Aircraft Recovery (TIGHAR) training school. Their departure date was originally scheduled for April 10, 1989; however, a native uprising was reported at Buin and the group was advised not to risk the trip. The expedition was rescheduled to depart in January 1990. Again, however, dissident elements on Bougainville had murdered several civilians, blew up a key bridge, and set fire to the airport terminal building. Despite these setbacks, the group still plans to visit the site.

Al Kauslick reported frequently from the Bougainville copper mine where he was working, but had to leave the area. He had kept the SYMA group informed about the situation and advised that no one attempt to arrange a visit to the area until the uprising is quelled. At this writing, with the wreckage and the area around the Betty bomber rapidly disintegrating, it is extremely doubtful that meaningful evidence will be found there that would forever settle the controversy. However, much credit is due George T. Chandler for organizing the expedition and for his efforts in seeking an unbiased decision based on irrefutable scientific evidence.

EPILOGUE

*I*T APPEARS THAT ALL OF THE CREDIBLE EVI-
dence that can be readily obtained to answer the question of who deserves credit
for Admiral Yamamoto's demise is currently in hand. In view of
reports of continuing deterioration of the Betty bomber's wreckage, it is unlikely that any subsequent visits to the site will yield
any new and definitive evidence that will change the facts as
shown herein.

It is undisputed that Capt. Thomas G. Lanphier, Jr., was an
exceptionally articulate pilot whose psychological motivations
during his wartime service and subsequent civilian positions
were directed toward self-aggrandizement and self-glorification.
Although brilliant in many respects, he tended to run roughshod
over opponents to his viewpoints, especially when it came to his
version of the Yamamoto shootdown. The author was witness to
his articulate justification for his actions and decisions during a
number of discussions about a TV series on the history of flight
that he was planning to produce.

Discounting Lanphier's apparent impulsions brought out in
this book, there are many aspects about the Yamamoto mission

that do not support his account. By his own admission, when he approached the two Betty bombers with Barber on his right wing, he turned 90 degrees in a climbing left turn directly into the line of flight of the three Zeros that were descending toward them. He claims to have blasted one Zero out of the sky as he continued his climb past them to 5,000 or 6,000 feet. There is no evidence to support this claim since all Zeros landed safely.

Meanwhile, Barber continued toward the two descending bombers. He overshot them briefly and momentarily lost sight of them as he banked and turned in the direction of their flight. When he rolled out of the bank, he quickly lined up on one bomber directly in front of him, not knowing if it was the lead bomber or not. He fired many shots from the rear of the bomber and is positive that he scored some hits. The bomber slowed down suddenly and he flew past it when it started to smoke. Looking back, he saw a black plume rising from the jungle as Zeros began attacking him from the rear.

Barber is unable to account for Lanphier's actions after Lanphier pulled up into the Zeros because he never saw his plane again until he returned to Guadalcanal. Lanphier claims that as he reached 5,000–6,000 feet going in the opposite direction from the bombers, he rolled over on his back, looked down, and saw a bomber skimming the treetops below. He then dove toward the target in a descending 270-degree high-speed left turn and caught up with the bomber, now at right angles to his aircraft after having apparently made a 360-degree left turn. He claims he fired and destroyed it and saw a wing tear off the bomber just before it plunged into the jungle. He also states that he saw Barber shoot down a bomber.

Barber believes this account could not be true. He sums up the logic of his claim succinctly: "We were miles down the track by the time he reached the top of his climb after passing the Zero. There was no possible way that he could have gotten around and back to that bomber before it crashed. He was going the other way. The bombers were going as fast as they could to get away. Lanphier later verified that I did, indeed, shoot down one bomber, but *nobody* ever verified Lanphier's alleged bomber shootdown."[1]

It is difficult to say how much time was involved in either

Barber's or Lanphier's actions; however, the distance Lanphier had to travel to make a 90-degree interception of the lead bomber after climbing into the Zeros in the opposite direction was much greater than the distance Barber had to fly to make his engagement with the bomber—unless the bomber made a 360-degree turn as Lanphier claimed. Even at the superior diving speeds of the P-38, it is highly unlikely that he could have caught up with it, especially at right angles, before it crashed into the jungle.

Although Lanphier, Barber, and Holmes each claimed a Betty bomber, it is undisputed that there were only two enemy bombers and the lead bomber carrying Yamamoto was the one that was shot down and crashed in the jungle. It also is accepted by the air force that, based on the 1988 statements of Kenji Yanagiya, the lone survivor of the six enemy fighters, no escorting Zeros were shot down. One of the escorting Zeros had to land at Shortland Island but its difficulty has never been ascertained. Yanagiya stated that all six Zeros returned to Rabaul later that day. This may be open to question but there are no other escorting Zero pilot survivors and it is unlikely that the surviving Zero pilot would have any reason to lie. If his testimony continues to be accepted, the only explanation of Barber's and Holmes's claims to have shot down two Zeros is that some Zeros did take off from Kahili to attempt to intercept the P-38s before the latter fled to Guadalcanal. A Japanese historian has reported that there is evidence that as many as sixteen fighters did become airborne from Kahili to challenge the P-38s. Several American pilots, including Lanphier, recall seeing great clouds of dust ascending from Kahili which were presumably made by aircraft taking off or warming up when the base was alerted by Yanagiya. Yanagiya has stated he believes some got airborne.

The second Betty bomber carrying Yamamoto's staff members crashed into the water off Moila Point. There were three survivors. Holmes, circling out over the water with his wingman, Lt. Ray Hine, saw the Betty and fired on it, but did not bring it down. This was witnessed by Barber. Barber claims he finished it off. The air force has given them each credit for one-half of a kill. Barber has no quarrel with this decision. Holmes does, but offers no proof that he deserves *sole* credit. The damage to

Barber's P-38 from the disintegrating bomber proves how close he was and certainly tends to confirm his report. The difference between the Barber and Holmes stories will probably continue, but few, if any, of Holmes's contemporaries believe his version.

Barber claims that he was attacked by Zeros as he pressed his strikes on the lead and staff bombers. The 104 bullet holes in his aircraft and propeller fired from the rear and the damage to his gondola and fuselage from the exploding staff bomber are affirmations of these encounters.

The proof that Lanphier always cited to anyone who doubted his claim was the mission report and the medal citations he allegedly wrote in 1943, and a 1945 War Department news release giving him sole credit for the lead bomber's shoot-down. What destroys his claim to fame is the testimony of the credible visitors who have inspected the wreckage for the express purpose of determining bullet damage and the direction from which bullets were fired. None have ever found *any* evidence that shows damage was inflicted on the lead bomber's right side caused by bullets being fired from right angles to the bomber's route of flight.

It must be assumed that these on-site observers, several of them non-Americans, had no personal stake in the outcome of their findings and were not biased in the dispute between Barber and Lanphier. Even though the wreckage has been disturbed and vandalized by souvenir hunters over the years, the holes in the fuselage showing that all firing was from the rear were still evident as late as the fall of 1988. Several photographs have been offered as verification.

Lanphier has his supporters; unfortunately, none of them are able to offer any physical evidence that will sustain his claim. Several of Lanphier's contemporaries take the position that even if no bullet holes are found in the wreckage that show he scored any hits from right angles, no one could say he didn't fire at the bomber; therefore, they say he should not be deprived of at least half credit. However, fighter pilots object vigorously to anyone getting credit for an aerial victory based solely on his word that he fired on an enemy plane.

Julius Jacobson, wingman for John Mitchell, the mission leader, believes that Lanphier deserves lasting praise for diverting the attention of the descending Zeros, thus allowing Barber to attack the two bombers. In addition, he and a few others believe it is still possible that Lanphier could have made the attack as he claimed but the evidence has not yet been uncovered.

It is admitted by most pilots who fought during those chaotic early days of aerial combat in the southwest Pacific that proof of victories was less than scientific. Confirmation of an aerial victory was usually obtained by statements of witnesses on the ground or in the air who had actually seen the enemy aircraft fall in flames, crash into the ground, or be abandoned in flight by its crew. Without gun cameras to record the action on many combat flights like the Yamamoto mission, it was one pilot's word against another's or one man's word against proof that he *didn't* shoot down an enemy aircraft. Sometimes, one pilot would confirm another's victory, provided he was accorded the same courtesy in return. And, of course, there were enemy aircraft claimed as shot down which eventually landed safely, damaged but not destroyed. Conversely, there were probably enemy aircraft considered damaged but which did not return safely to base.

Air force historians state that

> the word of the claimant has never been accepted as sufficient evidence to establish a victory credit. Some kind of confirmation, by a witness, by photography, or by other means, is necessary. Unfortunately, people do not always agree on the significance, validity, or sufficiency of the evidence pertaining to any particular claim. The evidence must be accepted and a credit must be awarded by competent authority before a victory can be regarded as official. This means that a man's score depends upon how many victories were *officially credited* to him, and not upon the number of enemy aircraft he may have actually destroyed.[2]

Since fighter pilots receive their impressions during microseconds in the heat of battle, it is understandable that they cannot always analyze and evaluate the damage they may have inflicted on an enemy aircraft. The Air Force Victory Credit Review Board cannot assign credit for a victory long after the fact when there is no confirmation from other pilots or proof of loss to the enemy ascertained through intelligence sources or postwar research.

Despite the passage of time, victory credits are corrected

periodically as new evidence becomes available. The latest official victory credit list for World War I, World War II, Korea, and Vietnam was published in 1988. Each of the previous listings of aerial victory credits was reviewed for accuracy and corrected when necessary. A number of errors were eliminated and the tabulations, according to the United States Air Force Historical Research Center, "have been made more accurate than ever before." However, even this list cannot be considered final, "for future research may yet uncover errors of omission or commission that will be corrected in future editions."[3]

The first attempt to give credit for aerial victories began in France following the Armistice on November 11, 1918. Historians of the Air Service, American Expeditionary Forces, published the first list in the "Thirtieth Report of Air Service Activities, AEF, for the Week Ending May 26, 1919." The list was revised in 1920, and again in 1931. Five historical studies addressed USAF aerial victory credits of all four wars in the ensuing years.

It is important to the fighter pilots who fought during America's four wars in the air to get proper credit for their victories, especially those who have destroyed five or more enemy aircraft to become an "ace." In the history of the flying arms of the military services, no group is more highly acclaimed than those fighter pilots who attained that goal. Because of their daring exploits, they have earned a place among the twentieth-century's most honored warriors.

The latest list of World War II victories included the most recent change for the April 18, 1943, mission because of the testimony of Kenji Yanagiya, the lone survivor of the six escorting Zeros. Since he stated that none of the escorting Zeros were shot down, the late Tom Lanphier lost his status as an ace. The official listing now shows him with 4.5 victories. He had claimed a total of 7 victories at the end of the war, including one aircraft he said he shot down while a passenger on a bombing mission. Since no other fighter pilots have ever been given credit for shooting down an enemy aircraft from a bomber's gunner position and the bomber crew refused to verify this kill, it is unlikely Lanphier could have ever pressed that claim successfully in order to maintain his status as an ace.

According to R. Cargill Hall, Chief, Research Division at the United States Air Force Historical Research Center, "presently, the Zeros claimed by Holmes and Barber on 18 April 1943 are presumed to have been based at Kahili, and remain on the listing." Therefore, both continue to be credited with a Zero each.[4]

Unfortunately for Holmes and Barber, the victory credits that have admitted them to the honored roll of aviation heroes could also be changed if it is later ascertained that no Zeros joined the battle from Kahili. And if it continues to be accepted that none of the six escorting Zeros were eliminated, the two Bettys would have been the only enemy aircraft downed that day.

Likewise, Holmes will not be able to claim his current 5.5 victory ace status if he is not given credit for a Zero shootdown yet retains credit for one-half of the staff bomber. If his half credit for the staff bomber were also discredited, his total would be reduced to four enemy aircraft.

Barber, now on the record as having downed five enemy aircraft, would end up with 5.5 credited victories if full credit were given for the Yamamoto bomber. However, if the Zero he claimed were discredited at a later date, he would have only 4.5 victories and would also lose his ace status.

Since it is reported that some Zeros were able to get airborne from Kahili and attack Barber and Holmes, credits for the Zeros they claimed that day will not be challenged by the Victory Credit Review Board.

The designation of "ace" is extremely important to the three pilots on the Yamamoto mission. All were admitted to membership in the American Fighter Aces Association, a brotherhood of pilots officially credited with five or more victories in any of the American wars. The term *ace* was first bestowed informally on members of the aero squadrons sent overseas with the American Expeditionary Forces during World War I. Most of the AEF members who became aces were pursuit pilots, for the men of the bombardment and observation units naturally had fewer opportunities to attack the enemy in the air.

According to a policy stated by the director of the Army Air Service on January 5, 1920:

> The U.S. Air Service does not use the term "ace" in referring to those who are credited officially with five or more aerial victories over enemy aircraft. It is not the policy

of the Air Service to glorify one particular branch of aeronautics, aviation, or aerostation at the expense of another. . . .

. . . The work of observation and bombardment is considered equally as hazardous as that of pursuit, but due to the fact that observation and bombardment pilots are not called upon to destroy enemy aircraft, it should not be allowed to aid in establishing a popular comparison of results merely by relative victories.

This policy was retained by the Air Corps, Army Air Forces, and U.S. Air Force. It was in effect in World War II, the Korean War, the Vietnam War, and remains true today. Nevertheless, people insist on using this title, and the air force never has prohibited, or discouraged, the informal and unofficial use of the title within its own organizations.

The word *ace* does appear frequently in air force publications, however. The word is defined in the *United States Air Force Dictionary* as "an expert pilot; specif., one credited with not less than five victories." In January 1962, when the air force published "A Preliminary List of U.S. Air Force Aces—1917–1953," neither Lanphier nor Barber was listed; Besby F. Holmes was credited with 5 victories; John W. Mitchell with 11. The 1988 list credits Holmes with 5.5 victories, Barber with 5.0, and Lanphier with 4.5. Mitchell is credited with 11 during World War II and 4 more during the Korean Conflict.

Despite the evidence presented thus far, the question of who deserves credit for the downing of Adm. Isoroku Yamamoto will no doubt continue to be debated. Just as the question of who shot down Manfred von Richthofen (the Red Baron), Germany's top ace with 80 victories during World War I, has never been resolved to the complete satisfaction of aviation historians, the credit for the Yamamoto shootdown may never be determined to everyone's satisfaction.

However, until any unassailable new evidence to the contrary is presented, either as a result of a visit to the wreckage site by members of the Second Yamamoto Mission Association or by others, it is the opinion of this writer that only one pilot can rightfully lay total claim to this epic shootdown.

His name is Rex T. Barber.

ACKNOWLEDGMENTS

PECIAL THANKS GO TO THE ONE PERSON who sustained a never-ending interest in this work and provided exceptionally valuable background and references: George T. Chandler, a World War II ace who flew fighters in the South Pacific. He had a special concern for ascertaining the truth about this historic mission and organized an expedition under the banner of the Second Yamamoto Mission Association to accumulate evidence and visit the wreckage site in the Bougainville jungle. His purpose was to determine, if at all possible, from which direction the bullets came that downed Japan's revered naval leader. If this could be determined positively, he felt that the long controversy over who *really* deserves the credit would be finally resolved. Knowing most of the participants, he felt a special obligation to determine beyond all doubt, fairly and scientifically, whose name or names should go down in the history books and be credited for the outcome of this epic fighter mission. He was ably assisted by Eugene M. Monihan, a World War II aviation historian and a specialist in producing paintings of historic air missions, who continually provided valuable background information and contacts.

The author is also indebted to the American survivors of the

Yamamoto mission for their encouragement and assistance in providing background and vital information about their flight and its aftermath. I am also grateful for the helpful suggestions and assistance rendered by the many archivists of the Office of Air Force History, the National Archives, the Marine and Navy Archives, and the National Air and Space Museum.

A debt of large proportions is owed to Bruce Smith, director, and James D. Bigley and Mrs. Helen Springall, dedicated archivists, at the Admiral Nimitz Museum in Fredericksburg, Texas, for their extraordinary help in providing documents and encouragement during my visit in 1988.

Special thanks go to Colonels John W. Mitchell, commander of the 339th Fighter Squadron, and Rex T. Barber, wingman for Captain Thomas G. Lanphier, Jr., for their patience in reviewing portions of the manuscript and providing constructive suggestions and photographs. They insisted on presenting only the facts in regard to their own actions as they recall them and would not speculate on the motivations of others. They willingly and promptly answered all questions during interviews, by letter, and by telephone.

The author also owes thanks to Joseph C. Pruett, who provided background information concerning the aftermath of the death of Yamamoto from the files of John Brannon, one of the defense attorneys during the Japanese War Crimes Trials of 1946-1947. Thanks also to Douglas Canning, one of the mission pilots, whose interest in photography led him to take many photos during his stint in the South Pacific. These photos enabled the author to gain the tenor of the difficult times and conditions faced by the pilots at Fighter Two on Guadalcanal at this point in Air Force history.

Terry Gwynn-Jones, an Australian writer/pilot, and Ross Channon, a New Zealand aviation archaeologist, generously provided descriptions and photos of the wreckage of Yamamoto's plane. Gwynn-Jones's candor and his forthright National Air and Space Museum presentation describing his visit to the wreckage site contributed an interesting and valuable viewpoint about the mission and its participants.

CHAPTER NOTES

1. "TALLEY HO! LET'S GET THE BASTARD!"

1. From presentation at "Yamamoto Retrospective" conducted by The Admiral Nimitz Museum Foundation, Fredericksburg, Texas, April 16, 1988.

2. Translation of Japanese Naval Message 006430, April 13, 1943 as transmitted by Message No. 4/131755/I.

3. Cited by Capt. J. N. Wenger, USN, in "A Lecture on Communications Intelligence" Washington, D.C., August 14, 1946.

4. Mitsuo Fuchida and Masatake Okumiya, *Midway: The Battle That Doomed Japan* (Annapolis: Naval Institute Press, 1955), pp. 73–74.

5. David Kahn, *The Codebreakers* (New York: The Macmillan Co., 1967), p. 598.

6. Edwin T. Layton, *"And I Was There"* (New York: William Morrow and Co., 1985), p. 475.

7. E. B. Potter, *Nimitz* (Annapolis: Naval Institute Press, 1976), p. 233.

8. CINCPAC Bulletin No. 395, 150249 April 1943. Also, Wenger lecture, op. cit., August 14, 1946.

9. Message No. 141916, April 14, 1943.

10. Wenger lecture, op. cit.

11. Message No. T2W 150643, April 15, 1943.

12. William F. Halsey, and Bryan Joseph III, *Admiral Halsey's Story* (New York: Whittlesey House, 1947), p. 155.

13. Message No. 160039, April 16, 1943.

14. Kahn, op. cit., p. 1074.

15. Layton, op. cit., p. 475.

16. David Bergamini, *Japan's Imperial Conspiracy* (New York: William Morrow and Co, 1971), p. 977.

17. Burke Davis, *Get Yamamoto* (New York: Random House, 1969), p. 122.

18. John Deane Potter, *Yamamoto: The Man Who Menaced America* (New York: The Viking Press, 1965), p. 304.

19. From presentation made by Capt. Roger Pineau, USNR (Ret) at Yamamoto Retrospective, Fredericksburg, Texas, April 16, 1988, and confirmed by telephone conversation with the author, January 4, 1989.

20. For the complete story of the Doolittle raid on Japan, see *The Doolittle Raid, Doolittle's Tokyo Raiders,* and *Four Came Home* by the author.

21. Theodore Taylor, *The Magnificent Mitscher* (New York: W. W. Norton and Co., 1954), pp. 150–151.

22. Robert Sherrod, *History of Marine Corps Aviation in World War II* (San Rafael, Calif.: Presidio Press, 1952), pp. 138–139.

2. THE CODEBREAKERS

1. Ronald H. Spector, *Eagle Against the Sun* (New York: The Free Press, 1985), p. 445.

2. Ladislas Farago, *The Broken Seal* (New York: Random House, 1967), p 46.

3. Ibid., p. 55.

4. Ibid., p. 63.

5. Ibid., p. 67.

6. Ronald Clark, *The Man Who Broke Purple* (Boston: Little, Brown and Co., 1977), p. 196.

7. Ibid., p. 99.

8. Ibid., p. 100.

9. Ronald Lewin, *The American Magic* (New York: Farrar Straus Giroux, 1982), p. 86.

10. W. J. Holmes, *Double-Edged Secrets* (Annapolis: Naval Institute Press, 1979), p. 54.

11. Clark, op. sit., p. 190

3. A MILLION-TO-ONE MISSION

1. Report of interview with intelligence officers, Washington, D.C., June 15, 1943.

2. Colonel Mitchell was interviewed extensively by the author during a reunion of the 70th Fighter Squadron at Valdosta, Georgia, October 16, 1988.

3. Ibid.

4. Ibid.

5. Ibid.

6. Ibid.

7. Ibid.

4. WHO WAS ADMIRAL YAMAMOTO?

1. John Deane Potter, *Yamamoto: The Man Who Menaced America* (New York: The Viking Press, 1965), p. 3.

2. Willard Price, "America's Enemy No. 2: Yamamoto," *Harper's Magazine*, Vol. 184. No. 1103, April 1942, p. 452.

3. Potter, op. cit, p. 10.

4. Ibid, p. 12

5. Hiroyuki Agawa, *The Reluctant Admiral* (Tokyo: Kodansha International Ltd., 1979), p. 2.

6. Price, op. cit., p. 458.

7. Willard Price, "Hidden Key to the Pacific," *National Geographic Magazine*. Vol. 82, June 1942, p. 21.

8. Ibid., p. 23.

9. Agawa, op. cit., p. 80.

10. Potter, op. cit., p. 20.

11. Ibid., p. 23.

12. Ibid., p. 24.

13. Ibid., p. 30.

14. Agawa, op. cit., p. 186.

15. Potter, op. cit., p. 36.

16. Ibid., p. 37.

17. Ibid., p. 54.

18. Matsuo Kato, *The Lost War* (New York: Alfred A. Knopf, 1970), p. 89.

19. Potter, op. cit. p. 128. Many historians doubt that Yamamoto actually said this. However, this wording was used in a letter dated January 24, 1941, to an acquaintance named Ryoichi Sasakawa. He added: "I wonder if our politicians who speak so lightly of a Japanese-American war have confidence as to the outcome and are prepared to make the necessary sacrifices?"

20. Agawa, op. cit., p. 260.

21. Ibid.

22. A. J. Barker, *Pearl Harbor* (New York: Ballantine Books, Inc.), p. 152.

23. Vice Adm. Homer N. Wallin, *Why, How, Fleet Salvage and Final Appraisal* (Washington, D.C., Naval History Division, 1968), p. 83.

24. Potter, op. cit., p. 129.

25. Ibid.

26. Agawa, op. cit., p. 300.

27. Masatake Okumiya and Jiro Horiyoshi, *Zero!* (New York: E. P. Dutton and Co., 1956), p. 160.

5. "BOGEYS! ELEVEN O'CLOCK HIGH!"

1. Interview, 70th Fighter Squadron Reunion, Valdosta, Georgia, October 16, 1988.

2. Ibid.

3. Ibid.

4. Ibid.

5. Yamamoto Retrospective, Fredericksburg, Texas, April 16, 1988.

6. Hiroyuki Agawa, *The Reluctant Admiral*. (Tokyo: Kodansha International, Ltd., 1979), p. 347.

7. Interview, Valdosta, Georgia, October 16, 1988.

8. Ibid.

9. Letter from Delford C. Goerke to the author, December 15, 1988.

10. Interview, Valdosta, Georgia, October 16, 1988.

11. Interview, Valdosta, Georgia, October 15, 1988.

12. Thomas G. Lanphier, Jr., three-part article, *The New York Times*, September 12–14, 1945.

13. Thomas G. Lanphier, Jr., six-part article, North American Newspaper Alliance, September 12–17, 1945.

14. Interview, Valdosta, Georgia, October 16, 1988.

15. Besby F. Holmes, "Who Really Shot Down Yamamoto?" *Popular Aviation*, March/April, 1967, p. 56.

16. Interview, Valdosta, Georgia, October 15, 1988.

17. Interview, Valdosta, Georgia, October 16, 1988.

18. Excerpted with permission from Thomas G. Lanphier, Jr., "I Shot Down Yamamoto," *Reader's Digest*, December 1966, p. 82. Copyright by the Reader's Digest Association, Inc.

19. Interview, Valdosta, Georgia, October 16, 1988.

6. "APRIL 18 SEEMS TO BE OUR DAY"

1. Interview, Valdosta, Georgia, October 16, 1988.

2. From Besby F. Holmes, "Who Really Shot Down Yamamoto?" *Popular Aviation*, March/April, 1967, pp. 62–63.

3. Interview, Valdosta, Georgia, October 16, 1988.

4. From note left at reception desk, Admiral Nimitz Museum, Fredericksburg, Texas, by Edward C. Hutcheson, October 6, 1979.

5. Letter from Roger J. Ames to George T. Chandler, September 8, 1988.

6. Letter from Joseph O. Young to George T. Chandler, September 11, 1988.

7. Letter from Bill Harris to the author, November 29, 1988.

8. Letter from Louis Kittel to the author, September 22, 1988.

9. Letter from Paul S. Bechtel to George T. Chandler, September 22, 1988.

10. Interview, Valdosta, Georgia, October 16, 1988.

11. Interview, Valdosta, Georgia, October 15, 1988.

12. Letter from Louis Kittel to the author, September 22, 1988.

13. Letter from Delton C. Goerke to the author, December 15, 1988.

14. Letter from Brooklyn Harris to George T. Chandler, May 29, 1988.

15. Letter from John E. Little to George T. Chandler, January 24, 1989.

16. Interview, Valdosta, Georgia, October 16, 1988.

17. Interview, Valdosta, Georgia, October 16, 1988.

18. Message No. 180229 Commander, Air Solomons to Commander, South Pacific, April 18, 1943.

19. From Rear Adm. William Augustus Read, "Condition Red on Guadalcanal, and the Shooting Down of Admiral Yamamoto," in *The Pacific War Remembered*, edited by John T. Mason, Jr. (Annapolis: Naval Institute Press, Oral History Collection, 1986), p. 166.

20. William F. Halsey and Joseph Bryan III, *Admiral Halsey's Story*. (New York: Whittlesey House, 1947), p. 157.

21. Message No. 180724, commander, Third Fleet to commander, Air Solomons, April 18, 1943.

22. Daily Summary, Commander in Chief, Pacific, April 17, 1943.

23. From Besby F. Holmes, "Who Really Shot Down Yamamoto?" *Popular Aviation*, March/April 1967, p. 64.

24. Interview, Valdosta, Georgia, October 15, 1988.

25. Letter from Fighter Intelligence Office, 13th Fighter Command Detachment, APO 709, Subject: Fighter Interception, to Commanding General, USAFISPA, April 18, 1943.

26. Message No. 240315, commander, South Pacific to commander in chief, Pacific, April 24, 1943.

27. 1st Endorsement to letter from commander, South Pacific to commander in chief, Pacific, April 26, 1943.

28. "Thirteenth Air Force, April–October 1943," Historical Study No. 120 prepared by Army Air Forces Historical Office, Headquarters, Army Air Forces, Washington, D.C., September, 1946.

29. Letter from Louis Kittel to the author, September 22, 1988.

7. THE OTHER SIDE OF THE STORY

1. Hiroyuki Agawa, *The Reluctant Admiral*. (Tokyo: Kodansha International, Ltd., 1979), p. 350.

2. Kenji Yanagiya stated in a 1988 interview at Fredericksburg, Texas, that not only were none of the six Zeros shot down, but also that none of the five that landed at Buin had any combat damage. He made no statement about the sixth Zero that landed at Shortland Island.

3. From Matome Ugaki's diary, as quoted in Masatake Okumiya and Jiro Horikoshi, *Zero!*, (New York: E. P. Dutton and Co., 1956), pp. 247–251.

4. Headquarters, Army General Staff, History Series No. 6, *History of World War II until June 1943*, (Tokyo: Asagumo Shimbunsha for the Japanese Self Defense Training Center, undated), pp. 368–369.

5. Agawa, op. cit., p. 358.

6. Letter from Shingo Suzuki to Rex T. Barber, September 10, 1984.

7. Agawa, op. cit., p. 358.

8. Letter from Shingo Suzuki to Rex T. Barber, June 14, 1985.

9. Report of autopsy by Lt. Comdr. Tabuchi, chief medical officer, First Base Unit, Buin, April 20, 1943.

10. Agawa, op. cit., p. 359.

11. Letter from Shingo Suzuki to John T. Wible, June 17, 1986.

12. Telegram 181109. Highest Priority, Confidential. Top Secret Ro–3 Code from Commandant, 6th Air Force to Commandant 11th Air Fleet, April 18, 1943.

13. Agawa, op. cit., p. 380.

14. Telegram No. 211757 from Chief of Personnel Bureau to commanders of all fleets. The message also announced the appointment by Emperor Hirohito of Admiral Mineichi Koga to be Commander in Chief, Combined Fleet, effective April 21, 1943.

8. "BULL" HALSEY RAGES

1. Interview, Valdosta, Georgia, October 16, 1988.

2. Ibid.

3. Letter from Rex T. Barber to the author, January 5, 1989.

4. Interview, Valdosta, Georgia, October 16, 1988.

5. Article submitted by J. Norman Lodge to U.S. Navy censors from "advanced Pacific base," May 11, 1943.

6. Interview, Valdosta, Georgia, October 15, 1988.

7. W. J. Holmes, *Double-Edged Secrets*. (Annapolis: Naval Institute Press, 1979), p. 136.

8. Message No. 242053, commander in chief, Pacific to commander, South Pacific, May 24, 1943.

9. From Rear Adm. William Augustus Read, "Condition Red on Guadalcanal, and the Shooting Down of Admiral Yamamoto," in *The Pacific War Remembered*, edited by John T. Mason, Jr. (Annapolis: Naval Institute Press, Oral History Collection, 1986).

10. Memorandum for commander, Aircraft, South Pacific Force, Subject: "Investigation concerning leakage of information concerning the fighter sweep of the Kahili area on April 18, 1943," dated May 30, 1943.

11. "Most Secret" letter from commander, Aircraft, South Pacific Force, to commander, South Pacific Force, June 10, 1943.

12. Memorandum from commander, Fleet Marine Force on Guadalcanal to Headquarters, Marine Aircraft South Pacific, Fleet Marine Force, June 1, 1943.

13. Letter from Lt. Gen. Millard F. Harmon to commander, South Pacific Area and South Pacific Force, Subject: "Safeguarding of Military Information" June 9, 1943.

14. Letter from Maj. Gen. Nathan F. Twining, to commander, Aircraft, South Pacific, Subject: "Investigation, Specific Information Desired Concerning" June 7, 1943.

15. Statement made at Headquarters, Thirteenth Air Force, attached to letter from Maj. Gen. Nathan F. Twining, June 2, 1943, addressed to commander, Aircraft, South Pacific, Subject: "Investigation, Specific Information Desired Concerning," June 7, 1943.

16. Letter from Lt. Gen. Millard F. Harmon to Lt. Gen. Henry H. Arnold, May 26, 1943.

17. Letter from Lt. Gen. Millard F. Harmon to Maj. John W. Mitchell, Subject: "Commendation," April 24, 1943.

18. Press release, War Department Bureau of Public Relations, Washington, D.C., June 17, 1943.

19. Letter from John W. Mitchell to the author, January 22, 1989.

20. William F. Halsey and Joseph Bryan III, *Admiral Halsey's Story*. (New York: Whittlesey House, 1946), p. 157. Lt. Charles C. Lanphier died of malnutrition on Rabaul while a prisoner-of-war on April 29, 1944. His death was not known until after the surrender.

21. Letter directed to subordinate commanders, prepared by Assistant Chief of Staff, Intelligence, for General Douglas MacArthur, January 28, 1944.

9. THE AFTERMATH

1. Walter Millis, ed., *The Forrestal Diaries*, (New York: Viking Press, 1951), p. 86.

2. Telegram from Thomas G. Lanphier, Jr., to Rex T. Barber, September 14, 1945.

3. Letter from Thomas G. Lanphier, Jr., to Rex T. Barber, written on "The Whittier" stationery, September 13, 1945.

4. Letter from Luther Kissick to Milton Miller, December 13, 1988.

5. Interview, Valdosta, Georgia, October 15, 1988.

6. Army Air Force Historical Office, *The Thirteenth Air Force, March–October 1943*, Historical Study No. 120. (Washington, D.C. Headquarters, Army Air Forces, September 1946).

7. Interview, Valdosta, Georgia, October 16, 1988.

8. Leonard Lyons, "Loose Leaf Notebook" column, *Washington Post*, September 17, 1945.

9. John W. Mitchell, from speech at Business and Professional Men's Luncheon, American Legion Post, San Antonio, Texas, January 8, 1946.

10. Quoted from news item, *Army Times*, May 4, 1946, p. 30.

11. Letter from Col. John W. Mitchell to Gen. Carl A. Spaatz, Chief of Staff, Army Air Forces, July 29, 1947.

12. *Air Force*, April 1946, p. 30.

13. Quoted from news item, *Air Force*, November 1947, p. 45.

14. W. F. Craven and J. L. Cate, eds., *The Pacific—Guadalcanal to Saipan*, Vol. IV. (Chicago: University of Chicago Press, 1950), p. 214.

15. Ibid., chapter notes for Chapter 7, p. 729.

16. Burke Davis, *Get Yamamoto*. (New York: Random House, 1969), pp. 207–208.

17. Letter from Murray Green to George T. Chandler, October 22, 1988.

18. From column by Joseph Alsop, *Washington Post*, September 26, 1959.

19. Interview, Valdosta, Georgia, October 15, 1988.

20. Letter from Joseph Alsop to Thomas G. Lanphier, Jr., November 14, 1984.

21. Interview with Rex T. Barber, Valdosta, Georgia, October 15, 1988.

22. Davis, op. cit., p. 185.

23. Kit C. Carter and Robert Mueller, "Combat Chronology," Air University, Maxwell Air Force Base, Alabama, 1973, p. 123.

24. This conclusion is confirmed in the latest victory credit listing prepared by Dr. Daniel L. Haulman and Col. William C. Stancik, USAFR, eds., *Air Force Aerial Victory Credits: World War I, World War II, Korea, and Vietnam*, United States Air Force Historical Research Center, Maxwell Air Force Base, Alabama, 1988.

25. Letter from Barrett Tillman to the author, July 24, 1988.

26. Interview by unnamed Japanese interviewer with Kenji Yanagiya, Sony Studios, Tokyo, Japan, June 13, 1975.

27. Interview, Valdosta, Georgia, October 16, 1988.

28. Obituary section of the (Portland, Oregon) *Oregonian*, November 30, 1987.

29. Letter from Brig. Gen. Michael J. Jackson, USAF (Ret) to Dr. Richard H. Kohn, Chief, Office of Air Force History, March 6, 1985.

30. Victory Credit Board of Review, United States Air Force Historical Research Center, Maxwell Air Force Base, Alabama, March 22, 1985.

31. Letter from Julius Jacobson to the author, February 27, 1989.

32. Letter from Judith Lanphier Strada to the author, November 10, 1988.

10. THE YAMAMOTO RETROSPECTIVE

1. Letter from Helen B. Springall to the author, January 27, 1988.

2. Elizabeth Longford, *Wellington: The Years of the Sword*. (New York: Harper and Row, 1969), p. 472.

3. Presentation by Dr. Joseph Dawson, Yamamoto Retrospective, Fredericksburg, Texas, April 16, 1988.

4. Presentation by Dr. Roger H. Beaumont, Yamamoto Retrospective, Fredericksburg, Texas, April 16, 1988.

5. Presentation by Dr. Paul Woodruff, Yamamoto Retrospective, Fredericksburg, Texas, April 16, 1988.

6. Presentation by Dr. Manuel Davenport, Yamamoto Retrospective, Fredericksburg, Texas, April 16, 1988.

7. Several pilots described the dust that rose from the Kahili airfield as caused by aircraft that were apparently taking off to intercept the P-38s. Barber also believes that several Zeros, other than the six escorts, were in the air by the time he went after the second bomber.

8. Presentation by Roger Ames, Yamamoto Retrospective, Fredericksburg, Texas, April 16, 1977.

11. WHO *REALLY* SHOT DOWN YAMAMOTO?

1. Thomas G. Lanphier, Jr., North American Newspaper Alliance, New York, N.Y., September 12, 1945.

2. Interview, Valdosta, Georgia, October 15, 1988.

3. Letter from General James H. Doolittle to the author, November 1, 1988.

4. James T. Wible, "The Yamamoto Mission," letter from Thomas G. Lanphier, Jr. to "a correspondent," published by The Admiral Nimitz Foundation, 1988.

5. Interview with former pilot of the 339th Squadron on Guadalcanal who prefers to remain anonymous, Valdosta, Georgia, October 16, 1988.

12. IN SEARCH OF HISTORY

1. Letter from D'E. C. Darby to Rex T. Barber, 1975.

2. Undated letter from D'E. C. Darby to Jack Ilfrey, Fighter Aces Association.

3. *GEO*, November, 1982, p. 19.

4. *Air Force*, April, 1985, p. 125.

5. Presentation at National Air and Space Museum, Washington, D.C., September 19, 1988.

6. Letter from Ross Channon to Larry W. Crestman, December 15, 1985.

7. Letter from Jack P. DeBoer to George T. Chandler, June, 1988.

8. Letter from Dr. Richard H. Kohn to George T. Chandler, March 22, 1989.

9. Letter from D'E. C. Darby to Rex T. Barber, October 27, 1988.

10. Aircraft Crash Investigation Report, G4M1, Serial No. 2756, by D'E. C. Darby, August 5, 1988.

11. Letter from George T. Chandler to the author, March 21, 1989.

12. Letter from R. Cargill Hall to George T. Chandler, May 11, 1988.

13. Interview by Richard Y. Nishiyama, Tokyo, Japan, August 10, 1989.

14. Resolution No. 302, 89th National Convention, Veterans of Foreign Wars, Chicago, Illinois, August, 1988.

15. Letter from Dr. Richard H. Kohn to Howard E. Vander Clute, Jr., September 16, 1988.

16. Letter from Dr. Richard H. Kohn to George T. Chandler, January 17, 1989.

EPILOGUE

1. Interview, Valdosta, Georgia, October 16, 1988.

2. USAF Historical Study No. 73, "A Preliminary List of U.S. Air

Force Aces, 1917–1953." USAF Historical Division, Research Studies Institute, Air University, Maxwell AFB, Alabama, 1962.

3. "Air Force Aerial Victory Credits: World War I, World War II, Korea and Vietnam," edited by Dr. Daniel L. Haulman and Col. Williams C. Stancik, USAFR. U.S. Air Force Historical Research Center, Maxwell AFB, Alabama, 1988.

4. Letter to the author from R. Cargill Hall, April 10, 1989.

BIBLIOGRAPHY

Agawa, Hiroyuki. *The Reluctant Admiral*. Tokyo: Kodansha International Ltd, 1979.

Barker, A. J. *Pearl Harbor*. New York: Ballantine Books, Inc., 1969.

Bergamini, David. *Japan's Imperial Conspiracy*. New York: William Morrow and Co., 1971.

Clark, Ronald. *The Man Who Broke Purple*. Boston: Little, Brown and Co., 1977.

Craven, Wesley F., and James L. Cate, eds. *United States Air Force in World War II; The Pacific—Guadalcanal to Saipan: August 1942 to July 1944*. Chicago: University of Chicago, 1950.

Davis, Burke. *Get Yamamoto*. New York: Random House, 1969.

Farago, Ladislas. *The Broken Seal*. New York: Random House, 1967.

Ferguson, Robert Lawrence. *Guadalcanal: The Island of Fire*. Blue Ridge Summit, Penn.: Aero, a division of TAB Books, 1987.

Fuchida, Mitsuo and Masatake Okumiya. *Midway: The Battle that Doomed Japan*. Annapolis: Naval Institute Press, 1955.

Glines, Carroll V. *The Doolittle Raid*. New York: Orion Books, 1988.

——. *Four Came Home*. Princeton: Van Nostrand Reinhold, 1967.

——. *Doolittle's Tokyo Raiders*. Princeton: Van Nostrand Reinhold, 1964.

——. *The Compact History of the United States Air Force*. New York: Hawthorn Books, Inc., 1973.

Gurney, Gene. *Five Down and Glory*. New York: Ballantine Books, Inc., 1958.

Halsey, William F. and Joseph Bryan, III. *Admiral Halsey's Story*. New York: Whittlesey House, 1947.

Holmes, W. J. *Double-Edged Secrets*. Annapolis: Naval Institute Press, 1979.

Hoyt, Edwin P. *Crossing the Circle*. New York: Van Nostrand Reinhold, 1982.

Kahn, David. *The Codebreakers*. New York: The Macmillan Co., 1967.

Layton, Edwin T. *"And I Was There."* New York: William Morrow and Co., 1985.

Lewin, Ronald. *The American Magic*. New York: Farrar Straus Giroux, 1982.

Miller, Thomas G., Jr. *The Cactus Air Force*. New York: Harper and Row, 1969.

Morison, Samuel E., *History of U.S. Naval Operations in World War II*. Boston: Atlantic-Little, Brown and Co., 1947.

Okumiya, Masatake and Jiro Horiyoshi. *Zero!* New York: E. P. Dutton and Co., 1956.

Potter, E. B. *Nimitz*. Annapolis: Naval Institute Press, 1976.

Potter, John Deane. *Yamamoto: The Man Who Menaced America*. New York: The Viking Press, 1965.

Prange, Gordon W. *At Dawn We Slept: The Untold Story of Pearl Harbor*. New York: McGraw-Hill Book Co., 1981.

————. *Miracle at Midway*. New York: McGraw-Hill Book Co., 1982.

Spector, Ronald H. *Eagle Against the Sun*. New York: The Free Press, 1985.

Taylor, Theodore. *The Magnificent Mitscher*. New York: W. W. Norton and Co., 1954.

Theobald, Robert A. *The Final Secret of Pearl Harbor*. New York: The Devin-Adair Co., 1954.

Toland, John. *The Rising Sun*. New York: Random House, 1970.

Wible, John T. *The Yamamoto Mission*. Fredericksburg, Texas: The Admiral Nimitz Foundation, 1988.

Wohlstetter, Roberta. *Pearl Harbor: Warning and Decision*. Stanford, California: Stanford University Press, 1962.

APPENDIX

Members of the 339th fighter squadron on the Yamamoto mission and their hometowns of record during World War II.

Maj. John W. Mitchell, squadron commander, Enid, Mississippi

ATTACK FLIGHT
Capt. Thomas G. Lanphier, Jr., Detroit, Michigan
1st Lt. Rex T. Barber, Culver, Oregon
1st Lt. Besby F. Holmes, San Francisco, California
1st Lt. Raymond K. Hine, Harrison, Ohio

TOP COVER FLIGHT
1st Lt. Roger J. Ames, Laramie, Wyoming
1st Lt. Everett H. Anglin, Arlington, Texas
1st Lt. Douglas S. Canning, Wayne, Nebraska
1st Lt. Delton C. Goerke, Syracuse, New York
1st Lt. Lawrence A. Graebner, St. Paul, Minnesota
1st Lt. Julius Jacobson, San Diego, California
Maj. Louis R. Kittel, Fargo, North Dakota
1st Lt. Albert R. Long, Taft, Texas
1st Lt. William E. Smith, Glendale, California
1st Lt. Eldon E. Stratton, Anderson, Missouri
2d Lt. Gordon Whittaker, Goldsboro, North Carolina

PILOTS OF THE MITSUBISHI A6M ZERO ESCORTING FIGHTER PLANES, 204TH KOKUTAI NAVAL AIR UNIT

Chief Petty Officer Yoshimi Hidaka
Lt. Takeshi Morizaki
Petty Officer 2nd Class Yasuji Okazaki
Flight Petty Officer Shoichi Sugita
Flight Petty Officer Toyomitsu Tsujinoue
Flight Petty Officer Kenji Yanagiya

FLIGHT CREW ON MITSUBISHI G4M BOMBER NO. 323, 205TH KOKUTAI NAVAL AIR UNIT

Flight Petty Officer Nobuo Hata, radio operator
Chief Flight Seaman Harumasa Kobayashi, gunner
Flight Warrant Officer Takeo Kotani, pilot
Chief Flight Seaman Akiharu Ohsaki, copilot
Flight Petty Officer Minoru Tanaka, observer
Flight Petty Officer Haruo Ueda, mechanic
Chief Flight Seaman Mitsuo Ueno, radio operator

PASSENGERS ON BOARD AIRCRAFT NO. 323

Comdr. Noboru Fukusaki, aide to Admiral Yamamoto
Rear Adm. Rokuro Takata, chief surgeon, Combined Fleet
Comdr. Kurio Toibana, staff officer
Adm. Isoroku Yamamoto, commander in chief, Combined Fleet

FLIGHT CREW ON MITSUBISHI G4M BOMBER NO. 326

Chief Flight Seaman Fumikatsu Fujimoto, copilot
Flight Petty Officer Isamu Hachiki, radio operator
Flight Petty Officer Hiroshi Hayashi, pilot
Flight Petty Officer Sukeichi Itoh, radio operator
Flight Petty Officer Nobuyuki Kuriyama, mechanic
Chief Flight Seaman Kaneyoshi Nomiyama, gunner
Flight Petty Officer Hiroaki Tanimoto, observer

PASSENGERS ON BOARD AIRCRAFT NO. 326

Comdr. Kaoru Imanaka, staff officer
Capt. Motoharu Kitamura, chief paymaster, Combined Fleet
Comdr. Suteji Muroi, staff officer
Comdr. Rinji Tomono, meteorology officer, Combined Fleet
Vice Adm. Matome Ugaki, chief of staff, Combined Fleet

INDEX

940.5426 Glines, Carroll
GLI   V., 1920-

The attack on
Yamamoto

$19.45   10/15/90

DATE

01 15 91